Entrepreneurship, Competitiveness and Local Development

Entrepreneurship, Competitiveness and Local Development

Frontiers in European Entrepreneurship Research

Edited by

Luca Iandoli

Department of Business and Managerial Engineering, University of Naples Federico II, Italy

Hans Landström

School of Economics and Management, Lund University, Sweden

Mario Raffa

Department of Business and Managerial Engineering, University of Naples Federico II, Italy

IN ASSOCIATION WITH THE ECSB

Edward Elgar
Cheltenham, UK • Northampton, MA, USA

Published by
Edward Elgar Publishing Limited
Glensanda House
Montpellier Parade
Cheltenham
Glos GL50 1UA
UK

Edward Elgar Publishing, Inc.
William Pratt House
9 Dewey Court
Northampton
Massachusetts 01060
USA

A catalogue record for this book
is available from the British Library

Library of Congress Cataloguing in Publication Data

Research in Entrepreneurship Conference (19th: 2005: Naples, Italy)
Entrepreneurship, competitiveness and local development: frontiers in European entrepreneurship research/edited by Luca Iandoli, Hans Landström, Mario Raffa.
p. cm.
Selected papers presented at the annual Research in Entrepreneurship (RENT) Conference, RENT XIX, which was held in Naples in November 2005.
Includes bibliographical references and index.
1. Entrepreneurship—Research—Europe—Congresses. 2. New business enterprises—Research—Europe—Congresses. I. Iandoli, Luca, 1972– . II. Landström, Hans. III. Raffa, Mario. IV. Title.
HB615.R48 2005
338'.04094—dc22

2007001399

ISBN 978 1 84720 327 4

Printed and bound in Great Britain by MPG Books Ltd, Bodmin, Cornwall

Contents

Contributors

Elena Aculai, Institute of Economy, Finance and Statistics (IEFS) of the Academy of Sciences of Moldova and the Ministry of Economy and Commerce of the Republic of Moldova, Chisinau, Moldova; eaculai@moldova.md.

Fabio Bertoni, Dipartimento di Ingegneria Gestionale, Politecnico di Milano, Italy; fabio.bertoni@polimi.it.

Stijn Bruyneel, Hasselt University, Research Center for Entrepreneurship and Innovation (KIZOK), Diepenbeek, Belgium; stijn.bruyneel@uhasselt.be.

Martin Carree, Maastricht University, Department of Organization and Strategy, Faculty of Economics and Business Administration, Maastricht, The Netherlands; m.carree@os.unimaas.nl.

Massimo G. Colombo, Dipartimento di Ingegneria Gestionale, Politecnico di Milano, Italy; massimo.colombo@polimi.it.

Pauline de Jong-'t Hart, EIM Business and Policy Research, Zoetermeer, The Netherlands; paj@eim.nl.

S. Gerhard Dijkstra, Faculty of Economics, University of Groningen, The Netherlands; gerharddijkstra@gmail.com.

Rudolf Dömötör, Institute for Entrepreneurship and Innovation, Vienna University of Economics and Business Administration, Austria; rudolf.doemoetoer@wu-wien.ac.at.

Jonas Gabrielsson, Centre for Innovation, Research and Competence in the Learning Economy (CIRCLE), Lund University, Sweden; jonas.gabrielsson@circle.lu.se.

Petra Gibcus, EIM Business and Policy Research, Zoetermeer, The Netherlands; pgi@eim.nl.

Luca Grilli, Dipartimento di Ingegneria Gestionale, Politecnico di Milano, Italy; luca.grilli@polimi.it.

Christopher Hader, Institute for Entrepreneurship and Innovation, Vienna University of Economics and Business Administration, Austria; christopher.hader@wu-wien.ac.at.

Luca Iandoli, Department of Business and Managerial Engineering, University of Naples Federico II, Italy; luca.iandoli@unina.it.

Nina Isakova, STEPS Centre at the National Academy of Sciences, Kiev, Ukraine; nisakova@hotmail.com.

Ron Kemp, EIM Business and Policy Research, Zoetermeer, and Netherlands Competition Authority, The Netherlands; r.g.m.Kemp@nmanet.nl.

Johan Lambrecht, Research Centre for Entrepreneurship, European University College Brussels (EHSAL) and Catholic University of Brussels (KU Brussel), Belgium; johan.lambrecht@ehsal.be.

Hans Landström, School of Economics and Management, Lund University, Sweden; hans.landstrom@fek.lu.se.

Clemens Lutz, Faculty of Management and Organization, University of Groningen, The Netherlands; c.h.m.lutz@rug.nl.

Colm O'Gorman, DCU Business School, Dublin City University, Ireland; colm.ogorman@dcu.ie.

Ludo Peeters, Hasselt University, Research Center for Entrepreneurship and Innovation (KIZOK), Diepenbeek, Belgium; ludo.peeters@uhasselt.be.

Diamanto Politis, Department of Business Administration, Lund University, Sweden; diamanto.politis@fek.lu.se.

Theo J.B.M. Postma, Faculty of Management and Organization, University of Groningen, The Netherlands; t.j.b.m.postma@rug.nl.

Mario Raffa, Department of Business and Managerial Engineering, University of Naples Federico II, Italy; mario.raffa@unina.it.

David Smallbone, Small Business Research Centre (SBRC), Kingston University, UK; d.smallbone@kingston.ac.uk.

Rebecca Stratling, Durham Business School, University of Durham, UK; r.stratling@durham.ac.uk.

Siri Terjesen, Brisbane Graduate School of Business, Queensland University of Technology, Australia; siriterjesen@yahoo.com.

Lorraine Uhlaner, Center for Entrepreneurship, Nyenrode Business Universiteit, Breukelen, The Netherlands; l.uhlaner@nyenrode.nl.

Jerry van Santen, Akzo Nobel Car Refinishes bv, Department BU-Color, Sassenheim, The Netherlands; jerry.vansanten@akzonobel.com.

Bram Wauters, Research Centre for Entrepreneurship, European University College Brussels (EHSAL) and Catholic University of Brussels (KU Brussel), Belgium; bram.wauters@ehsal.be.

Friederike Welter, School of Economic Disciplines, University of Siegen, Germany; welter@uni-siegen.de.

Frits H. Wijbenga, Durham Business School, University of Durham, UK; f.h.wijbenga@durham.ac.uk.

Foreword

It gives me great pleasure to present the second volume in a new series of selected papers from the annual Research in Entrepreneurship (RENT) conference; in this case, from RENT XIX, which was held in Naples in November 2005. Since the first RENT conference in Brussels in 1987, the conference has grown in terms of both the number of participants and reputation, to become recognized as one of the leading conferences in its field globally. RENT is organized through a partnership between the European Institute for Advanced Studies in Management (EIASM) and the European Council for Small Business and Entrepreneurship (ECSB).

The aim of this book, and the series on which it is based, is to present a selection of papers from the RENT conference, to provide a 'shop window' on current European research in the entrepreneurship field. I would personally like to thank the editors of this volume for the dedicated and speedy way in which the contributions were selected and reviewed. I am sure that the book will become a valued addition to the growing international literature on entrepreneurship.

David Smallbone
President, ECSB

Introduction: entrepreneurship, competitiveness and local development

Luca Iandoli, Hans Landström and Mario Raffa

INTRODUCTION

The Research in Entrepreneurship (RENT) conference is an annual international research meeting for scholars and practitioners in the field of entrepreneurship and small business management, promoted by the ECSB (European Council for Small Business and Entrepreneurship) and the EIASM (European Institute for Advanced Studies in Management). Starting from the RENT conference in Copenhagen in 2004, an anthology containing the best papers presented at RENT conferences is published yearly thanks to the joint effort of the RENT Scientific Committee and the local conference organizers. This book in particular contains a group of 11 contributions selected among the 131 accepted for presentation at the RENT conference hosted at the University Federico II in Naples (Italy) in November 2005. The anthology is representative of the main research areas that are of interest to a community of scholars, which is undoubtedly the leading research community in entrepreneurial and small business studies in Europe and one of the most representative ones at the international level.

The RENT conference has undergone a remarkable growth during the last 20 years. As a consequence it has experienced a marked increase in heterogeneity of approaches, research topics and theoretical backgrounds. This increasing diversity undoubtedly represents a valuable resource. At the same time a need for a unitary view and the search for point of contacts between different approaches seems to emerge. As with any growing and evolving research field, entrepreneurship studies also need to manage a trade-off. It is necessary to preserve internal diversity to foster innovation and at the same time to find a common background, shared values and a common language to ensure that the different research 'souls' are able to talk to each other and cross-fertilize the debate. In our opinion, two possible directions to manage this trade-off have been proposed at the 2005 RENT conference.

The first is related to the conference theme: 'Entrepreneurship, Competitiveness and Local Development'. In the following we present some considerations about the relationship between entrepreneurship and local development, and introduce a competence-based framework to entrepreneurship aimed at proposing a unitary view of some of the main research challenges for sustaining small firms and local development.

The second direction was addressed by Hans Landström from Lund University in his keynote speech, when he outlined the long history of entrepreneurship as a research discipline, identified the most influential thinkers on entrepreneurship research and argued that a more coherent picture and unitary view of entrepreneurship can be gained if one looks at its roots and evolution. In other words, he claims that history matters and in order to move the field of entrepreneurship research forward we need to look backward.

The next section contains a summary of Landström's speech. Then we outline the main research topics addressed in the papers presented at the 2005 conference through a competence-based framework to entrepreneurship research for local development. Finally we illustrate the organization of the book and present the chapters contained in this anthology.

A HISTORY OF ENTREPRENEURSHIP RESEARCH

This historical retrospect will start with a short summary of early thinking on entrepreneurship leading to a discussion about Joseph Schumpeter – his thoughts and life. Next, the change of entrepreneurship research from a topic within the discipline of economics to a behavioural science, with David McClelland as one of the pioneering exponents for this new approach, will be elaborated. Finally, the emergence of a research field of its own will be discussed: the turbulence in society during the 1960s and 1970s, the seminal work by David Birch, and the characteristics of entrepreneurship as an emergent field of research.

Early Thinking on Entrepreneurship

Despite its relatively recent ascent to acceptance as an academic field, entrepreneurship research has a long tradition (Landström, 2005). Although the term 'entrepreneur' has been used in the French language since the twelfth century, the feudal system operating in the European world at the time hampered the development of entrepreneurship and innovation. Gradually, during the Middle Ages, the situation changed, especially in countries such as Italy, France and southern Germany, which became the driving forces behind European economic development. Emerging cities created a breeding ground for entrepreneurship, especially among the merchant class who processed raw material and marketed the finished goods. By the eighteenth century, feudalism had been eliminated, and legal and institutional conditions had greatly changed with the burgeoning of the joint stock company and the development of a banking system (Wennekers and Thurik, 1999). Entrepreneurship and innovation thrived.

It was the writings of the Irish-born banker (who lived in Paris), Richard Cantillon (circa 1680–1734), whose *Essai Sur la Nature du Commerce en Général* was published posthumously in 1755, that gave the concept of entrepreneurship an economic meaning and the entrepreneur a role in economic development. However, for a long period 'classical' economic theory, originating in Adam Smith's well-known work *Inquiry into the Nature and Causes of the Wealth of Nations* (1776 [1994]), dominated the intellectual development of economic science – an economic theory that did not emphasize the entrepreneurial function in the economy. Only a few economists were successful in breaking that trend, and authors such as Jean-Baptiste Say (1767–1832), Jeremy Bentham (1748–1832) and John Stuart Mill (1806–73) should be mentioned in this respect.

At the end of the nineteenth century, the European discussion of entrepreneurship found an audience in the United States, which by that time was well on the way to becoming a major industrial power. Some of the American economists who developed the discussion about entrepreneurship during this period were Francis Walker, Fredrick Hawley and John Bates Clark. Perhaps the best-known author among them was Frank Knight (1885–1972), who in his thesis *Risk, Uncertainty and Profit* (1916, revised 1921) makes a distinction between risk and uncertainty, where uncertainty is unique and uninsurable and he argues that the skills of the entrepreneur lie in the ability to handle the uncertainty that exists in any given society.

Joseph Alois Schumpeter

The late nineteenth and early twentieth centuries were characterized by the emergence of an industrial society, and the building of the modern enterprise. Many authors claimed to see the death of small firms in the economy. It was against this background that the thoughts of Joseph Schumpeter (1885–1950) were developed. Schumpeter was inspired by Gustav Schmoller, who in his analysis of the historical–economic development, was convinced that there existed a unique and central factor in all economic activity – the entrepreneur – who is a key figure due to his/her ability as a creative organizer. Schumpeter's seminal work was *Theorie der Wirtschaftlichen*

Entwicklung (1912, second edition 1926) or *The Theory of Economic Development* (1934), which is the English translation of the second edition. The first and second editions are rather different, in that the latter is more streamlined and Schumpeter attempted to relate his work to the mainstream of economic thinking at that time. In the book, Schumpeter tried to develop an entirely new economic theory based on change – as opposed to equilibrium. The basic assumption was that economic growth resulted not from capital accumulation but from innovations, or 'new combinations'. Once Schumpeter had recognized the crucial role of innovation in economic growth, he understood that innovation had to be implemented by someone, and this ability to break the established practice was primarily related to the individual entrepreneurs. In Chapter 2 of the book, he discusses the function of the entrepreneur as an individual who tends to break the market's equilibrium by introducing innovations into the system – entrepreneurs who were characterized by the desire and the will to found private kingdoms (power and independence), the will to conquer (succeed) and the joy of creating (getting things done).

Schumpeter was highly productive: during his career he wrote nine major books, more than 200 papers and 90 book reviews. If we look at his production of scientific works it could be regarded as very fragmented, but throughout his career there is a very clear line of thought – to build a new economic theory built on 'newness'. It might also be important to put this idea into the context of his career and his life (Box I.1).

All his misfortunes, not least during the 1920s – his abrupt dismissal as finance minister in Austria, his own financial problems as a consequence of too risky investments, and the fact that his mother died in 1926, followed a couple of months later by his wife and son (Josef) – made him very pessimistic and melancholic, and to some extent self-destructive. His wife and mother became a personal cult, and he buried himself in his work and much travelling.

Schumpeter is often regarded as difficult to understand. One reason for this is that he was a very bad pedagogue – his arguments were not always easy to follow, and he wrote in a rather complex way (for example he seldom cited other authors, he used long sentences, and he defined his terms explicitly). He was also to a considerable extent a 'one-man band' in the sense that he was never part of a 'school of thought' and he had no followers among his PhD students.

It should be added that Schumpeter never received any strong recognition among economists, and his influence on policy was rather limited – he was totally absorbed by the Keynesian revolution in 1936 and Keynes's *General Theory of Employment, Interest and Money* (1936). Keynes's reasoning was more normative and emphasized to a greater extent the role

BOX I.1 THE CAREER OF JOSEPH SCHUMPETER

1883	Born an only child on 8 February in Triesch (today in Slovakia). His father was a factory owner, but died when Joseph was four years old
1893	Joseph and his mother moved to Vienna
1901–06	*Study of Law and Economics at the University of Vienna* Several of the world's most famous economists were working at the Department of Law at that time, such as Carl Menger, Eugen von Böhm-Bawerk, Friedrich von Wieser and Gustav Schmoller
1906	Doctorate (Dr Juris) in Law (23 years old)
1906	Post-doctorate at London School of Economics
1907–08	Practised law at the International Mixed Tribunal in Cairo
1909	Associate Professor ('habilitation' degree) at the University of Vienna
1909–11	Teacher in economics at the University of Chervotsky (Ukraine)
1911–21	*Professor at the University of Graz*
1913–14	Visiting Professor at Columbia University in New York
1919	Finance minister in a Social Democratic government in Austria, but was abruptly replaced after seven months
1921–24	*President of the Biedermann Bank in Vienna* Used his wealth to invest in outside speculations, but during the crisis of 1924 in Austria the bank failed and he became bankrupt
1925–32	*Professor of Economics at the University of Bonn*
1926	His mother died (in June), and his wife and son died in childbirth (in August)
1927–28	Visiting Professor at Harvard University
1931	Visiting Professor at Tokyo College of Commerce
1932–50	*Professor of Economics at Harvard University*
1939	Became an American citizen Schumpeter had a very conservative political attitude. At the outbreak of the Second World War, the FBI investigated him for pro-Nazi leanings, but there was no evidence that he had any sympathies for Nazism
1950	Died on the night of 7–8 January 1950, at the age of 66

Sources: Swedberg (1994); Reisman (2004).

of the government, and the Great Depression during the 1930s made Schumpeter's theory irrelevant and even wrong.

However, Schumpeter's reasoning has remained a basic point of reference for many of his successors, both those who follow his tradition of regarding the entrepreneur as an innovative pathbreaker (for example, Dahmén, 1950; Leibenstein, 1968; Baumol, 1968, 1990) and for those economists who put forward alternative interpretations of the entrepreneur (for example, members of the Austrian school represented by Friedrich von Hayek, Ludwig von Mises, and more recently, Kirzner, 1973).

From Economic to Behavioural Science

Despite some exceptions of entrepreneurship research within the discipline of economics, for a long time entrepreneurship continued to be largely overlooked in economic science models – models often based on a strong equilibrium paradigm in which there seems to be little room for the entrepreneur (Baumol, 1968). In addition, after the Second World War it was important to stimulate individuals to start businesses and get development in society under way, and in the 1950s the availability of entrepreneurial ability was considered a vital factor in economic development. It was tempting to try to find an individual profile leading to entrepreneurial success (or failure). We must also keep in mind that during the war there was a strong development of (and confidence in) psychological instruments that could be helpful in selecting people for certain tasks, for example, to be a fighter pilot, an officer in command and so on. Following this line of thinking, it would be possible to identify and encourage those personalities appropriate to engage in an entrepreneurial career. However, economists could not play a useful role in identifying and developing this ability. Instead, behavioural science researchers, and especially psychologists, saw an open field and increasingly assumed responsibility for continuing the theoretical development on entrepreneurship. The point of departure in this respect was: why do some individuals tend to start their own business whereas others do not? The answer was: it depends on the fact that some individuals have certain qualities that others lack.

David McClelland

Even though we could find many pioneering exponents for the behavioural approach in entrepreneurship research, perhaps the best-known researcher among behavioural scientists with an interest in entrepreneurship is David McClelland, who was one of the first to present empirical studies in the field of entrepreneurship that were based on behavioural science theory. In his pioneering work *The Achieving Society* (1961), McClelland discussed the question: why are certain societies more dynamic than others? For McClelland, the premise was that the norms and values that prevail in any given society, particularly with regard to the need for achievement (nACH) are of vital importance for the development of the society. By means of a large number of experimentally constructed studies, he demonstrated the link between a country's need for achievement and its economic development. He concluded that countries that are economically more developed are characterized by a stronger focus on institutional norms and openness towards other people and their values, as well as communication between people. It is in this context that entrepreneurs have been recognized as an important driving force for development. Entrepreneurs are people who have a high need for achievement coupled with strong self-confidence, independent problem-solving skills and who prefer situations that are characterized by moderate risk, while accepting individual responsibility.

McClelland was regarded as one of the leading researchers in personality and motivation psychology, and during his career he wrote 16 books and about 185 scientific papers. Best known are his books *Personality* published in 1951, which was used as a textbook as late as the 1980s, and *Human Motivation* (1987), in which he summarized much of his thinking on human personality and motivation. (Box I.2.)

Throughout McClelland's career he was guided by his motto 'if something exists, it exists in some amount and can be measured' and that a theory cannot be accepted until tested by rigorous quantitative measurements. In addition, it is possible to identify some salient themes in McClelland's production that characterize his research on human motivation:

BOX I.2 THE CAREER OF DAVID MCCLELLAND

1917	Born on 20 May in New York, one of five children of a Methodist college president. His religious background (he later became an active Quaker) may explain his interest in solving 'real-world' problems, and his desire to help the socially maladjusted in society
1942	PhD at Yale University
1941–56	Wesleyan University in Connecticut
1956–87	Professor at Harvard University
1998	Died 27 March 1998

- a commitment to measurement – everything could be measured and transformed into numbers;
- a fascination with Sigmund Freud and the unconscious – he studied the underlying dimensions in the personality that motivate behaviour, and he believed that the motivations should crystallize into concrete behaviour; and
- a belief that motivations can be changed – during his career he developed different education programmes for altering people's motivational profiles.

McClelland's contributions meant that the personal qualities of the entrepreneur occupied a prominent position in entrepreneurship research during the 1960s and 1970s, and there are a large number of studies that try to identify the particular qualities of the entrepreneur (see summaries in Brockhaus, 1982 and Delmar, 2000), such as the need for achievement, risk-taking propensity, locus of control, overoptimism, and desire for autonomy.

. . . to a Management Science

After the Second World War, Keynesian economic theory, suggesting increased government interventions to manage cyclical fluctuations, seemed to be working, and there was a positive economic development in society. The importance of entrepreneurship and small businesses seemed to fade away, and many scholars supported Schumpeter's declaration (1942) that 'what we have got to accept is that the large-scale establishment has come to be the most powerful engine of progress' (p. 106). The notion that large-scale production and a social order with strong collectivistic elements were conducive to economic development was firmly established among social scientists at the time.

It was in the mid-1970s that the world economy first began to show signs that large systems were not always superior in promoting technological development. The 'twin oil' crises triggered an appraisal of the role of small firms. Many large companies were hit by severe economic difficulties, and unemployment became a major problem in many Western societies. Large companies were increasingly seen as inflexible and slow to adjust to new market conditions. Carlsson (1992) found two explanations for a greater interest in smaller firms: (i) a fundamental change in the world economy, related to the intensification of global competition, the increase in the degree of uncertainty, and greater market fragmentation, and (ii) changes in the characteristics of technological progress. As a consequence, new areas of interest emerged and topics such as entrepreneurship, innovation, industrial dynamics and job generation (Acs, 1992) came to dominate the political debate. This development received additional support from politicians such as Ronald Reagan in the US and Margaret Thatcher in the UK, who pursued a policy strongly in favour of promoting small business and entrepreneurship.

David Birch

It was in this context that entrepreneurship research *per se* began to develop. David Birch, in his pathbreaking report *The Job Generation Process* (1979), found that the majority of employment opportunities in the US were created by small and young firms – not large companies. Birch was interested in understanding how jobs were created. The main problem was to obtain adequate data – existing databases were not equipped to cope with large longitudinal data. Birch and his research group used Dun & Bradstreet data in the US from 1969 to 1976, making considerable efforts to facilitate the analysis of the data over time. The study focused on job creation, and some interesting findings emerged. For example, migration of firms from one region to another played a negligible role, and job losses seemed to be about the same everywhere. Thus, it was not the rate of closures, which varied from one region to another, but rather the rate of job replacements that was crucial for the growth or decline of a region. Birch found that the majority of new jobs were created by firms – often independent and young firms – with 20 or fewer employees. The conclusion was that it was not the large firms in the economy that created new jobs, but the small and young firms.

The report (54 pages) sold only 12 copies; however its influence was enormous, not least on policy makers, but it also had a huge impact on the research community. Although it has been a source of considerable controversy and criticism, it has nevertheless provided the intellectual foundation for research throughout the world to incorporate young and small firms into the analyses of economic development, and many of the findings have been verified in a host of later studies. (Box I.3.)

Birch was not alone in his interest in entrepreneurship and small businesses, a large number of enthusiastic researchers with different backgrounds and different interests began to pour into this new and promising area. The growth of entrepreneurship as an academic field had begun.

The Emergence of an Academic Field

In the 1980s we can find an increasing interest in entrepreneurship and small business among scholars, especially in management studies, who became

BOX I.3 THE CAREER OF DAVID BIRCH

1937	Born 1937
1959	MSc in nuclear reactor design at Harvard University
1962	MBA at Harvard University
1962–66	Research engineer at the General Astronautics and Jet Propulsion Laboratory
1966	PhD in economics at Harvard Business School
1966–74	Harvard Business School
1974–93	MIT Center for Urban Studies (Director of MIT Program on Jobs, Enterprises and Markets)
1983–2000	CEO and President at Cognetics (consulting firm)

interested in entrepreneurship – leading to the start of a community of entrepreneurship teachers and researchers. This early development was to a high degree characterized by:

- Discovery-orientated research, that is, a focus on providing descriptions and insights about a phenomenon that was previously unfamiliar. The level of methodological sophistication and theoretical analysis in most of the studies was quite low. Churchill (1992) made an analogy with the six blind men and the elephant, stating that it was an unstructured exploration of the elephant – the researchers discovered that this animal was different, that it was composed of a number of unusual parts, and that it was quite large.
- Importation of knowledge, that is, entrepreneurship research had not developed an identity of its own. Instead, it was strongly influenced by the mainstream discipline's terms, concepts, models and methods – mainly from scholars with roots in 'management studies'.
- Individualism, that is, the research community was small and fragmented. Entrepreneurship research was, to a great extent, dependent on individual initiatives and projects.

Interestingly, in the early 1990s there was a systematic shift from an interest in the entrepreneur as an individual (entrepreneurial traits) to contextual and processual aspects of entrepreneurship. In this respect, the pioneering work by William Gartner deserves to be mentioned. As early as 1988, Gartner claimed that '"Who is the entrepreneur?" is the wrong question', arguing that more relevant questions were 'How are new organizations created?' (Gartner, 1988). Even if this development towards a process-orientated approach has taken time, Gartner's ideas are now firmly anchored within entrepreneurship research.

In addition, since the 1990s we have seen an exponential growth of entrepreneurship research – independent of measures used (number of researchers, articles, conferences and so on) – and we know a lot more today about entrepreneurship than we did 20 years ago. In this respect we can identify some influential trends in the development of entrepreneurship research, for example:

- an influx of more theory-driven approaches;
- a change from fragmentation of research towards specialization (with emerging 'tribes');
- international 'isomorphism' (Aldrich, 2000), including a stronger 'normal science approach' in entrepreneurship research;
- increased internal orientation in research; and
- identifiable research community, role models and core researchers.

History Matters!

In the development and maturity of entrepreneurship research, with an increased specialization, increased internal orientation, and core research, there is a stronger need for history:

- it is necessary for knowledge accumulation within the field, that is, knowledge accumulation requires an extensive groundwork;
- some topics in entrepreneurship research recur from time to time, and we do not need to invent the wheel every time we start a project; and
- some of the best and most influential works were written in the early days of entrepreneurship research.

In order to move our field forward we need to look backward!!!

A RELATIONAL VIEW TO RESEARCH AND PRACTICE IN ENTREPRENEURSHIP

Looking at the contributions to the RENT XIX conference in Naples 2005 (Iandoli and Raffa, 2005), the main theme for the conference was 'Entrepreneurship, Competitiveness and Local Development'. The intention of the Scientific Committee was to drive scholars' attention towards the widely acknowledged role played by entrepreneurs and small firms in fostering economic development in emerging as well as in developed countries.

Here we want to introduce the conference's main theme and make some comments from recent perspectives to entrepreneurial studies, which see the relationship between entrepreneurs, local context and development in a multidisciplinary and holistic way.

It is well known that the creative and destructive action of entrepreneurs has been considered as one of the main drivers for value creation in the capitalist economy (Schumpeter, 1934) and as the main source for radical innovation in mature markets, when incumbents have exhausted their capability to look for emerging markets (Christensen, 1997). Following such assumptions, recent policies have been developed to promote entrepreneurship as a key leverage for local development. Some models, for example, the 'Learning Region', widely adopted by major international institutions such as the Organisation for Economic Cooperation and Development (OECD) and the European Union are inspired by this vision and based on the following assumptions:

1. regions and territories are required to assume a proactive and autonomous attitude towards the promotion of the growth and development of local industrial systems by exploiting and enhancing local idiosyncratic resources and competencies; and
2. growth is the result of the local capability to construct, develop, foster and integrate local networks of resources, relationships and competencies.

The Learning Region perspective is clearly inspired to the resource-based view – RBV (Barney, 1991; Conner, 1991), in which competitive advantage is related to firms' capability to acquire and develop rare and inimitable resources. Such resources have been classified as natural, infrastructural, technological, financial and human. The RBV criticizes Michael Porter's approach (Porter, 1990), which traces back competitive advantage to structural reasons related to industry characteristics. By reducing the role of structural explanation of competitive advantage, the RBV founds entrepreneurial success on uniqueness and exceptions, including the entrepreneur's subjectivity.

A more recent perspective, the relational view, tries to escape from the juxtaposition between a structural versus individual explanation of competitive advantage, and assumes social networks and relational issues as more comprehensive and crucial competitive factors (Dyer and Singh, 1998). According to the relational view, the analysis of the relationships between firms is a critical research issue for understanding the creation of competitive advantage. According to this perspective, firms' relationships are constructed on four potential sources: (i) relation-specific asset; (ii) knowledge-sharing routines; (iii) complementary resources and capabilities; and (iv) effective governance.

Industrial districts, firm clusters and Japanese *keiretsu* are examples of networks that nurture their competitive advantages on relational assets. Furthermore, the competitiveness of such networks is strongly influenced by location and geographic proximity. In other words, companies belonging to such embedded networks base a significant part of their competitive advantage on their membership to a local business community.

According to Uzzi (1996) firms can be embedded in such networks in which 'the structure and quality of social ties among firms shape economic action by creating unique opportunities and access to those opportunities' (p. 675). The relationship between embeddedness and performance is problematic: if embeddedness is too weak or too strong, then firms experience lower performances, in the former case because they are unable to exploit relational assets, in the latter because excess of embeddedness brings about closure towards novelty and inability to innovate.

In the relational view perspective and by assuming embeddedness as a driver for firm performance, traditional categories of analysis and research subjects need to be reframed in a more systemic way. Many papers presented at the RENT XIX conference, especially those more coherent with the conference theme, appear to be aware of this necessity.

Through a review of the papers accepted for presentation we have looked for both dominant and emerging research issues and tried to reframe them into a holistic view in which social ties, relationships between firms and embeddedness within a local business community represent a possible perspective of analysis to explain the relationship between entrepreneurship and competitiveness. In particular we want to focus readers' attention on the following aspects:

- the local context as socio-geographic entity;
- the importance of knowledge flow and creation in local networks;
- organizational models and management issues for small firms operating within local networks; and
- the role of entrepreneurs within networks.

The Local Context as Socio-geographic Entity

Research on small business management, especially those adopting an institutionalist view (Scott, 1995), underlines the influence on entrepreneurial action of the territory, meant as a social, cultural and geographic whole. Culture, local entrepreneurial tradition, norms and values of a community produce remarkable effects on the motivations and managerial style of entrepreneurs as well as on the ways in which firms interact and aggregate (Becattini, 2000; Rullani, 2002).

It is important to remark that the dependence of small firms on their territory is not only cultural but also structural. Small firms are incomplete economic actors, which depend much more than large companies on the external environment for the acquisition of critical resources, such as professional capabilities, knowledge and financial assets. What matters is that such assets can be better described and understood bearing in mind their relational nature. The strength of the relationship between firms and their territory represents a force that may hinder globalization and internationalization processes.

Papers presented at the RENT conference that may be classified in this research stream focus on the following topics: global entrepreneurship and internationalization, company growth and survival, developing economies, industrial districts and clusters, social capital, supporting policies for small business and the role of regional governments for local development.

The Importance of Knowledge Flow and Creation in Local Networks

Research on firm networks has investigated the role of knowledge in influencing network performance and individual behaviour. Soda et al. (2004) outline the effects on outcomes of enduring patterns of relationships and comment that 'a past network with its accumulated relational experience becomes a kind of "network memory" that cannot be ignored as it may project a structural overhang over the present, much like a shadow of the past' (p. 893).

Uzzi (1996) relates firm network performance to embeddedness, that is, the capability of a social network to develop dense and strongly interconnected relationships among firms based on mutual trust, reputation, resources sharing and complementarity (Dyer and Singh, 1998). Successful patterns of actions and interactions give rise to tacit knowledge embedded in routines (Nelson and Winter, 1982).

Papers that can be classified in this cluster, representing perhaps the most numerous category, focus on topics such as alliances, interaction with universities and public research (academic spin-off, research-based venture, and so on), regional innovation systems, knowledge sharing in firm networks, start-up, innovation management, network theory and small firms in the extended enterprise.

Organizational Models and Management Issues for Small Firms Operating within Local Networks

Small firms are characterized by blurred organizational borders (Raffa and Zollo, 2000) because of their higher dependency on external resources through a number of different ways. In other words, some kinds of resources can be said to belong to a firm with a certain degree of membership. The organizational model of small firms tends to be fuzzy and loosely coupled, and this ensures high organizational flexibility. Adaptation and rapidity are the result of loosely coupled organizational models characterized by a lack of formalization, weak coordination, and strong overlapping between entrepreneurial and managerial behaviours (Hansoff, 1975; Marchini, 1995). Small businesses are themselves networked organizations moving in a wider relational and knowledge network. Such organizational and strategic characteristics make problematic the adoption of traditional management approaches developed in large companies by small firms. Second, the management of a dense network of relationships based on the sharing and exchange of assets requires the development of ad hoc tools and new management attitudes.

Papers that can be classified in this stream deal with the following research subjects: family business, management systems for small firms, knowledge sharing, creation and management, human resource and intellectual capital management, decision making, accounting, planning and control, information technology diffusion, adoption and implementation, and finance (loans, venture capital).

The Role of Entrepreneurs within Networks

The analysis of entrepreneurs' subjectivity and individual characteristics is a traditional research stream in the small business management research agenda. Actually, in small businesses the entrepreneur plays a major role in shaping organizational lay-out and firm strategy (Schollhammer and Kuriloff, 1979; Stanworth et al., 1989). Both organization and firm strategy are constructed around an entrepreneur's action. Entrepreneurial action develops from an entrepreneur's perception and sense-making of opportunities and threats. Plans, coordination and resource allocation all depend on this perceived world. Firm governance tends to be based more on intuition and entrepreneurial cognition rather than on formalization and planning. As a consequence, decision making is strongly influenced by individual characteristics of entrepreneurs such as traits, motivation, cognitive bias, intuition and gender. Decisions are seldom communicated and discussed with other managers and employees, and entrepreneurs very often tend to centralize both operative and strategic responsibilities.

Papers that can be classified in this cluster focus on topics such as entrepreneur training and learning, gender and diversity, traits and attitudes, cognitive issues, motivation and leadership.

ENTREPRENEURIAL ACTION IN EMBEDDED LOCAL NETWORKS

In the embeddedness perspective, the local context, intended as a mix of physical, social and cultural assets, plays a major role in shaping entrepreneurs' behaviour and firm performance. On the other hand, this perspective is not deterministic if one conceives entrepreneurial action as the result of a sense-making process (Weick, 1979), in which the entrepreneur scans the context, frames environmental clues into opportunities and threats, enacts possible patterns of action and activates accessible resources within the network (Fayolle and Bruyat, 2002; Johannisson, 2002; Stam, 2002). In this way, both objectivist and subjectivist research approaches to entrepreneurship find a higher synthesis that acknowledges the idiosyncratic and situated nature of entrepreneurship, but at the same time considers entrepreneurial behaviour as a combination of structural/social constraints and individual initiative.

By making sense of the local environment, entrepreneurs frame problems in terms of two kinds of critical situations (Capaldo and Iandoli, 2005): those related to the management of the relational assets and those concerning the management of internal assets (Figure I.1).

According to the model proposed in Figure I.1, entrepreneurial action is the construction of satisfying solutions to perceived critical situations.

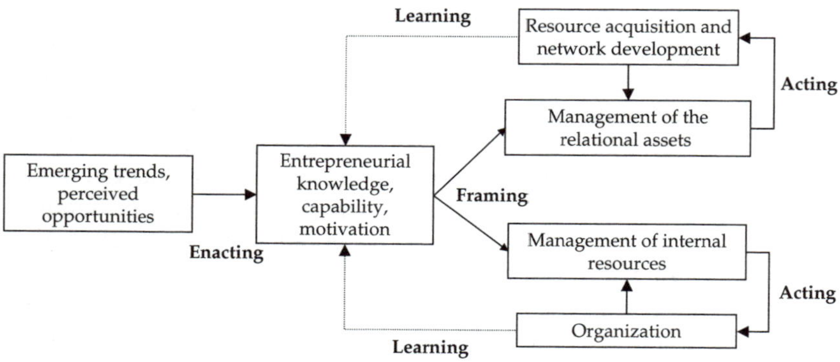

Source: Adapted from Capaldo and Iandoli (2005).

Figure I.1 A model for entrepreneurial action

Such solutions pertain both to action on the context aimed at managing and developing relational assets, and action on the firm, aimed at allocating and coordinating resources and processes (Davidsson, 2001). Thus, what characterizes entrepreneurial action is not only creativity and opportunity seizing but a variable mix of exploration and administration, whose composition may be influenced by many factors such as an entrepreneur's individual characteristics, cultural issues and structural variables.

In a perspective based on action and sense-making, the distinction between the 'what to do' (strategy) and the 'how to do' (organization) becomes blurred. This lack of distinction explains the loosely coupled character of small-firm organization in which decisional responsibilities and operations are not separated. In such conditions, strategy collapses into action and organization into organizational improvisation (Weick, 1998). Through time, strategy and action in small firms are modelled around predefined or imitable models such as recipes and routines (Nelson and Winter, 1982) and are constrained by an environment perceived as a set of opportunities, threats and accessible resources.

The different theoretical perspectives evoked above and ranging from a knowledge-based theory of the firm (Penrose, 1959; Fransman, 1994; Grant, 1996) to RBV and the relational view can find a possible synthesis into the concept of 'entrepreneurial competence' (Capaldo et al., 2005). Entrepreneurial competence can be defined as the capability of entrepreneurs to face effectively a critical situation by making sense of environmental constraints and by activating relational and internal specific resources.

In a competence-based view of entrepreneurship, the context becomes relevant not only as a set of objective constraints and available resources but also as both an individual construction shaped by an entrepreneur's perceptions and intuitions, and a social construction influenced by embeddedness. Entrepreneurial competence is then the entrepreneur's capability to notice what others do not see but also to exploit embedded relational resources through a mix of openness and embeddedness. For the research purpose, competencies can be assumed as conjectures aimed at explaining superior performance and at describing entrepreneurial behaviour.

As shown by Figure I.1, entrepreneurial action starts from and ends with entrepreneurial competencies. Literature about competence management, developed in other fields such as human resource management, can be evoked to better characterize the concept of entrepreneurial competence in terms of three fundamental dimensions (Boyatzis, 1983): knowledge, skills and motivations. Although several competency models have been proposed in the literature and there is no dominant agreement about competency definition, this proposal can be justified on the basis of the following reasons:

1. Emphasis on knowledge, intended above all as technical and specialized knowledge, is acceptable given the usual strong involvement of entrepreneurs in technical activities; this is true particularly in emerging and hi-tech industries where small firms' founders are technical entrepreneurs.
2. Emphasis on skills permits us to take into account the tacit, routine and situated nature of entrepreneurial capabilities. If any work knowledge can be assumed to have a tacit component, the tacit face of the entrepreneurial activity is even more relevant, because such activity is strongly based on action and learning by doing in ill-structured high discretionary work situations, such as the ones usually experienced by entrepreneurs.
3. Motivation has been widely acknowledged as a fundamental element of entrepreneurial behaviour (Stanworth et al., 1989; Davidsson, 1995; Bird, 1989); the proactive nature of entrepreneurial action is based on deep motivational factors ranging from personal characteristics (self-esteem, sense of achievement and so on) to strong social commitment. Motivation, considered as a determinant of action, represents the energy needed to activate and nurture knowledge and skills and to transform them from potentialities to working capabilities. Motivation is the wishful side of entrepreneurial competence.

We think that entrepreneurial competencies can constitute a research object that can attract the interest of scholars with different backgrounds and following different research perspectives or interested in different management or policy issues concerning small business and entrepreneurship. The relational view, thanks to its holistic vision of entrepreneurial behaviour, can favour the convergence and the comparison of different points of view, thus increasing the potential for joint research projects. Finally, managerial implications entailed by a competence-based view of entrepreneurship can attract the attention of practitioners and institutions interested in enhancing and supporting small business development.

ORGANIZATION OF THE BOOK

The aim of this book is to collect and present the best papers presented at the RENT XIX conference co-organized by the Department of Business and Managerial Engineering – ODISSEO, University of Naples Federico II, ECSB and EIASM, hosted at the University of Naples Federico II on 17–19 November 2005.

Further clarification may be needed at this point about the selection process. More than 250 papers and abstracts from more than 30 countries were submitted to the conference. After a review process performed by the members of the Scientific Committee, 131 papers were accepted for presentation with an acceptance rate of about 50 per cent. After the conference a gross list of 45 papers was defined, starting from the recommendation of session chairpersons. These then underwent a first review round managed by the editors of this book, at the end of which 15 were selected and sent out for a second review round to the members of the editorial board. At the end of this stage, 11 were selected and reviewed by the authors. They appear in this book in alphabetical order of first author initial. In the following we introduce them briefly.

In Chapter 1, Fabio Bertoni, Massimo Colombo and Luca Grilli analyse the causality relation between venture capital (VC) financing and growth in the number of high-tech small-firm employees through a longitudinal dataset relating to a sample composed of 537 Italian companies. The results of the econometric analysis performed by the authors strongly support the argument that VC financing spurs firm growth. Conversely, only weak evidence is provided that firm growth leads to a greater likelihood of obtaining VC.

Stijn Bruyneel, Martin Carree and Ludo Peeters (Chapter 2) search for a relation between the employment status of the individual and his or her probability of becoming an entrepreneur. Data from the Belgian Global Entrepreneurship Monitor (GEM) are used in a logistic regression model. It was found that unemployed Belgians were less likely to become an entrepreneur. However, merely claiming that unemployed individuals who are involved in a start-up act out of necessity has been found to be an incomplete account of the decision process. No relationship with age, gender, risk or education emerges from the study.

Gerhard Dijkstra, Ron Kemp and Clemens Lutz (Chapter 3) investigate the relationship between entry barriers and real entry and show that some barriers seem to influence the starter ratio more strongly. Remarkably, from their study it emerges that several of the most important perceived barriers do not restrict real entry rates. This result contains an interesting lesson for policy makers. They should not address important barriers *per se*, but scrutinize the effects of barriers that seem to restrict real entry.

Rudolf Dömötör and Christopher Hader (Chapter 4) compare traditional entrepreneurial traits and entrepreneurial attitudes with regard to their ability to predict future entrepreneurial behaviour. The practical benefit of such a comparison would be the ability to use these instruments more effectively in predicting future entrepreneurship and in training future entrepreneurs. On the basis of an empirical study the authors show that attitudes represent better predictors of entrepreneurial intent than do entrepreneurial traits.

Jonas Gabrielsson and Diamanto Politis (Chapter 5) develop theory-driven hypotheses on entrepreneurial decision making and empirically test them on a sample of entrepreneurs in order to increase the understanding of causal and effectual decision making in entrepreneurial settings. They develop exploratory measures to assess the extent to which entrepreneurs are involved in causal and effectual modes of decision making and integrate concepts and models from career theory into the entrepreneurship field to understand how different career motives may guide and constrain future entrepreneurs' decision making.

Petra Gibcus, Pauline de Jong-'t Hart and Ron Kemp (Chapter 6) examine the determinants of growth of start-ups in the Netherlands by distinguishing between environmental and internal determinants (entrepreneurial and organizational) of growth through a longitudinal dataset containing 10 years of information on start-ups. Their study shows that several determinants seem to have a positive effect on growth, among which are the ambition to expand, unfulfilled needs, networking and organizational learning through employees.

Siri Terjesen and Colm O'Gorman (Chapter 7) explore female involvement in the supply of, and demand for, new venture finance in Ireland in order to understand whether there are differences in the financing of new ventures planned by female and male nascent entrepreneurs. Given the paucity of research on female entrepreneurship activity, they report the demographic profiles and aspects of personal context of the entrepreneurs and informal investors and seek to explain why it is that Irish females, as compared to Irish males, have a lower demand for entrepreneurial finance and are less involved in informal investment activity.

Lorraine Uhlaner and Jerry van Santen (Chapter 8) examine the relationship between organization contextual variables and knowledge management (KM) practices in small and medium-sized enterprises (SMEs). The proposed research model is explored empirically using a sample of 16 Dutch technology-based SMEs. Size and membership with a trade organization and/or having a large supplier are all found to predict certain KM practices. In contrast to expectations, a strong positive relationship is found between the family business variable and certain enabling practices. A positive relationship is found especially between degree of formalization of capturing and locating practices and quality performance.

Bram Wauters and Johan Lambrecht (Chapter 9) focus on refugee entrepreneurship. The aim of this chapter is to examine the current situation regarding refugee entrepreneurship in Belgium. The authors tested five motivational theories for becoming an entrepreneur among refugees and found that the main motive was hope of facilitating integration into the host society. Reasons that also apply to native entrepreneurs, such as being one's own boss (the entrepreneur model), also score high. Negative motives (a way out of unemployment) score low in this form of self-reporting.

Friederike Welter, David Smallbone, Nina Isakova and Elena Aculai (Chapter 10) explore similarities and differences between male and female entrepreneurs, and their businesses and strategies in different transition environments. Their analysis illustrates that in a transition context there are more similarities than differences, essentially because the difficult nature of the external environment facing entrepreneurs is a dominant influence. Overall, the results emphasize the need to look at entrepreneurship within its social and economic context, which also might explain differences that are often taken as gender related.

Frits Wijbenga, Theo Postma and Rebecca Stratling (Chapter 11) propose a multi-theoretical approach to investigate the role of venture capitalists (VCs) in the strategy development and evaluation process of the entrepreneurial firm and to understand whether the VC enhances the entrepreneurial firm's control systems and accordingly contributes to entrepreneurial firm performance. The results indicate that VCs play an enabling role for effective use of firms' control systems, facilitating stability and efficiency. Furthermore, VC services facilitate the entrepreneurial firm's utilization of cost control and incentive and reward systems and have an indirect effect on organizational performance. The results also suggest that VCs tend to pay too little attention to the establishment of quality systems in entrepreneurial firms.

ACKNOWLEDGEMENTS

We wish to thank Odd Jarl Borch, Hermann Frank, Bengt Johannisson, Asko Miettinen, Monder Ram, Peter Rosa, David Smallbone and Friederike Welter for their valuable work as reviewers of the contributions contained in this book – their efforts have definitely contributed to raising the overall quality standard.

Moreover, we wish to thank Asko Miettinen (Tampere University of Technology), Antti Paasio (Turku School of Economics, Finland), David Smallbone (Kingston University, UK), Roy Thurik (Erasmus Universiteit Rotterdam, The Netherlands), Gerry Van Dyck (EIASM, Brussels, Belgium) and José M. Veciana (Universidad Autonoma de Barcelona, Spain), members of the RENT 2005 Scientific Committee, for their valuable work in selecting the 131 papers accepted for presentation at the conference, which represented the starting-point for the preparation of this book.

REFERENCES

Acs, Z.J. (1992), 'Small business economics: a global perspective', *Challenge*, **35**, 38–44.

Aldrich, H.E. (2000), 'Learning together: national differences in entrepreneurship research', in D.L. Sexton and H. Landström (eds), *The Blackwell Handbook of Entrepreneurship*, Oxford: Blackwell, pp. 5–25.

Barney, J.B. (1991), 'Firm resources and sustained competitive advantage', *Journal of Management*, **17**, 99–120.

Baumol, W.J. (1968), 'Entrepreneurship in economic theory', *American Economic Review*, **58** (2), 64–71.

Baumol, W.J. (1990), 'Entrepreneurship: productive, unproductive and destructive', *Journal of Political Economy*, **98** (5), 893–921.

Becattini G. (2000), *Il distretto industriale*, Turin: Rosenberg & Sellier.

Birch, D.L. (1979), *The Job Generation Process*, Cambridge, MA: MIT Program on Neighborhood and Regional Change.

Bird, B. (1989), *Entrepreneurial Behavior*, Glenview, IL: Scott Foresman & Co.

Boyatzis, R.E. (1983), *The Competent Manager*, New York: Wiley.

Brockhaus, R. (1982), 'The psychology of the entrepreneur', in C.A. Kent, D.L. Sexton and K.H. Vesper (eds), *Encyclopedia of Entrepreneurship*, Englewood Cliffs, NJ: Prentice-Hall, pp. 39–71.

Capaldo, G. and L. Iandoli (2005), 'Un apporccio metodologico basato sulle competenze per la rilevazione dei fabbisogni formativi nelle piccole imprese', in G. Capaldo, L. Iandoli and P. Montobbio (eds), *Piccole Imprese e Competenze*, Naples: ESI, pp. 15–24.

Capaldo, G., L. Iandoli and C. Ponsiglione (2005), 'Entrepreneurial competencies and training needs of small firms: a methodological approach', *Piccola Impresa/Small Business*, **2**, 115–35.

Carlsson, B. (1992), 'The rise of small business: causes and consequences', in W.J. Adams (ed.), *Singular Europe: Economy and Policy of the European Community after 1992*, Ann Arbor, MI: University of Michigan Press, pp. 145–69.

Christensen, C.M. (1997), *The Innovator's Dilemma*, Boston, MA: Harvard Business School Press.

Churchill, N.C. (1992), 'Research issues in entrepreneurship', in D.L. Sexton and J.D. Kasarda (eds), *The State of the Art of Entrepreneurship*, Boston, MA: PWS-Kent, pp. 579–96

Conner, K.R. (1991), 'A historical comparison of resource-based theory and five schools of thought within industrial organization economics: do we have a new theory of the firms?', *Journal of Management*, **17**, 121–54.

Dahmén, E. (1950), *Svensk industriell företagsverksamhet*, Stockholm: IUI.

Davidsson, P. (2001), 'Towards a paradigm for entrepreneurship research', paper presented at the RENT XV conference, Turku, 22 November.

Delmar, F. (2000), 'The psychology of the entrepreneur', in S. Carter and D. Jones-Evans (eds), *Enterprise and Small Business*, Harlow: Pearson Education, pp. 132–54.

Dyer, J.H. and H. Singh (1998), 'The relational view: cooperative strategy and sources of interorganizational competitive advantage', *Academy of Management Review*, **23** (4), 660–79.

Fayolle, A. and C. Bruyat (2002), 'A conceptual and methodological framework to study, using the modelling of complex system, the foundation and the develop-

ment processes of innovative business activities', paper presented at the RENT XVI conference, Barcelona, 21–22 November.
Fransman, M. (1994), 'Information, knowledge, vision and theories of the firm', *Industrial and Corporate Change*, **3** (2), 1–45.
Gartner, W.B. (1988), ' "Who is an entrepreneur?" is the wrong question', *American Journal of Small Business*, Spring, 11–32.
Grant, R.M. (1996), 'Toward a knowledge-based theory of the firm', *Strategic Management Journal*, **17**, 109–22.
Hansoff, H.I. (1975), 'The state of practice in management systems', Working Paper 75, EIASM, Brussels.
Iandoli, L. and M. Raffa (2005), *Entrepreneurship, Competitiveness and Local Development*, Naples: Edizioni Scientifiche Italiane.
Johannisson, B. (2002), 'Entrepreneurship as breaking and making sense-learning beyond boundaries', paper presented at the RENT XVI conference, Barcelona, 21–22 November.
Keynes, J.M. (1936 [1973]), *General Theory of Employment, Interest and Money*, New York: Harcourt Brace.
Kirzner, I.M. (1973), *Competition and Entrepreneurship*, Chicago: Chicago University Press.
Knight, F.H. (1916 [1921]), *Risk, Uncertainty and Profit*, New York: Houghton Mifflin.
Landström, H. (2005), *Pioneers in Entrepreneurship and Small Business Research*, New York: Springer.
Leibenstein, H. (1968), 'Entrepreneurship and development', *American Economic Review*, **58**, 72–83.
Marchini, I. (1995), *Il governo della piccola impresa*, Vols I and II, Urbino: Aspi/InsEdit.
McClelland, D.C. (1951), *Personality*, New York: Holt, Rinehart & Winston.
McClelland, D.C. (1961), *The Achieving Society*, Princeton, NJ: van Nostrand.
McClelland, D.C. (1987), *Human Motivation*, Cambridge: Cambridge University Press.
Nelson, R.R. and S.G. Winter (1982), *An Evolutionary Theory of Economic Change*, Cambridge, MA: The Belknap Press of Harvard University Press.
Penrose, E.T. (1959), *The Theory of the Growth of the Firm*, Oxford: Basil Blackwell.
Porter, M. (1990), *The Competitive Advantage of Nations*, New York: Free Press.
Raffa, M. and G. Zollo (2000), *Economia del software. Elementi introduttivi*, Naples: Edizioni Scientifiche Italiane.
Reisman, D. (2004), *Schumpeter's Market: Enterprise and Evolution*, Cheltenham, UK and Northampton, MA, USA: Edward Elgar.
Rullani, E. (2002), 'Il distretto industriale come sistema adattivo complesso', in Quadrio Curzio and M. Fortis (eds), *Complessità e Distretti Industriali*, Bologna: Il Mulino, pp. 65–110.
Schollhammer, H. and A.H. Kuriloff (1979), *Entrepreneurship and Small Business Management*, Chichester: Wiley.
Schumpeter, J.A. (1912), *Theorie der Wirtschaftlichen Entwicklung*, Leipzig: Duncker & Humblot.
Schumpeter, J.A. (1934), *The Theory of Economic Development*, Cambridge, MA: Harvard University Press.
Schumpeter, J.A. (1942), *Capitalism, Socialism and Democracy*, New York: Harper & Row.

Scott, W.R. (1995), *Institutions and Organizations: Foundations for Organizational Science*, Thousand Oaks, CA: Sage.
Smith, A. (1776 [1994]), *The Wealth of Nations*, E. Cannan (ed.), New York: Modern Library.
Soda, G., A. Usai and A. Zaheer (2004), 'Network memory: the influence of past and current networks on performance', *Academy of Management Journal*, **47** (6), 893–906.
Stam, E. (2002), 'Theorizing entrepreneurship in context', paper presented at the RENT XVI conference, Barcelona, 21–22 November.
Stanworth J., S. Blythe, B. Granger and C. Stanworth (1989), 'Who becomes an *International* entrepreneur?', *Small Business Journal*, **8** (1), 11–22.
Swedberg, R. (1994), *Schumpeter: Omskapande förstörelse och entreprenörskap*, Stockholm: Ratio.
Uzzi, B. (1996), 'The sources and consequences of embeddedness for the economic performance of organizations', *American Sociological Review*, **61**, 674–98.
Weick, K.E. (1979), *The Social Psychology of Organization*, 2nd edn, Reading, MA: Addison Wesley.
Weick, K.E. (1998), 'Improvisation as a mindset for organizational analysis', *Organization Science*, **9** (5), 543–55.
Wennekers, S. and R. Thurik (1999), 'Linking entrepreneurship and economic growth', *Small Business Economics*, **13** (1), 27–55.

1. Venture capital financing and the growth of new technology-based firms: what comes first?

Fabio Bertoni, Massimo G. Colombo and Luca Grilli

INTRODUCTION

It is generally acknowledged by the economic literature that new firms, especially new technology-based firms (NTBFs), greatly contribute to the static and dynamic efficiency of the economic system (see, for instance, Audretsch, 1995). A conspicuous body of empirical studies has analysed the determinants of their post-entry performances (for a survey, see Colombo and Grilli, 2005). This literature generally shows that firms financed by venture capital (VC) grow faster than their non-VC-backed counterparts.

However, this evidence is compatible with two fundamentally different arguments. On the one hand, the positive correlation between VC financing and firm growth is generally interpreted as evidence that this type of financing spurs growth. Studies in financial economics argue that due to capital market imperfections, it is difficult for NTBFs to obtain the external financing they need. Even though this reasoning especially applies to debt financing, the cost of external equity capital may also be very high for NTBFs. Hence, in accordance with the 'financing hierarchy' hypothesis (Fazzari et al., 1988), NTBFs generally resort to personal capital to finance operations. In turn, lack of adequate funds may hinder a firm's growth (Carpenter and Petersen, 2002a, 2002b). As a corollary, VC financing may be instrumental in removing these binding financial constraints.

On the other hand, rapidly growing firms are also more likely both to demand and to obtain VC. In other words, there may be a reverse causality with a firm's growth attracting VC.

In this chapter we analyse the causality relation between VC financing and growth in the number of a firm's employees. For this purpose, we take advantage of a longitudinal dataset relating to a sample composed of 537

Italian NTBFs. We first estimate survival data analysis models to check whether (lagged) growth of the number of employees influences the likelihood of subsequently obtaining VC financing. Then we estimate fixed-effects (FE) and generalized method of moments (GMM) panel data models to check whether (lagged) dummy variables capturing VC financing drive the subsequent growth of the number of employees.

The results of the econometric analysis strongly support the argument that VC financing spurs a firm's growth. Conversely, only weak evidence is provided that this growth leads to a greater likelihood of obtaining VC.

The chapter is structured as follows. The next section summarizes the literature about the relationship between growth and VC. Thereafter follows a section that describes the sample and sampling procedure, and some descriptive statistics. A further section deals with the effect of a firm's growth (and other firm- and industry-specific characteristics) on the likelihood of obtaining VC, and then a model of the effect of VC financing on a firm's growth is presented. The last section elaborates on the causality relationship between VC and growth and concludes the chapter.

THE RELATIONSHIP BETWEEN A FIRM'S GROWTH AND VC FINANCING

There are basically three reasons why VC financing should spur the growth of the participating NTBF. The first argument relates to the 'scouting' function performed by VC investors. In fact, due to lack of a track record, the scarcity of publicly available information, and the inherent complexity of the business of most NTBFs, these firms suffer from information asymmetries that make external financing problematic. According to this argument, VC investors are better able to distinguish between 'good' and 'bad' investment opportunities than are other investors (Chan, 1983; Zacharakis and Meyer, 1998, 2000). Therefore, due to their superior screening capabilities they can spot the 'hidden value' of an NTBF and provide it with adequate financing, thus removing the financial constraints that would otherwise inhibit growth.

The second argument relates to the 'monitoring' function performed by VC investors and the reduction of *ex post* information asymmetries. In fact, the ongoing involvement of the VC investor in the participating firm has the effect of keeping management 'under pressure', giving it the correct incentives to exert effort.[1] According to this view, VC investors contribute to performance by improving a firm's corporate governance.

Finally, in addition to providing financing to and improving the corporate governance of participating companies, VC investors perform a 'coaching' function. In fact, they provide advisory services and management support relating to financial, administrative, marketing, and other strategic issues where NTBFs typically lack the necessary competencies (Sapienza, 1992; Sapienza et al., 1996; Casamatta, 2003). They also add value to the participating company indirectly, as this company benefits from the network of business contacts of the investor. The positive signal that VC conveys to outsiders also makes it easier for the NTBF to team up with other firms that possess complementary resources and capabilities.

In accordance with the above arguments, the empirical literature has generally highlighted a positive relationship between VC financing and the growth of NTBFs.[2] For instance, Jain and Kini (1995) compare the post-issue performance of a sample of VC-backed IPO (initial public offering) firms with those of a matched sample of non-VC-backed IPO firms and find that both sales and cash flows grow faster for the former. Manigart and Van Hyfte (1999) use a similar methodology to study the growth rate of Belgian VC-backed firms; they find that, if growth is measured by the number of employees, there is no significant difference between VC-backed and non-VC-backed firms; however, if growth is measured on total assets or cash flows, VC-backed firms exhibit a significantly higher performance. Audretsch and Lehmann (2004) analyse a sample of 341 firms that went public on the Neuer Markt between 1997 and 2002; their OLS (ordinary least squares) and quantile regressions show that firms that obtained VC financing grow at a higher rate than firms that are financed by other intermediaries (for instance, banks).

Nevertheless, the evidence mentioned above is also compatible with an opposite causality relationship. In fact, VC investors typically seek promising investment opportunities in young high-tech companies with the intention of realizing a sizeable capital gain. A firm's rapid growth may signal the existence of this kind of opportunity, thus attracting VC. In addition, the demand for VC financing is likely to be greater from fast-growing firms, while for slow-growing firms the personal capital provided by founders, their family and friends may suffice. According to this view, it is a firm's growth that determines VC financing and not the other way round.

Some previous empirical works tried to deal with the bias engendered by the potentially endogenous nature of VC financing. The likelihood of obtaining VC may depend on observed and unobserved factors that also affect growth. Failure to control for the endogeneity bias possibly generated by unobserved heterogeneity across firms may have led to inconsistent estimates in previous studies. Engel (2002) resorts to a two-step estimation procedure to deal with the endogeneity problem. He first considers the effect that firm-specific variables have on the probability of obtaining VC financing. Then he analyses the growth rate, measured by the number of employees, of 1071 start-up firms in Germany between 1991 and 1998, while introducing in the regressions inverse Mill ratio-type control factors. He concludes that even when controlling for endogeneity, VC-backed firms have, on average, a growth rate 170 per cent higher than non-VC-backed firms. A similar methodology is used by Colombo and Grilli (2005), who obtain similar results relating to Italian high-tech start-ups.

Previous studies generally do not use longitudinal datasets. A notable exception is the work by Davila et al. (2003). By means of an event study research design on monthly data, the authors analyse whether VC financing results in superior growth in the number of employees. Focusing attention on VC-backed US high-tech firms, they report that in the six-month period surrounding the financing event, firms that received VC financing on average grew at a higher rate than those that did not get it in the same period. In addition, they find that growth increases significantly in the same month in which financing actually occurred and in the preceding month. Finally, through logit estimates they show that employee growth is not a predictor of VC financing.

Similar results are obtained by Balboa et al. (2006), who compare the absolute growth (both in terms of sales and employees) of 250 Spanish VC-backed companies with a matched sample of non-VC-backed ones. They find that, although VC-backed firms do not differ significantly from matched firms in the years before the investment, they grow significantly more in the following years.

In this chapter we are interested in analysing the causality relationship between VC financing and the growth of a firm's employees. We add to the existing literature in several ways. First, we use longitudinal yearly data relating to a large sample composed of 537 Italian NTBFs (most of which are not listed) that operate in high-tech sectors in manufacturing and services. Second, we use a survival data analysis model to test whether lagged firm growth positively affects the likelihood of obtaining VC financing. Third, we use FE and DIF-GMM panel data models to test whether a firm's growth is stimulated by access to VC financing; in this way we are better able than other previous studies to control for unobserved heterogeneity across firms and other sources of endogeneity biases.

THE SAMPLE

In this chapter we consider a sample of 537 Italian NTBFs. Sample firms were established in 1980 or later, were independent at founding time and remained so at 1 January 2004 (that is, they are not controlled by another business organization even though other organizations may hold minority shareholdings) and operate in the following high-tech sectors in manufacturing and services: computers, electronic components, telecommunication equipment, optical, medical and electronic instruments, biotechnology, pharmaceuticals, advanced materials, aerospace, robotics and process automation equipment, multimedia content, software, Internet services (e-commerce, ISP: Internet service provider, web-related services), and telecommunication (TLC) services. The sample of NTBFs was extracted from the RITA (Research on Entrepreneurship in Advanced Technologies) database, developed at the Politecnico di Milano. The development of the database went through a series of steps.

First, Italian firms that complied with the above criteria relating to age and sector of operations were identified. For the construction of the target population a number of sources were used. These included lists provided by national industry associations, on-line and off-line commercial firm directories, and lists of participants in industry trades and expositions. Information provided by the national financial press, specialized magazines, other sectoral studies, and regional chambers of commerce was also considered. Altogether, 1974 firms were selected for inclusion in the database. For each firm, a contact person (that is, one of the owner-managers) was also identified. Unfortunately, data provided by official national statistics do not allow us to obtain a reliable description of all Italian NTBFs.[3] Second, a questionnaire was sent to the contact person of the target firms either by fax or by e-mail. The first section of the questionnaire provides detailed information on the human capital characteristics of the firm's founders. The second section comprises further questions concerning the characteristics of the firm, including its access to VC financing and its post-entry performance. Finally, answers to the questionnaire were checked for internal coherence by competent personnel and were compared with published data (basically data provided by the firm's annual reports and financial accounts) if they were available. In several cases, phone or face-to-face follow-up interviews were made with the firm's owner-managers. This final step was crucial in order to obtain missing data and ensure that data were reliable.[4]

The sample used in the present work consists of all RITA firms for which we were able to create a complete dataset. Two χ^2 tests show that there are no statistically significant differences between the distributions of the sample firms across industries and regions and the corresponding distribution of the population of 1974 RITA firms from which the sample was obtained ($\chi^2(4) = 3.39$ and $\chi^2(3) = 4.87$, respectively).

The sample is quite large and it exhibits considerable heterogeneity as to the relevant explanatory variables.[5] Note, however, that there is no presumption that this is a random sample. First, in this domain representativeness is a slippery notion as new ventures may be defined in different ways (see, for instance, Birley, 1987; Aldrich et al., 1989; Gimeno et al., 1997). Second, as was mentioned above, in the absence of reliable official statistics, it is very difficult to identify unambiguously all Italian NTBFs. Therefore, one cannot check *ex post* whether the sample used in this work is representative. Third, only firms that have survived up to the survey date could be included in the sample.[6] In principle, attrition may generate a sample selection bias that is difficult to control. As long as failure rates of new firms decrease with the human capital of founders and the benefit of VC financing, the impact of human capital variables on the likelihood of a firm gaining access to this source of financing and the impact of this latter event on the firm's growth might actually be greater than that highlighted by our empirical analysis. None the less, our sample has many interesting characteristics that were missing in those used by most of the previous empirical studies on firms' access to VC financing and its impact on firm performance. First, information in our dataset on the human capital of the founding team is very detailed and fine-grained. Second, we deal with a large number of (mainly unlisted) firms while most of the previous studies are based either on smaller samples (Manigart and Van Hyfte, 1999; Sapienza et al., 1996; Hellmann and Puri, 2000, 2002; Davila et al., 2003; Audretsch and Lehmann, 2004; Bottazzi et al., 2004) or are limited to a particular typology of firms, namely: listed companies (Bottazzi and Da Rin, 2002; Audretsch and Lehmann, 2004), firms that outsourced human resource needs (Davila et al., 2003), and young and large firms located in Silicon Valley (Hellmann and Puri, 2000, 2002).

DESCRIPTIVE STATISTICS

The characteristics of the Italian financial system are quite unfavourable to VC financing in comparison with those of Anglo-Saxon countries. For instance, in Italy the ratio of the market value of listed firms to GDP in 2001 was 48.2 per cent (41.7 per cent in 2004) (source: Consob), while it was 138.0 per cent in the USA and 151.4 per cent in the UK (source: OECD, Financial Market Trends, October 2004). The difference was even larger at the beginning of the 1990s. For instance, Rajan and Zingales (2003) show that in 1990, the ratio of the market value of listed firms to GDP was 13 per cent in Italy, while it was 54 per cent in the USA and 84 per cent in the UK. Conversely, the ratio of bank deposits to GDP was 40 per cent in Italy, 33 per cent in the UK and only 19 per cent in the USA. Accordingly, the Italian VC industry is still quite undeveloped. Early-stage equity financing was almost nonexistent up to the mid-1990s. It increased considerably in the 1995–2000 period, reaching a peak of €540 million in 2000, equal to 0.046 per cent of GDP (source: AIFI, Italian Association of Private Equity Investors). Nevertheless, not all this amount was invested in NTBFs. Since 2001, early-stage financing has experienced a dramatic decline and it almost vanished in 2004, when there were only 50 investments in 36 companies; the total invested amount was only €23 million, that is 0.002 per cent of GDP.[7]

Our data show that the number of NTBFs that received VC financing during their lifetime is 55 (10.2 per cent of the sample). None of these firms had access to any VC financing before 1994. Their distribution across industries and regions of the country is highlighted in Table 1.1.

Internet & TLC services and Biotech & Pharmaceutics have the greatest share of financed firms (16.6 per cent and 10.0 per cent, respectively), ICT manufacturing shows a lower percentage (8.5 per cent), while firms that operate in the Automation & Robotics (6.0 per cent) and Software (5.1 per cent) sectors are those that are less likely to obtain VC financing. Turning to the geographical distribution, no significant difference emerges in the share of VC-backed firms across the Northwest (10.6 per cent), Northeast (11.1 per cent) and the Centre (10.9 per cent) of Italy, while the South has the lowest percentage (7.0 per cent).

Table 1.1 Distribution of NTBFs and VC-backed firms by industry and geographic area

	No. of firms	No. of VC-backed firms	% of VC-backed firms
Industry			
Internet & TLC services	193	32	16.6
Software	156	8	5.1
ICT manufacturing	118	10	8.5
Biotechnology & Pharmaceutics	20	2	10.0
Automation & Robotics	50	3	6.0
Total	537	55	10.2
Area			
Northwest	256	27	10.6
Northeast	117	13	11.1
Centre	92	10	10.9
South	72	5	7.0
Total	537	55	10.2

ACCESS TO VC FINANCING

In this section we investigate the determinants of NTBF access to VC financing. The aim is to test whether (lagged) growth in the number of employees positively affects the likelihood of obtaining VC financing. The next subsection describes the models and variables, followed by a subsection that reports the results.

Specification of the Model

As a first step to examining the determinants of VC financing, we analyse NTBF access to this source of financing; in order to take into account the right-censored nature of the sample (firms which did not receive any VC financing within the survey period) we resort to a survival model.[8] In particular, we define the duration as the lifetime between 1994 (or the year of the firm's foundation if after 1994) and the year when the firm was financed by a VC investor for the first time.

The probability distribution of duration can be specified by the distribution function $F(t)=\Pr(T<t)$, which specifies the probability that the duration variable T is less than some value t, where t: $1994 \leq t \leq 2003$. The hazard function is defined as $h(t)=f(t)/S(t)$, where $f(t)$ is the probability density function and $S(t)$, which is equal to $1-F(t)$, is the survival function. The hazard function gives the instantaneous rate of receiving VC financing, given that this has not been granted up to t. As a preliminary non-parametric analysis, Figure 1.1 presents the plot of the hazard function computed by the Kaplan–Meier estimator, which reveals a decreasing hazard rate and therefore a negative duration dependence.

This graphical analysis suggests that we should model duration and survival through a Weibull distribution, so:

$$S(t)=\exp[-(\lambda t)^{\alpha}] \tag{1.1}$$

and

$$h(t)=\lambda\alpha(\lambda t)^{\alpha-1}, \tag{1.2}$$

where $\lambda=\exp(-\beta' x)$, x is a set of time-varying covariates and β are the estimated parameters. In this specification, the hazard function is monotonically decreasing in duration (negative duration dependence) if $\alpha<1$.

The set of explanatory variables of NTBF access to VC financing is illustrated in Table 1.2. The key variable is the one-period lagged growth rate of the number of employees of a firm (*LGrowth*). If this variable

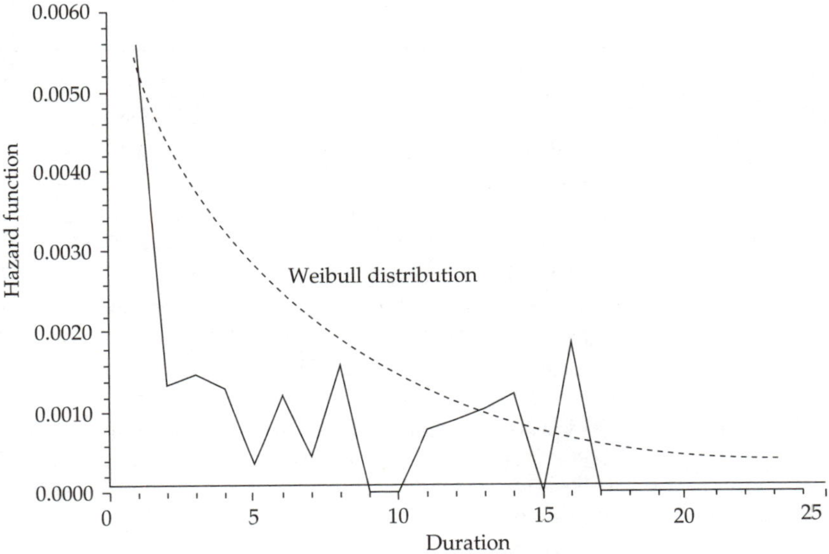

Figure 1.1 Non-parametric hazard function

exhibits a positive coefficient in the estimates, we deduce that rapidly growing NTBFs are more likely to attract VC investors than are other firms. The explanatory variables include a large set of firm- and industry-specific controls. In fact we introduce in the regressions measures of the *generic* (*Education*, *Otherworkexp*) and *specific* human capital[9] possessed by the founding team (*Specworkep*, *DManager*, *DEntrepreneur*), measures of the size and innovative performance of the firm (*LSize*, *DPatent*), a variable that reflects the importance of innovative motivations for the creation of the firm (*DInnomotive*),[10] a variable that captures the presence of a salaried manager among the firm's personnel (*DSalaried Manager*), and a variable that captures access by the firm to public direct financial aid (*DPublic Subsidy*). Finally, there are also proxies of the propensity of VC to invest in the sector (*VCSector*) and in the geographical area (*VCArea*) in which the NTBF operates.

Results

Results obtained by the survival model are shown in Table 1.3. The most interesting result is that growth in the number of employees is only a weak predictor of subsequent access to VC financing. The coefficient of *LGrowth*, though positive, is not statistically significant at conventional

Table 1.2 Explanatory variables of NTBF access to VC

Variable	Description
Education	Average number of years of education of founders
Specworkexp	Average number of years of work experience of founders in the same sector of the start-up before the firm's foundation
Otherworkexp	Average number of years of work experience of founders in other sectors than that of the start-up before the firm's foundation
DManager	Firms with one or more founders with a prior management position in a company with more than 100 employees
DEntrepreneur	Firms with one or more founders with previous self-employment experience
DInnomotive	Firms where all founders declared that the wish to exploit an innovative technology was the main motive for the creation of the firm
DSalaried Manager	Firms that at $t-1$ had a salaried manager
DPatent	Firms that at $t-1$ have applied for a patent at least once during their lifetime
DPublic Subsidy	Firms that at $t-1$ have received a public direct financial subsidy at least once during their lifetime
LSize	Logarithm of the size of the firm at $t-1$ measured by the number of employees (including owners that have an active role in the management of the firm)
LGrowth	Logarithm of the growth of the size of the firm measured by the number of employees (including owners that have an active role in the management of the firm) between $t-2$ and $t-1$
VCSector	Ratio of the share accounted for by the sector of the new firm out of the total number of high-tech firms that obtained VC, 1997–2003 (source: AIFI) to the share accounted for by the same sector out of the total number of Italian high-tech firms in 2003 (source: RITA Directory)
VCArea	Ratio of the share accounted for by the geographical area in which the new firm is located out of the total number of high-tech firms that obtained VC financing over the period 1997–2003 (source: AIFI) to the share accounted for by the same geographical area out of the total number of Italian high-tech firms in 2003 (source: RITA Directory)

Note: *VCSector* and *VCArea* are defined as follows. First, we considered the total number of high-tech firms that obtained VC over the 1997–2003 period (source: AIFI). Let VCS_j and VCA_k indicate the shares accounted for by sector *j* and geographical area *k* out of this number. Let S_j and A_k be the estimated shares accounted for by sector *j* and geographical area *k* out of the total number of Italian NTBFs in 2003 (source: RITA Directory). Then: $VCSector_j = VCS_j/S_j$ and $VCArea_k = VCA_k/A_k$.

Table 1.3 Determinants of NTBF access to VC

		Weibull survival regression
a_0	Constant	−11.074 (3.203)***
a_1	*LGrowth*	0.137 (0.104)
a_2	*LSize*	0.657 (0.372)*
a_3	*DSalaried Manager*	1.250 (0.473)***
a_4	*DPatent*	−0.944 (1.162)
a_5	*DPublic subsidy*	−1.737 (0.920)*
a_6	*Education*	0.023 (0.063)
a_7	*Specworkexp*	−0.015 (0.036)
a_8	*Otherworkexp*	0.013 (0.034)
a_9	*DEntrepreneur*	1.003 (0.525)*
a_{10}	*DManager*	1.454 (0.963)
a_{11}	*DInnomotive*	2.539 (1.048)**
a_{12}	*VCSector*	0.184 (0.074)**
a_{13}	*VCArea*	0.452 (0.181)**
	α	0.716 (0.227)***
	Log-likelihood	−250.111

Note: * $p<0.10$; ** $p<0.05$; *** $p<0.01$. Standard deviations in parentheses. No. of observations is 4029.

confidence levels. In other words, once firm- and industry-specific control variables are taken into account, past growth does not significantly influence the financing decision by VC investors. This result suggests that the investment decision is not based on past growth. Interestingly, Davila et al. (2003) find similar results: in their study of US start-up firms they find that VC firms do not select start-ups with a differential level of headcount growth prior to the first round of financing.

This result is particularly important for the analysis of the causality relationship between growth and VC financing. As we mentioned before, the mere existence of a positive relationship between the presence of VC and growth is not, by itself, proof that this form of financing spurs growth. The result could simply be driven by the propensity of VC investors to finance firms that already grow at a fast rate. However, the results shown in Table 1.3 prove that this is not the case for Italian NTBFs. Once industry- and firm-specific control variables are taken into account, VC is not more likely to invest in firms that are growing more rapidly.

Some interesting results also come from the coefficients of the control variables. First, the only human capital characteristic that significantly affects the access to VC financing is prior entrepreneurial experience by founders. Second, firms whose founders aimed at commercially exploiting an innovative idea are more likely to be financed by VC investors. This may mean that VC investors select firms on the basis of entrepreneurs' goals and that these latter are able to credibly convey this information.[11] In addition, Table 1.3 shows that the grant of public financing (that is, financing and subsidies obtained from the state or local governing bodies) reduces the likelihood of a firm obtaining VC. This is most likely not due to a supply-side effect (that is, a negative signal conveyed to VC investors) but rather to a demand-side effect (that is, firms which were granted public money will have less incentive to seek costly external equity financing). Our findings also indicate that firm size is an important determinant of VC financing. This result, which is consistent with Fried and Hisrich (1994), confirms that VC activity entails some fixed costs (for instance: screening, due diligence, *ex post* monitoring): fixed VC costs are more likely to offset gross capital gains if the firm is small in size. Finally, geographic and industry control variables are significant, meaning that VC tends to polarize: a firm is more likely to obtain VC financing the more this type of financing has been provided to other firms operating in the same region and industry. It is also worth stressing that the estimate for the α coefficient in Table 1.3 is smaller than unity. This means that as time goes by a firm is less likely to receive VC financing, other things being equal.

EFFECTS OF VENTURE CAPITAL ON A FIRM'S GROWTH

In this section we focus on the effect of VC financing on the growth rate of the number of a firm's employees. We describe the methodology of the econometric analysis, as well as the results.

Specification of the Model

The impact on firm growth of receiving VC financing is investigated through the estimation of the following augmented Gibrat law-type dynamic FE model with distributed lags:

$$\begin{aligned} LSize_{i,t} = {} & \beta_1 LSize_{i,t-1} + \beta_2 LAge_{i,t-1} + \beta_3 DVC_{i,t-1} \\ & + \beta_4 DVC_{i,t-2} + \beta_5 DVC_{i,t-3} + \beta_6 DPatent_{i,t-1} \\ & + \beta_7 DPatent_{i,t-2} + \beta_8 DPatent_{i,t-3} + \gamma W_i + \varepsilon_{i,t} \end{aligned} \quad (1.3)$$

where $LSize_{i,t}$ and $LSize_{i,t-1}$ are the logarithms of the size of the firms measured by the number of employees (including owners active in the firm) at time t and $t-1$ respectively; $LAge_{i,t-1}$ is the logarithm of the age of the firms at time t–1; $DVC_{i,t-s}$ are dummy variables that take one if at time $t-1$, $t-2$ and $t-3$ NTBFs had access to VC financing; $DPatent_{i,t-s}$ are dummy variables that take one if at time t–1, t–2 and t–3 firms have been granted one or more patent; W_i are unobservable firm-specific time-invariant characteristics of the firms and $\varepsilon_{i,t}$ is a random disturbance.

Note that since model (1.3) includes a lagged dependent variable as one of the regressors, the usual approach to estimating an FE model through the least squares dummy variable estimator (LSDV) is likely to produce a biased estimate of the parameters, with the bias increasing as T becomes smaller (see Nickell, 1981). Hence, we also resort to the DIF-GMM procedure suggested by Arellano and Bond (1991).

Results

Table 1.4 shows the results of the FE and DIF-GMM models relating to the determinants of the (logarithm of) the number of employees for firms in our sample.[12]

The key result of the estimates relates to the coefficients of the VC lagged dummy variables, which are all positive and statistically significant at 99 per cent. In other words, VC financing does spur growth in the number of employees. The increase is greater in the first year after the first round of

Table 1.4 Effect of VC on NTBF growth

		FE model	GMM model
β_1	*LSize* (−1)	0.526 (0.015)***	0.432 (0.043)***
β_2	*LAge*	0.251 (0.023)***	0.297 (0.039)***
β_3	*DVC* (−1)	0.363 (0.058)***	0.456 (0.119)***
β_4	*DVC* (−2)	0.322 (0.058)***	0.204 (0.063)***
β_5	*DVC* (−3)	0.316 (0.065)***	0.160 (0.057)***
β_6	*DPatent* (−1)	0.141 (0.074)*	0.062 (0.083)
β_7	*DPatent* (−2)	−0.089 (0.093)	0.028 (0.043)
β_8	*DPatent* (−3)	−0.087 (0.079)	−0.019 (0.041)
	Adjusted R^2	0.907	–
	AR (1)	–	−6.896***
	AR (2)	–	−0.6419
	Sargan	–	115.7 (103)

Note: * $p<0.10$; ** $p<0.05$; *** $p<0.01$. Standard deviations in parentheses. No. of observations is 3072 for the FE model and 2544 for the GMM model. Logged dependent variable and *DVC* (−1) are endogenous.

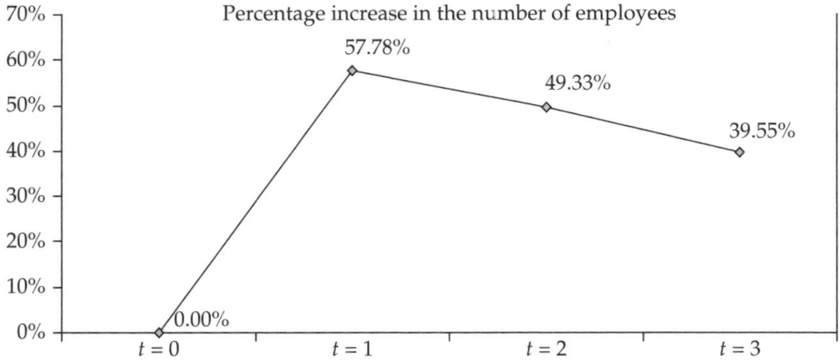

Note: The vertical axis shows the percentage difference in firm size (measured by the number of employees) between a VC-backed firm and a twin firm having the same (average) characteristics at time $t = 0$ but receiving no VC financing. Calculation is based on the DIF-GMM column in Table 1.4.

Figure 1.2 Impact of VC financing on NTBF size (based on DIF-GMM estimation)

financing is obtained, smaller in the second year, and still smaller in the third year. To better exemplify this, we report in Figure 1.2 the predicted increase in firm size due to the occurrence of VC financing.

We start, at time $t = 0$, with a firm having average characteristics (that is, having continuous control variables set to their mean values and dummy variables set to zero). Then, building on the DIF-GMM estimates in Table 1.4, we compare the change in size due to financing occurring in year $t = 0$. At time $t = 1$ the number of employees of the benchmark firm is 57.78 per cent higher if it receives VC. At time $t = 2$ the number of employees of a VC-backed firm is 49.33 per cent higher than its non-VC-backed counterpart. At time $t = 3$ the figure goes down to 39.55 per cent. In other words, Figure 1.2 shows that the effect of VC on growth is significant and enduring over time.

It is worth stressing that, as shown in the previous section, VC-backed firms did not have a significantly higher growth rate prior to external financing. Thus, our results strongly support a direct causality relationship between VC investment and growth.

As to the remaining variables in Table 1.4, the coefficient associated with firm size is significantly smaller than 1. This is consistent with most of the empirical literature in the Gibrat's law investigation (see, for example, Evans, 1987) and confirms that smaller firms tend to grow faster than larger firms. Second, firms' age positively affects growth. In other words, in contrast to Jovanovic (1982) and Evans (1987) but consistently with

Shanmugam and Bhaduri (2002), younger firms grow more slowly than older ones.[13]

CONCLUDING REMARKS

The aim of this study is to analyse the causality relationship between VC financing and the growth of NTBFs. Previous literature emphasizes the benefits that VC financing may have on the performance of investee firms, due to the 'scouting', 'monitoring' and 'coaching' role performed by these investors. Nevertheless, the empirical evidence supporting this view is quite scarce. More importantly, failure by most previous studies to control effectively for the endogenous nature of VC investments may have led to biased results. In particular, there may well be a reverse causality relationship, with VC investors being attracted by NTBFs that exhibit superior growth performance. Therefore, in order to be able to detect the real added value associated with VC financing, a more robust methodology, accounting for a two-way causality relationship, is needed.

In this work, we have estimated a series of econometric models that are aimed at highlighting both whether the growth in the number of employees of firms positively affects the likelihood of obtaining VC financing through survival data analysis models, and whether access to VC financing spurs firms' growth after the first round of financing through FE and DIF-GMM panel data models. For this purpose, we have taken advantage of a new longitudinal dataset relating to a large sample of Italian high-tech young firms that operate in manufacturing and service sectors. Our results clearly support the argument that VC financing drives firms' growth, while no evidence is found of the existence of an opposite causality relationship.[14] Once industry- and firm-specific control variables are taken into account, VC investment is not more likely to occur in firms that are growing more rapidly. On the other hand, the effect of VC on growth is positive and statistically significant; in other words, VC financing does spur growth in the number of employees. The marginal increase in firm size is greatest in the first year after the first round of financing is obtained, smaller in the second year, and still smaller in the third year. Overall our results confirm that VC plays a fundamental role for NTBFs, even in a country in which VC is relatively underdeveloped (if compared to Anglo-Saxon countries).

It is important to acknowledge that the VC industry is complex and heterogeneous and is composed of various players who are characterized by different financing strategies and objectives. It will thus be interesting, in future extensions of this work, to further characterize VC players and test whether there are substantial differences in both the *ex ante* characteristics of their investee firms and in the *ex post* effect on firm performance.

ACKNOWLEDGEMENT

Support from Venture Fun PRIME project is gratefully acknowledged.

NOTES

1. Monitoring is performed in several ways: venture capitalists ask for a seat on the board of directors, measure the firm's performance accurately and regularly, and set pay-for-performance remuneration packages for managers and key employees.
2. A related stream of the literature analyses the effect of VC on innovation, with mixed results (Kortum and Lerner, 2000; Hellmann and Puri, 2000; Engel and Keilbach, 2007; Ueda and Hirukawa, 2003).
3. The main problem is that in Italy most individuals who are defined as 'self-employed' by official statistics are actually salaried workers with atypical employment contracts. Unfortunately, on the basis of official data such individuals cannot be distinguished from entrepreneurs who have created a new firm.
4. Note that for only three firms the set of owner-managers at survey date did not include at least one of the founders of the firm. For these firms, information relating to the human capital characteristics of the founders was checked through interviews with the firm's personnel so as to be sure that it did not relate to current owner-managers.
5. Heterogeneity is partly determined by different technological trajectories, which could make generalization difficult. To address this issue we include several industry- and firm-specific control variables in our econometric models.
6. Davila et al. (2003) also acknowledge a similar bias produced by survivorship. To the best of our knowledge, the only study in the literature that partially overcomes this problem is the one by Manigart et al. (2002).
7. These figures refer exclusively to AIFI members; so they are likely to underestimate the actual amount of VC financing. In particular, they do not include most investments made by non-financial firms. For further details on the Italian VC industry, see Bertoni et al. (2006).
8. For a comprehensive treatment of the techniques of duration analysis, see Lawless (1982) and Keifer (1988).
9. See Becker (1975) for such a distinction and Colombo et al. (2004) for its empirical application.
10. The questionnaire provides information as to the main motive of each individual founder for the firm's creation. *Innomotive* is a dummy variable that indicates whether all the members of the founding team declared that the wish to exploit an innovative technology was the main motive for the creation of the firm.
11. This notwithstanding, note the insignificant coefficient of the *DPatent* variable.
12. Other control variables (for instance: number of patents, presence of a manager, grant of public financing, listing on a stock market) have been included in an extended version of the model but are omitted here as their coefficients are not significantly different from zero.
13. It should be pointed out that, since firms in our sample are never older than 25 years, results should not be generalized to older firms.
14. Interestingly Balboa et al. (2006) find similar evidence for VC-backed firms in Spain, although using a different methodology and without focusing exclusively on NTBFs.

REFERENCES

Aldrich, H.E., A. Kallenberg, P. Marsden and J. Cassell (1989), 'In pursuit of evidence: sampling procedures for locating new businesses', *Journal of Business Venturing*, **4**, 367–86.

Arellano, M. and S. Bond (1991), 'Some tests of specification for panel data: Monte Carlo evidence and an application to employment equations', *Review of Economic Studies*, **58**, 277–97.

Audretsch, D.B. (1995), *Innovation and Industry Evolution*, Cambridge, MA: MIT Press.

Audretsch, D.B. and E.E. Lehmann (2004), 'Financing high-tech growth: the role of debt and equity', *Schmalenbach Business Review*, **56**, 340–57.

Balboa, M., J. Martì and N. Zieling (2006), 'Does venture capital really improve portfolio companies' growth? Evidence from growth companies in Continental Europe', Proceedings of the European Financial Management Conference, Madrid, 28 June–1 July.

Becker, G.S. (1975), *Human Capital*, New York: National Bureau of Economic Research.

Bertoni, F., M.G. Colombo, A. Croce and E. Piva (2006), 'A review of the venture capital industry in Italy', in G.N. Gregoriou, M. Kooli and R. Kraeussl (eds), *Venture Capital in Europe*, Amsterdam: Elsevier, pp. 129–43.

Birley, S. (1987), 'Finding the new firm', S.M Working Paper, Cranfield, UK.

Bottazzi, L. and M. Da Rin (2002), 'Venture capital in Europe and the financing of innovative companies', *Economic Policy*, **17**, 229–70.

Bottazzi, L., M. Da Rin and T. Hellmann (2004), 'Active financial intermediation: evidence on the role of organizational specialization and human capital', IGIER Working Paper 266, Innocenzo Gasparini Institute for Economic Research, Milan.

Carpenter, R.E. and B.C. Petersen (2002a), 'Capital market imperfections, high-tech investment, and new equity financing', *Economic Journal*, **112**, F54–F72.

Carpenter, R.E. and B.C. Petersen (2002b), 'Is the growth of small firms constrained by internal finance?', *Review of Economics and Statistics*, **84**, 298–309.

Casamatta, C. (2003), 'Financing and advising: optimal financial contracts with venture capitalists', *Journal of Finance*, **58**, 2059–86.

Chan, Y.S. (1983), 'On the positive role of financial intermediation in allocation of venture capital in market with imperfect information', *Journal of Finance*, **35**, 1543–68.

Colombo, M.G., M. Delmastro and L. Grilli (2004), 'Entrepreneurs' human capital and the start-up size of new technology-based firms', *International Journal of Industrial Organization*, **22**, 1183–211.

Colombo, M.G. and L. Grilli (2005), 'Founders' human capital and the growth of new technology-based firms: a competence-based view', *Research Policy*, **34**, 795–816.

Davila, A., G. Foster and M. Gupta (2003), 'Venture capital financing and the growth of startup firms', *Journal of Business Venturing*, **18**, 689–708.

Engel, D. (2002), 'The impact of venture capital on firm growth: an empirical investigation', Discussion Paper 02–02, Centre for European Economic Research (Zentrum für Europäische Wirtschaftsforschung – ZEW), Mannheim, Germany.

Engel, D. and M. Keilbach (2007), 'Firm level implications of early stage venture capital investment: an empirical investigation', *Journal of Empirical Finance*, **14**, 150–67.

Evans, D.S. (1987), 'The relationship between firm growth, size and firm age: estimates for 100 manufacturing industries', *Journal of Industrial Economics*, **35**, 567–82.

Fazzari, S.M., R.G. Hubbard and B.C. Petersen (1988), 'Financing constraints and corporate investment', *Brooking Papers on Economic Activity*, **1**, 141–205.

Fried, V.H. and R.D. Hisrich (1994), 'Towards a model of venture capital-investment decision-making', *Financial Management*, **23**, 28–37.

Gimeno, J., T. Folta, A. Cooper and C. Woo (1997), 'Survival of the fittest? Entrepreneurial human capital and the persistence of underperforming firms', *Administrative Science Quarterly*, **42**, 750–83.

Hellmann, T. and M. Puri (2000), 'The interaction between product market and financing strategy: the role of venture capital', *Review of Financial Study*, **13**, 959–84.

Hellmann, T. and M. Puri (2002), 'Venture capital and the professionalization of start-up firms: empirical evidence', *Journal of Finance*, **57**, 169–97.

Jain, B.A. and O. Kini (1995), 'Venture capitalist participation and the post-issue operating performance of IPO firms', *Managerial and Decision Economics*, **6**, 593–606.

Jovanovic, B. (1982), 'Selection and the evolution of industry', *Econometrica*, **50**, 649–70.

Keifer, N. (1988), 'Economic duration data and hazard functions', *Journal of Economic Literature*, **26**, 646–79.

Kortum, S. and J. Lerner (2000), 'Assessing the contribution of venture capital to innovation', *Rand Journal of Economics*, **31** (4), 674–92.

Lawless, J.F. (1982), *Statistical Models and Methods for Lifetime Data*, Toronto: Wiley.

Manigart, S. and W. Van Hyfte (1999), 'Post-investment evolution of Belgian venture capital backed companies: an empirical study', in P. Reynolds, W. Bygrave, S. Manigart, C. Mason, G. Meyer, H.J. Sapienza and K. Shaver (eds), *Frontiers of Entrepreneurship Research*, Wellesley, MA: Babson College.

Manigart, S., K. Baeyens and W. Van Hyfte (2002), 'The survival of venture capital backed companies', *Venture Capital*, **4**, 103–24.

Nickell, S. (1981), 'Biases in dynamic models with fixed effects', *Econometrica*, **49**, 1417–26.

Rajan, R. and L. Zingales (2003), 'The great reversals: the politics of financial development in the twentieth century', *Journal of Financial Economics*, 69, 5–50.

Sapienza, H.J. (1992), 'When do venture capitalists add value?', *Journal of Business Venturing*, **7**, 9–27.

Sapienza, H.J., S. Manigart and W. Vermeir (1996), 'Venture capital governance and value added in four countries', *Journal of Business Venturing*, **11**, 439–69.

Shanmugam, K.R. and S.N. Bhaduri (2002), 'Size, age and firm growth in the Indian manufacturing sector', *Applied Economics Letters*, **9**, 607–13.

Ueda, M. and M. Hirukawa (2003), 'Venture capital and productivity', Working Paper, University of Wisconsin, USA, September.

Zacharakis, A.L. and G.D. Meyer (1998), 'A lack of insight: do venture capitalists really understand their own decision process?', *Journal of Business Venturing*, **13**, 57–76.

Zacharakis, A.L. and G.D. Meyer (2000), 'The potential of actuarial decision models: can they improve the venture capital investment decision?', *Journal of Business Venturing*, **15**, 323–46.

2. Unemployment in a model of entrepreneurship in Belgium: empirical evidence from the Global Entrepreneurship Monitor

Stijn Bruyneel, Martin Carree and Ludo Peeters

INTRODUCTION

Over the past few years, entrepreneurship[1] has become a central target for policy makers and economic researchers. Recently, several studies have identified the contribution of entrepreneurship to unemployment reduction and economic growth. However, unemployment has also been identified as an antecedent of entrepreneurship. The relationship between previous unemployment status and entrepreneurship has led to the opposing concepts of necessity- and opportunity-based entrepreneurship. Although both concepts have been widely accepted, empirical evidence has produced mixed results so far. One possible explanation for this flaw in the empirical literature is the impact of the *level* at which research has been conducted. Unemployment can be an antecedent of entrepreneurship at the individual, regional or national level. Although the impact of entrepreneurship is expected to be different depending on the level of analysis, most studies do not acknowledge this difference. We look at entrepreneurship from an *individual* perspective, in search of a possible relation between the employment status of the individual and his or her probability of becoming an entrepreneur. We question whether individuals are driven by unemployment when they decide to start up their own firm, or whether they are just as likely to start their own firm as their employed counterparts.

We make use of the Global Entrepreneurship Monitor (GEM), which provides a unique dataset for testing the influence of the employment status on the probability of becoming an entrepreneur. The most recent publicly available Belgian data for 2001 will be used in a logistic regression model. With an entrepreneurial rate of only 3.4 per cent of all individuals, Belgium was the 'least entrepreneurial country' in the database (Manigart et al., 2001). Although slightly increased to 3.9 per cent in 2005, Belgium is still one of the least-performing countries (Minniti et al., 2005). The low entrepreneurial activity makes Belgium an exceptional case to examine.

The chapter begins with a non-comprehensive overview of the antecedents of entrepreneurship. The role and impact of variables such as relative earnings differences, demography, self-efficacy, education, network and initial occupation are given broad attention. Next, we test the influence of the explanatory variables by making use of simple logistic regressions. The results from the maximum-likelihood estimation, policy implications and concluding remarks are presented in the last sections.

THEORETICAL BACKGROUND

The decision process of an individual who is about to set up a new firm is a major focal point in entrepreneurial theory. This theory tries to gain more knowledge on the dynamics of an individual becoming an entrepreneur. This individualistic perspective is rationalized by the mere fact that behind every new firm lies the work of an individual (Gartner and Carter, 2003). The core of this individual approach is to provide more insight into the forces driving an individual to start up a new firm. This approach is already apparent in the work of Knight (1921), where individuals can either be 'self-employed', 'wage-employed' or 'unemployed'. A standard explanation for the occupational choice[2] is the relative wage differences between these occupations, which make individuals move from one state to another. Vivarelli (1991), among others, finds empirical support for the importance of a higher income expectation from self-employment, as a determinant of entry into self-employment. Evans and Leighton (1990), however, qualify the prospect of a higher wage as an antecedent and show that the unemployed individual who starts a new firm, earns *less* than an unemployed individual who prefers to stay unemployed. This result can partly be explained by the fact that self-employed individuals have the tendency to under-report their profits. Moreover, we cannot expect a new firm to reap large profits in its first years. Nevertheless, this debate indicates that earnings differences between the different occupational choices cannot be the sole foundation of a solid entrepreneurial theory. Moreover, Ilmakunnas and Topi (1999) showed that past profits in the Finnish manufacturing industry fail to explain entry, and Dolton and Makepeace (1990) found that relative earnings differences did not play any role in the self-employment decision of UK graduates.

In an attempt to refine the profile of the entrepreneur, a broad range of antecedents can be introduced in the theoretical model. Based on the available microeconomic information, data on work status, rate of risk aversion,

Table 2.1 Antecedents and their expected effects on entrepreneurship

Antecedents	Direction of change
Age	?
Female gender	–
Risk averse	–
Network	+
Education	?
Self-efficacy	+
Unemployed	?

Note: '+' ('–') indicates a positive (negative) relationship, while an undetermined outcome in the literature is indicated with a question mark.

age, gender, educational attainment, self-efficacy and dimension of personal network are discussed in the following section. Unfortunately, the database does not contain data on other important antecedents, such as access to capital (Blanchflower and Oswald, 1998), industry differences (Vivarelli, 1991), and entrepreneurial experience (Rotefoss and Kolvereid, 2005).

An overview of the antecedents and their relation with entrepreneurship as found in the literature is presented in Table 2.1. It indicates the expected sign attached to the coefficients of the respective explanatory variable.

Before discussing the antecedents, a remark must be made concerning the applied definition of entrepreneurship. Although the exact definition is still an important debate in the economics literature, some consensus exists as regards the *measurement*. Most studies make use of (i) surveys, where nascent entrepreneurs are recognized as owner-managers who have executed some entrepreneurial activities, or (ii) existing databases including registrations of self-employed individuals. In the following overview of the antecedents, the referenced papers are all studies applying a comparable definition of entrepreneurship either characterized by self-registration or as an owner-manager who has undertaken some entrepreneurial actions.

Unemployment

One of the most debated determinants of entrepreneurship is unemployment. The influence of unemployment has been investigated at three levels: individual, regional and national.[3] At all these levels the contradicting 'push and pull' hypotheses have been proposed (Meager, 1992). In general, the push theory predicts a positive relation between the unemployment rate and the number of new firms (Gilad and Levine, 1986; Evans and Jovanovic, 1989; Evans and Leighton, 1990; Storey, 1991, 1994; Ilmakunnas and Topi,

1999; Ritsilä and Tervo, 2002). A higher unemployment rate means that fewer individuals can become employed, and thus are forced into entrepreneurship. Depressed market conditions would imply that individuals who are experiencing the threat of unemployment are more likely to start a new business (Storey, 1991). The pull theory, on the other hand, suggests that the prosperity, coinciding with low unemployment rates, pulls the individual towards entrepreneurship. A favourable economic environment attracts more individuals than an unfavourable one. The unemployment rate and the number of new firms are thus expected to be negatively related (Storey, 1994; Arenius and Minniti, 2005). Last but not least, some studies find no relation between unemployment and the number of new firms (Carree, 2002).

Following the individualistic approach (Gartner and Carter, 2003), the opposing push and pull hypotheses have a different content. The unemployment rate, reflecting existing market conditions, is replaced by the employment status of the individual as an antecedent of entrepreneurship. Focusing on this individual level, the push theory expects unemployed individuals to have a greater propensity to become an entrepreneur (Ritsilä and Tervo, 2002). These 'necessity' entrepreneurs are dissatisfied with their current situation of unemployment. They prefer setting up a new firm rather than staying unemployed and living off unemployment benefits. The pull theory, on the other hand, claims that unemployed individuals are less prone to start a new firm. Their desire to work for themselves, their ambition and (perhaps) their talent to capture new business opportunities are less pronounced. According to the pull hypothesis, employed individuals are better equipped and therefore more prone to starting a new firm, and are thus viewed as 'opportunity' entrepreneurs.

Although these definitions are widely accepted, the complexity of the relationship goes beyond the necessity–opportunity distinction. The positive relationship between unemployment and entrepreneurship predicted by the push hypothesis does not always mean that unemployed individuals act out of necessity. The mere fact that people are unemployed when starting a new firm might be because they resigned from their previous job to have more time to invest in the start-up. The same spurious significance is present with the pull hypothesis. Employed individuals who are in fact starting a new business might be acting out of necessity or out of discontent with their present occupation.

Table 2.2 gives an overview of the reasons behind the decision of the Belgian respondents to become an entrepreneur. It is based on Belgian GEM data for 2001. The GEM survey included the following question in order to gain more detailed insight into the drive behind entrepreneurship: 'Are you involved in this start-up to take advantage of a business opportunity or because you have no better choice for work?'

Table 2.2 Employment status and the necessity–opportunity distinction

Drivers of entrepreneurship	Employed (%)	Unemployed (%)
Opportunity	45	30
Necessity	14	30
Combination	24	20
Undecided/Don't know	17	20

The respondents were asked to choose one of the following answers: (a) take advantage of business opportunity, (b) no better choice for work, (c) combination of both of the above, or (d) other reasons. It appeared that 30 per cent of the unemployed who were involved with a start-up acted out of necessity, and 30 per cent out of opportunity. One-fifth of the respondents operated out of a combination of the above. This shows that a more careful interpretation of the push hypothesis is needed, given that just as many unemployed individuals become an entrepreneur because they see an opportunity, as those who are necessity entrepreneurs. Of the employed individuals involved in a start-up, 45 per cent acted on the basis of a new opportunity, whereas 14 per cent could be considered as necessity entrepreneurs. Having a job and starting a new firm out of necessity seem to go hand in hand in many instances. Those who are employed might, for instance, fear unemployment in the near future. Therefore, they try to start a new firm and state that, although employed, they had no better option for work than a start-up. To base the difference between necessity and opportunity entrepreneurs on the employment status of the individual is thus incorrect, and provides an incomplete picture of unemployment as a driver of entrepreneurship.

Risk Aversion

Differences in risk aversion might be a way to explain the differences between agents, as proposed by Kihlstrom and Laffont (1979). Storey (1994) shows that the variance of the average earnings from self-employment is large, implying a larger risk attached to self-employment. Individuals who are more willing to take risks are thus more likely to become an entrepreneur (Arenius and Minniti, 2005).

Gender

Demographic characteristics, such as gender, can supply a means to further define the entrepreneur. The greater feel for responsibility towards family and children and societal pressure disapproving of female entrepreneurship, make it more difficult for females to engage in entrepreneurship successfully. Consequently, a negative influence of female gender is typically found in the literature (Evans and Leighton, 1990; Blanchflower, 2000; Delmar and Davidsson, 2000; Blanchflower et al., 2001; Davidsson and Honig, 2003; Arenius and Minniti, 2005). An exception comes from Rotefoss and Kolvereid (2005), who failed to find a significant gender effect for self-employed individuals. However, evidence from more recent data might indicate that female entrepreneurship is on the increase.

Age

Reynolds et al. (2004) concluded that entrepreneurship is mainly an option for males aged between 25 and 34. Similar results emerge from Delmar and Davidsson (2000), who showed that entrepreneurs are aged mainly between 25 and 34. Such a non-linear relation is the result of two different linear effects. On the one hand, the motivation and energy of individuals decreases by age (Delmar and Davidsson, 2000; Davidsson and Honig, 2003; Arenius and Minniti, 2005; Rotefoss and Kolvereid, 2005). On the other hand, the experience of the individuals increases by age, indicating that older people have a higher probability of becoming an entrepreneur (Blanchflower, 2000; Blanchflower et al., 2001).

Education

The influence of the individual's educational attainment is still unclear. Education is often viewed as a proxy for human capital, and hence a higher educational attainment often leads to a higher probability of becoming an entrepreneur (Evans and Leighton, 1990; Davidsson and Honig, 2003). Conversely, entrepreneurs possess a broad range of talents which are not always the result of a higher educational attainment, but rather of specific training (Delmar and Davidsson, 2000). Kolvereid and Moen (1997) exemplify this, by showing the positive influence of a major in entrepreneurship. Education is thus linked to entrepreneurship (Reynolds et al., 2004), but a distinction between level and type of education must be made. Moreover, highly educated individuals are more attractive as employees, reinforcing the expected ambiguous effect. Mixed results are presented by Arenius and Minniti (2005), where either no relation or a positive one is presented, depending on the applied model.

Self-efficacy

Although originally proposed as an antecedent of intentional behaviour (Ajzen, 1991; Kolvereid, 1996), self-efficacy has also been used as an explanatory variable of entrepreneurship (Arenius and Minniti, 2005). Self-confident individuals are assumed to perform better, increasing the probability that their intentional effort results in a start-up (ibid.). In an attempt to distinguish entrepreneurs from managers, Chen et al. (1998) use self-efficacy as an explanatory variable and find a positive effect. It should be noted, however, that the concept suffers from hindsight bias when used as a determinant of entrepreneurship. It can be expected that entrepreneurs evolving through the business-development process are confirmed in their ability to start a firm.

Network

Due to informational spillovers and role-model effects, being a member of an extensive network increases the probability of becoming an entrepreneur. It can be expected that individuals who are familiar with the 'entrepreneurial community' have a higher probability of becoming an entrepreneur (Davidsson and Honig, 2003). Knowing other entrepreneurs has been shown to contribute significantly (Arenius and Minniti, 2005).

EMPIRICAL ANALYSIS

Data

Our analysis is based on the Global Entrepreneurship Monitor database.[4] GEM started in 1999 and gathered entrepreneurial information from all over the world. The most recent edition of the annual GEM report dates from 2005 and has been compiled by over 200 scholars and researchers from 35 countries (Minniti et al., 2005). We use the Belgian adult population survey of more than two thousand adults. The most recent, publicly available data relate to 2001.

Variables

The respondents from the interview were asked whether they are involved in a new firm, the starting process of a nascent firm, or both. An individual is registered as a 'nascent entrepreneur' if he/she has performed managerial tasks, owns all or part of the nascent firm and has been paying wages, salaries or any payment in kind for a period no longer than three months. When the firm has paid wages or salaries for between three and 42 months at the time of the survey, the individual is regarded as an 'infant entrepreneur'.

Unfortunately, Belgian entrepreneurial activity is very low. Out of the 2038 observations, only 69 individuals claim to be a nascent and/or an infant entrepreneur. Based on these figures, Belgium has the lowest rate of entrepreneurial activity in the GEM report of 2001. Such a low score makes it difficult to estimate the influence of the various antecedents. Therefore entrepreneurship will be measured by the probability of being an entrepreneur without further specification of nascent or infant entrepreneurship.[5]

The variable *self* takes the value of 1 when the individual is concerned with a start-up, a new firm or both. When the individual is not involved in any entrepreneurial activity, the variable takes the value 0. Each individual was also asked about their present employment status. The respondents were subdivided into two groups: working and not working. An important note regarding the content of the 'not working' category must be made. This category concerns all individuals who are not working, which includes students, retired or disabled persons, homemakers, housewives and the unemployed. In the rest of the chapter the term 'unemployed individuals' refers to the larger category of not working individuals. The variable *unemployment* codes 1 when the individual is not working at the time of the interview, and 0 otherwise. When investigating the influence of the employment status, the GEM database allows us to control for certain characteristics of the individual. Therefore, we are able to use data on gender, age and education. *Gender* is 0 for a male individual and 1 if the individual is female. The variable *age* is the age of the respondent at the time of the interview. The educational attainment of the individual is subdivided into three categories: some secondary education or less, a secondary qualification, and a post-secondary degree. Unfortunately, more detailed information on the type of education is not available. Two dummy variables were created to capture educational attainment; *second* and *post-second*. The reference category consists of individuals with some secondary education or less.

Information about the network can also be derived from the answers to the GEM interview. The respondents were asked whether they personally know another entrepreneur.[6] Personally knowing other entrepreneurs widens the network and makes it easier to start up a new firm. The variable *network* shows a value of 1 when the respondent claimed to personally know other entrepreneurs and a value of 0 otherwise. Unfortunately, GEM does not provide quantified information on the expected income of the employment status of the individual. As we shall show later, we do not really need information on the expected income, since the income related to the employment choice depends to a large extent on the individual's characteristics. Although difficult to measure and standardize, information on the risk aversion of the individual is indirectly provided in the GEM database. Respondents were asked whether fear of failing would prevent them from engaging in a business start-up. The answers are captured in the variable *risk*. The respondents were questioned about confidence in their own ability. This provides us with information about self-efficacy, and is taken up in the variable *selfeff*.

Estimation

Starting from these answers, we attempt to predict the probability that a specific individual will become an entrepreneur. More specifically, we are concerned with the dependence of the probability of becoming an entrepreneur on the initial employment state X. As mentioned previously, opposing theories on the influence of unemployment have been proposed. Standard entrepreneurial theory examines these hypotheses while controlling for wage differences $(Y_{i,SE} - Y_{i,EM})$ and $(Y_{i,SE} - Y_{i,UN})$ and individual characteristics such as age, gender, education and network (represented by the matrix Z).

A simple logit model seems an appropriate way of testing our hypothesis (Menard, 2002). The goal is to estimate the coefficients of the following equation:

$$P\left[U_{i,SE} > \max(U_{i,EM}, U_{i,UN}) = \frac{e^{\alpha' x_i}}{1 + e^{\alpha' x_i}}\right] \tag{2.1}$$

where $\alpha' x_i = \alpha_0 + \alpha_1'[Y_{i,SE} - \max(Y_{i,EM}, b)] + \alpha_2'X + \alpha_3'Z$ and b the unemployment benefit which is assumed equal across individuals.

A practical problem arises when quantifying the wage differences between the different employment choices. However, the expected wage coming from self-employment and employment strongly depends on the individual characteristics. Age, gender and educational attainment largely determine the wage that an individual can expect from employment and self-employment:

$$Y_{i,SE} = g(Z) \tag{2.2}$$

$$Y_{i,EM} = h(Z). \tag{2.3}$$

In addition, we assume the wage from unemployment b to be equal across individuals. Because the variance of the unemployment benefit over the individuals is approximately zero, it can be captured by the intercept of the equation. Therefore, the probability of becoming an entrepreneur can be written solely in terms of the individual characteristics X and Z:

$$P[U_{i,\,SE} > \max(U_{i,\,EM}, U_{i,\,UN})] = \frac{e^{\alpha_0 + \alpha_1'X + \alpha_2'Z}}{1 + e^{\alpha_0 + \alpha_1'X + \alpha_2'Z}} \quad (2.4)$$

since $g(Z)$ and $h(Z)$ are assumed to be linear for reasons of simplicity. Using the data available from the GEM database, we come to the following regression specification:

$$P(self = 1) = \frac{e^{\beta' x_i}}{1 + e^{\beta' x_i}}, \quad (2.5)$$

where:

$$\beta' x_i = \beta 0 + \beta_1 \cdot gender + \beta_2 \cdot age + \beta_3 \cdot second + \beta_4 \cdot postsecond + \beta_5 \cdot network + \beta_6 \cdot employment + \beta_7 \cdot risk + \beta_8 \cdot selfeff.$$

RESULTS

Table 2.3 gives an overview of the summary statistics of the variables. As previously stated, the entrepreneurship rate is low as indicated by the low mean of the variable *self*. The individuals are close to evenly spread over the employment categories. With an average of 0.52, slightly more of the respondents are unemployed at the time of the interview. The individual is on average 48 years old. Males and females are equally represented in the dataset. The majority of respondents do not personally know another entrepreneur, and are not frightened off by the threat of failure. Half of

Table 2.3 Descriptive statistics

Variables	Mean	Minimum	Maximum	Std. dev.
Self	0.04	0	3	0.50
Unemployment	0.52	0	1	0.50
Age	48.54	18	92	17.26
Gender	0.53	0	1	0.50
Network	0.25	0	1	0.43
Risk	0.30	0	1	0.46
Second	0.14	0	1	0.35
Post-second	0.50	0	1	0.50
Selfeff	0.28	0	1	0.45

Table 2.4 Entrepreneurial activity and employment status

Entrepreneurial activity	Employed	Occupational choice unemployed	Total
No activity	933	1036	1969
Nascent	40	10	50
Infant	15	2	17
Both	2	0	2
Total	990	1048	2038

them have a post-secondary degree. Of the other half, a minority have a secondary degree, leaving the rest with less than a secondary degree. About one-third of the respondents believe in their own entrepreneurial skills.

A first look at the influence of the employment status is given in Table 2.4. It can easily be seen that the majority of entrepreneurs are currently employed in another firm. As mentioned before, the number of nascent entrepreneurs is limited to 69 out of 2038 individuals. Only 12 of them were unemployed at the time of the interview. Since they are evenly spread according to their employment status, it can be concluded that the unemployed are underrepresented in the group of the entrepreneurial active individuals.

Table 2.5 reports the results of our maximum likelihood estimation. Before going into a detailed discussion of the influence of the explanatory variables, the overall fit of the model will be analysed. As indicated by the LR-statistic[7] and its *p*-value, adding the independent variables to our regression allows a better prediction of entrepreneurship. Our logistic regression model fits the data better than a model that consists of only the intercept β_0 (further labelled the 'constant model'). How much better the logistic model performs can be derived from the McFadden R^2. With a value of 18.7 per cent, the logistic model represents a moderate improvement in terms of fit. Table 2.6 presents the predictive efficiency of the model. The table is based on the calculated probability that each individual becomes an entrepreneur. These estimates are then compared to the observed data. When using a cutting point[8] of 0.50, the upper-left part of Table 2.6 shows that zero cases are classified as an entrepreneur (Predicted = 1). This represents a correct classification of 96.4 per cent of all the cases. Compared to the constant model, there is no improvement of the predictive power. In an attempt to estimate a higher number of entrepreneurs correctly, the cutting point was decreased. As can be seen from the other parts in Table 2.6, this leads to an increase in the number of correctly classified entrepreneurs. For cutting points of, respectively, 0.20, 0.15 and 0.10, the percentage of correctly classified entrepreneurs increases to, respectively,

Table 2.5 Results from the logistic regression

Variables	Coefficient β	*z*-statistic	Exp(β)
Constant	−3.946***	−6.155	0.019
Gender	0.106	0.373	1.112
Age	−0.004	0.398	0.996
Second	−0.263	−0.552	0.769
Post second	−0.220	−0.629	0.803
Network	0.872***	3.103	2.392
Unemployment	−1.155***	−2.975	0.315
Risk	−0.350	−1.130	0.705
Selfeff	1.941***	5.937	6.966
Self=0		1833	
Self=1		65	
LR-statistic		105***	
McFadden R^2		0.187	

Note: *** Significant at 1%; ** significant at 5%; * significant at 10%.

Table 2.6 Predictive power

Predicted	Observed		Total	Predicted	Observed		Total
$p=0.50$	0	1		$p=0.20$	0	1	
0	1833	65	1898	0	1819	62	1881
1	0	0	0	1	14	3	17
Total	1833	65	1898	Total	1833	65	1898
% Correct	100	0	96.58	% Correct	99.24	4.62	96.00
% Incorrect	0	100	3.42	% Incorrect	0.76	95.38	4.00
Total gain[a]	0	0	0	Total gain[a]	−0.76	4.62	−0.58
Predicted	Observed		Total	Predicted	Observed		Total
$p=0.15$	0	1		$p=0.10$	0	1	
0	1713	42	1755	0	1674	32	1706
1	120	23	143	1	159	33	192
Total	1833	65	1898	Total	1833	65	1898
% Correct	93.45	35.38	91.46	% Correct	91.33	50.77	89.94
% Incorrect	6.55	64.62	8.54	% Incorrect	8.67	49.23	10.06
Total gain[a]	−6.55	35.38	−5.11	Total gain[a]	−8.67	50.77	−6.64

Note: [a] The row 'Total gain' is the change in the percentage of correct estimates compared to the constant model.

4.6, 35.4 and 50.8 per cent. However, more errors are now made regarding the non-entrepreneurs. Since the last effect is relatively stronger, the overall performance of the model decreases. This can be seen from the negative values in the row representing the total gain. Although we found a significant LR-statistic and a moderate R^2, the logistic model fails as a classification model.

We now turn to the interpretation of the logistic regression coefficients. The employment status is significantly correlated with entrepreneurial activity. Unemployed individuals have a lower probability of being an entrepreneur than employed individuals. Being unemployed changes the odds[9] of being an entrepreneur by 0.32. This means that the probability of an unemployed individual becoming an entrepreneur is about three times lower. An employed male of age 30, who does not personally know an entrepreneur, believes in his own skills and has a post-secondary degree, has an 8.7 per cent probability of engaging in entrepreneurship. An individual with the same characteristics, but unemployed at the time of the interview, has a probability of only 2.9 per cent.

Personally knowing an entrepreneur and believing in one's own skills is positively and strongly related to entrepreneurship. Knowing another entrepreneur has an increasing effect of 2.39 on the odds of being an entrepreneur. Self-efficacy has the strongest impact on entrepreneurship. The odds of being an entrepreneur are multiplied by a factor of 6.97 when the individual is self-confident about his/her skills and entrepreneurial talent. An important note to make, however, is the inability to appoint the causal direction of the relationship. It is not possible to say whether network and self-efficacy drive entrepreneurial activity or vice versa. It is easy to reason that successful progress in the start-up process stimulates individuals in their belief about their entrepreneurial abilities. As discussed earlier, self-efficacy suffers from hindsight bias. Similarly, individuals might be brought into contact with other entrepreneurs as a consequence, and not a cause, of entrepreneurship.

As a general result, demographic variables such as age, gender and education, fail to explain entrepreneurship. The insignificance of age can partly be assigned to the existence of different effects of age on entrepreneurship. As discussed earlier, younger people are expected to be more motivated, while older ones are probably more experienced. Given these two opposing effects, it is difficult to discriminate between them in the dataset. In an attempt to find a significant relationship between age and entrepreneurship, age was also included as a quadratic term in the regression. However, this quadratic term proved to be insignificant. In another attempt, the individuals were classified into several age categories, with a five-year spread. The following age categories turned out to have a significantly higher probability of becoming entrepreneurs, 20–24, 30–34, 40–44, 55–59 and 60–64. It is difficult to discern a systematic age pattern in these categories. Apart from saying that individuals younger than 20 and older than 64 are less likely to become an entrepreneur, no more specific relation can be seen. This result only confirms the result of the base model, where age is not linearly related to entrepreneurial activity. Unfortunately, the result of this extension did not improve the original model. Apparently, the entrepreneurial individuals are evenly spread over the age pyramid.

Educational attainment, when classified into secondary and post-secondary education, fails to discriminate entrepreneurs from other individuals. This result, however, does not mean that education is not an important antecedent of entrepreneurship. Due to the 'crudeness' of the measure applied in the GEM survey, it was to be expected that finding a significant relation would be difficult. A different result might possibly show up when more detailed information on the level and type of education is provided.

Quite surprising is the failure of gender as an explanatory variable. In this dataset, women are just as likely as men to engage in entrepreneurship. It must be noted that possible gender effects might be intermediated through other explanatory variables such as network and self-efficacy.

The last insignificant variable is risk attitude. Individuals who think they should not pursue any entrepreneurial intention due to the high risk of failure, turn out to be no different from others. Although potentially indicative, it must be stressed that the variable *risk* is not an appropriate measure of risk attitude.

DISCUSSION AND POLICY IMPLICATIONS

From the results of the regression analysis it cannot be concluded that unemployed individuals start their own firm to escape their situation of unemployment. Our results suggest the opposite relation, where the unemployed are less likely to become entrepreneurs.

Based on the traditional push–pull opposition, one might argue for the introduction of pushing measures, such as a reduction in unemployment benefit or a decrease in the period in which individuals have the right to a benefit. However, as previously indicated in Table 2.2, the role of unemployment as a driver of entrepreneurship is not a one-sided distinction between necessity and opportunity. Unemployed individuals can also be pulled into entrepreneurship. As a stimulating measure, the appeal of entrepreneurship for unemployed individuals could therefore be increased. More positive measures such as a reduction in the workload and a more equal social security system for the self-employed could also be proposed.

If one wants to increase the pool of nascent entrepreneurs, the unemployed should be positively stimulated to abandon their current situation and proceed into self-employment. However, in order to make such policy statements, more insight into the different categories of the unemployed are required. Students, retired or disabled individuals, housewives, homemakers and the unemployed probably need diverse forms of attention and require different stimulating measures.

A shortcoming of the present research is the lack of more detailed information on educational attainment, country and time differences. First, more detailed information on educational attainment might be at hand. Second, since the entry decision is time and space dependent (Storey, 1994), the above results may not be generalized as such. The analysis could be enhanced by adopting longitudinal data. It can be expected that the drive of unemployed individuals is time dependent. They might have different drivers for entrepreneurship depending on the condition of the economic environment. The inclusion of other countries might also be valuable. Country differences may be an important factor in explaining entrepreneurial differences.

Access to more recent GEM data could also improve the analysis at different points. An advantage of more recent GEM editions is that they collect information about the entrepreneurial intentions of individuals where a clear distinction is made between latent, nascent and infant entrepreneurs. It would be a contribution to the entrepreneurship literature to see more clearly which individuals drop out during this process. More specifically, the differences in dropout rates between unemployed and employed individuals could be of major interest. A clearer picture of the entrepreneurial process would be possible.

As policy makers are interested in stimulating unemployed individuals into self-employment, it is presupposed that unemployed individuals have the same skills to make new firms perform well. If we want to learn more about the impact of unemployment, we should therefore include the last step in the entrepreneurial process. We should compare the survival and growth rates of new firms. Are the firms established by unemployed individuals more or less likely to be successful than firms started by employed individuals? If the performance of firms created by unemployed individuals is significantly lower, then it would not make sense to stimulate the unemployed into entrepreneurship.

More insight into the length of the unemployment period could also refine inferences about the impact of unemployment, since we would be able to distinguish between people who are temporarily unemployed when starting their own firm, and individuals who are unemployed for a longer period. A difference among these unemployment groups has already been suggested by Evans and Jovanovic (1989). Also, Alba-Ramirez (1994) showed that the duration of unemployment significantly affects an individual's decision to become an entrepreneur.

CONCLUSION

Unemployed Belgians were found less likely to become an entrepreneur. However, merely claiming that unemployed individuals who are involved in a start-up or a new firm act out of necessity has been found to be an incomplete account of the decision process. Similarly, employed nascent entrepreneurs have other reasons than opportunity. We were not able to find any relationship with age, gender, risk or education. On the other hand, in line with entrepreneurship literature, we found a clear positive effect of network and self-efficacy.

ACKNOWLEDGEMENTS

An earlier version was presented at the PhD seminar: 'New perspectives on entrepreneurship' in September 2005 which was organized by the Bodø Graduate School of Business and the Nordland Research Institute. The comments by participants in the seminar have been a great help in accomplishing this chapter. We should like to thank an anonymous referee as well as Marc Tiri and Lars Kolvereid who provided valuable comments.

NOTES

1. Although aware of the debate concerning the definition of entrepreneurship, we have chosen not to contribute to this research area. We define entrepreneurship as the formation of new firms as a result of individual actions, neglecting other aspects of entrepreneurship.
2. 'Occupational choice' might not be the best chosen concept since at least some of the unemployed do not choose to be unemployed. However, the concept is widely accepted in the economics literature and, therefore, it is kept as a recognizable concept.
3. Most often these hypotheses are tested at one of these levels. One rare exception is made in an article by Ritsilä and Tervo (2002), who test the pull and push hypotheses at all three levels.
4. For more information on GEM, see Reynolds et al. (2005) and www.gemconsortium.org.
5. Because an individual can be involved in a start-up and a new firm simultaneously, some individuals are recognized as a 'nascent' as well as an 'infant' entrepreneur.
6. The exact formulation of the question is as follows: 'You know someone personally who started a business in the past 2 years.' Some caution must be taken when interpreting the answers to this question. Individuals involved in a start-up might deliberately seek out entrepreneurs with whom to exchange information in order to improve their chances of success.

7. The LR-statistic compares the log-likelihood of the complete model with that of the base model, which consists only of an intercept as the independent variable. Based on the difference in log-likelihoods, the LR-statistic is calculated. The LR-statistic can be interpreted as a χ^2 statistic. By doing so, it provides a test for the null hypothesis that $\beta_1 = \beta_2 = \ldots = \beta_k$.
8. A cutting point of 0.50 means an individual whose probability of becoming an entrepreneur (based on the regression results) is higher than 50 per cent and is classified as an entrepreneur.
9. The odds of being an entrepreneur are: Prob[*self*=1)/(1 − Prob(*self*=1)]. Since Prob(*self* = 1) = $(e^{\beta' x_i})/(1+ e^{\beta' x_i})$ it can be proved that the odds are equal to $exp(\beta)$.

REFERENCES

Ajzen, I. (1991), 'The theory of planned behaviour', *Organizational Behaviour and Human Decision Processes*, **50** (2), 1–63.

Alba-Ramirez, A. (1994), 'Self-employment in the midst of unemployment: the case of Spain and the United States', *Applied Economics*, **26**, 189–204.

Arenius, P. and M. Minniti (2005), 'Perceptual variables and nascent entrepreneurship', *Small Business Economics*, **24**, 233–47.

Blanchflower, D.G. (2000), 'Self-employment in OECD countries', *Labour Economics*, **7**, 471–505.

Blanchflower, D.G. and A.J. Oswald (1998), 'What makes an entrepreneur?', *Journal of Labor Economics*, **16** (1), 26–60.

Blanchflower, D.G., A. Oswald and A. Stutzer (2001), 'Latent entrepreneurship across nations', *European Economic Review*, **45**, 680–91.

Carree, M.A. (2002), 'Does unemployment affect the number of establishments?', *Regional Studies*, **36** (4), 389–98.

Chen, C.C., P.G. Green and A. Crick (1998), 'Does entrepreneurial self-efficacy distinguish entrepreneurs from managers?', *Journal of Business Venturing*, **13**, 295–316.

Davidsson, P. and B. Honig (2003), 'The role of social and human capital among nascent entrepreneurs', *Journal of Business Venturing*, **18**, 301–31.

Delmar, F. and P. Davidsson (2000), 'Where do they come from? Prevalence and characteristics of nascent entrepreneurs', *Entrepreneurship and Regional Development*, **12**, 1–23.

Dolton, P. and G. Makepeace (1990), 'Self-employment among graduates', *Bulletin of Economic Research*, **42** (1), 35–53.

Evans, D.S. and B. Jovanovic (1989), 'An estimated model of entrepreneurial choice under liquidity constraints', *Journal of Political Economy*, **97** (4), 808–27.

Evans, D.S. and L.S. Leighton (1990), 'Small business formation by unemployed and employed workers', *Small Business Economics*, **12**, 319–30.

Gartner, W.B. and N.M. Carter (2003), 'Entrepreneurial behavior and firm organizing processes', in Z.J. Acs and D.B. Audretsch (eds), *Handbook of Entrepreneurship Research*, New York: Springer, pp. 19–221.

Gilad, B. and P. Levine (1986), 'A behavioral model of entepreneurial supply', *Journal of Small Business Management*, **24** (4), 45–53.

Ilmakunnas, P. and J. Topi (1999), 'Microeconomic and macroeconomic influences on entry and exit of firms', *Review of Industrial Organization*, **15**, 283–301.

Kihlstrom, R.E. and J.-J. Laffont (1979), 'A general equilibrium entrepreneurial theory of firm formation based on risk aversion', *Journal of Political Economy*, **81** (4), 719–48.
Knight, F. (1921), *Risk, Uncertainty and Profit*, Boston, MA: Houghton Mifflin.
Kolvereid, L. (1996), 'Prediction of employment status choice intentions', *Entrepreneurship Theory and Practice*, **21** (1), 47–57.
Kolvereid, L. and Ø. Moen (1997), 'Entrepreneurship among business graduates: does a major in entrepreneurship make a difference?', *Journal of European Industrial Training*, **21** (4), 154–60.
Manigart, S., B. Clarysse, H. Crijns and H. Goossens (2001), *GEM 2001 Executive Report for Belgium and Flanders*, Ghent: E.M. Kauffman Foundation, Vlerick Leuven Gent Management School.
Meager, N. (1992), 'Does unemployment lead to self-employment', *Small Business Economics*, **4** (4), 87–103.
Menard, S. (2002), 'Applied logistic regression analysis', *Quantitative Applications in the Social Sciences*, 2nd edn, no. 106, Beverly Hills, CA: Sage University Papers.
Minniti, M., W.D. Bygrave and E. Autio (2005), *GEM 2005 Executive Report*, Wellesley, MA: Babson College and London: London Business School.
Reynolds, P., N. Bosma, E. Autio, S. Hunt, N. De Bono, I. Servais, P. Lopez-Garcia and N. Chin (2005), 'Global Entrepreneurship Monitor: data collection design and implementation 1998–2003', *Small Business Economics*, **24**, 205–31.
Reynolds, P.D., N.M. Carter, W.B. Gartner and P.G. Greene (2004), 'The prevalence of nascent entrepreneurs in the United States: evidence from the Panel Study of Entrepreneurial Dynamics', *Small Business Economics*, **23**, 263–84.
Ritsilä, J. and H. Tervo (2002), 'Effects of unemployment on new firm formation: micro-level panel data evidence from Finland', *Small Business Economics*, **19**, 31–40.
Rotefoss, B. and L. Kolvereid (2005), 'Aspiring, nascent and fledging entrepreneurs: an investigation of the business start-up process', *Entrepreneurship and Regional Development*, **17**, 109–27.
Storey, D. (1991), 'The birth of new firms – does unemployment matter? A review of the evidence', *Small Business Economics*, **3**, 167–78.
Storey, D. (1994), *Understanding the Small Business Sector*, London: Routledge.
Vivarelli, M. (1991), 'The birth of new enterprises', *Small Business Economics*, **3**, 215–23.

3. Do entry barriers, perceived by SMEs, affect real entry? Some evidence from the Netherlands

S. Gerhard Dijkstra, Ron Kemp and Clemens Lutz

INTRODUCTION[1]

Entries of new firms into the market foster the dynamics in the economy. Entrants have an equilibrating function, as firms will enter the market if profits are above the long-run competitive level. Entrants are also considered as important agents of change, as new firms may introduce new products or production processes. The upshot is that entry contributes to allocative as well as dynamic efficiency in the market (Audretsch and Thurik, 2001). However, several mechanisms can prevent firms from entering the market and hamper the process of allocative and dynamic efficiency. Consequently, barriers to entry are one of the major issues in entrepreneurship and competition policy.

In Blees et al. (2003) the results of a comprehensive literature study on entry barriers have been published: the theoretical background and the operating mechanisms are discussed. The report describes in total 37 structural and strategic barriers to entry and discusses the expected specific effects on small businesses. The literature study concludes that small entrants suffer more from barriers to entry than do large entrants (often existing companies active in another product or geographical market) and provides us with the argument to focus this study on small and medium-sized enterprises (SMEs). For example, it is argued that barriers related to advertising, brand name, capital requirements, cost of operating abroad, high wages, research and development (R&D) and selling expenses are less restrictive for large entrants. However, the existence of barriers does not necessarily mean that the problem is widespread, nor does it test whether there is a relationship between the barriers and real entry. It is expected that important barriers will have a stronger effect on real entry.

Several authors stress the need for empirical evidence on extant barriers to entry (Scherer, 1988; Geroski et al., 1990; Bunch and Smiley, 1992; Karakaya, 2002). As Singh et al. (1998, p. 230) argue, there are many theoretical models but empirical evidence in support of them is rather weak. Subsequently, they raise the question: 'how important empirically are the types of strategic behaviour, which have been modelled [theoretically] so copiously?'

Although entry barriers are discussed in a large body of literature, empirical studies that measure the effect on real entry are quite rare. Most econometric investigations of entry barriers have regressed the profit rate rather than entry. Orr (1974) observes that there are theoretical reasons for questioning the assumed strong relationship between entry barriers (at present) and profits (historical instead of expected figures) and refers to the gap between true and measured profits. This chapter follows a different approach and addresses the direct relationship between perceived entry barriers and real entry. We expect that SMEs considering entry ponder the importance of different entry barriers and, in particular, their perceptions with regard to these entry barriers. First we identify the major entry barriers as perceived by firms. Subsequently, we analyse whether these perceptions affect the real starter ratio observed in different sectors and provinces. In general, entry barriers will have a negative effect on real entry. However, not all barriers will lead to low start-up ratios. Several sectors in the entrepreneurial economy operate in a turbulent and demanding environment (Audretsch and Thurik, 2001). These attributes may be considered as an entry barrier that restricts entry, but also as new opportunities that encourage start-ups. The latter effect may neutralize the former. However, not all barriers are harmless. We aim at identifying these barriers by testing the relationship between perceived barriers and real entry.

From a policy perspective this is a relevant issue as entrepreneurship and new ventures are encouraged to reduce unemployment and to increase the dynamics in the economy. The existence of entry barriers is a potential threat for the effectiveness of these policies. In the Netherlands several policy changes have been debated, and some have been implemented to reduce the barriers to entry that start-ups were facing as a result of existing rules and regulations.

The next section starts with a concise overview of the literature on entry barriers. The concept is defined and the method to measure the importance of entry barriers is presented in the third section. Subsequently the sample and the questionnaire are discussed. In total, 1164 Dutch firms have been interviewed. The fourth and fifth sections discuss the empirical findings, and the final section concludes.

LITERATURE REVIEW

A large body of literature discusses the importance of entry barriers. Two different traditions can be distinguished: industrial organization (for example, Bain, 1956; Stigler, 1968; Von Weizsaecker, 1980) and strategic management (for example, Porter, 1980, 1985; Singh et al., 1998; Robinson et al., 2001). The first tradition focuses on the industry as the unit of analysis, strives for efficiency and identifies harmful barriers for economic development. Various models are developed to show how entry barriers affect the behaviour of firms and the performance of the industry. One of the main issues concerns the question whether government policy is needed to neutralize the effects of the barriers. The second tradition takes the firm as the unit of analysis and assesses entry barriers as a resource to create competitive advantage for individual firms. In line with this approach, superior strategies should create sustainable competitive advantage. In other words, a firm should make use of entry barriers that deter new competitors in the firm's market.

The contradictory assessment of the value of barriers to entry is related to the unit of analysis and the role that competition is expected to play in the two traditions. At the firm level it is indeed important to develop resources that are difficult for competitors to copy (Barney, 1991; Rangone, 1999). A reduction of competitive forces is generally in the interest of incumbent firms. However, from a welfare economic point of view, this should not lead to social costs, as a reduction of competitive forces may hamper the allocative and dynamic efficiency of the industry. The latter argument is put forward by Von Weizsaecker (1980) to justify public policies. This study does not focus on the role of competition and the assessment of social costs. The objective of this research is to identify important entry barriers perceived by firms (Yip, 1982; Smiley, 1988; Karakaya and Stahl, 1989; Singh et al., 1998). It aims at recognizing the major constraints that hamper firms in making their entry decision. The unit of analysis is the firm.

In line with the two traditions, two types of barriers can be distinguished: structural and strategic barriers to entry. The structural barriers stem from market structure characteristics and are widely discussed in the tradition of industrial organization. Bain (1956) introduced the concept of 'barriers to new competition'. This concept is based on the assumption that competition is key in the operation of industries and that any artificial barrier to competition may reduce the efficient allocation of resources in the industry. Bain stressed the importance of structural characteristics that hamper market entry of potential competitors: economies of scale, technological advantages, absolute cost advantages and so on.[2] The conclusion of this research is that entry-deterrent mechanisms limit the intensity of competition and may enable incumbent firms to raise prices and to realize supernormal profits. The Chicago school (Stigler, 1968) contributed to the debate on barriers to entry by stressing the importance of cost asymmetry between incumbents and potential entrants: the research should not focus on supernormal profits but on the question whether the conditions of entry for the incumbents were less difficult than those for the new entrants. The importance of this argument becomes clear when the advantages of economies of scale are interpreted. According to the Chicago school, scale economies do not represent a barrier to entry if they imply penalties for companies operating at suboptimal levels of production. A third approach that stems from this tradition focuses on the welfare effects and defines barriers to entry as a difference in cost structures which provokes a distortion in the use of economic resources from a social point of view (Von Weizsaecker, cited in Geroski et al., 1990, p. 10). A discussion of the specific difficulties of these approaches is beyond the scope of this chapter. However, what is important is to understand that the different approaches lead to different definitions of entry barriers. We conclude that Bain's perspective provides the broadest scope, while the other two approaches consider additional requirements in order to identify the 'real' barriers that hamper the efficient allocation of resources in the economy.

The strategic management tradition stresses the importance of strategic barriers. Barriers to entry not only result from structural characteristics of the market but also can be created as a result of strategies of individual firms that reduce the threat of new entrants. Following Barney (1991, p. 99), firms are advised to 'obtain sustained competitive advantages by implementing strategies that exploit their internal strengths, through responding to environmental opportunities, while neutralizing external threats and avoiding internal weaknesses'. Porter (1980, pp. 9–13) does not define the concept but specifies seven major sources of barriers to entry: economies of scale, product differentiation, capital requirements, switching costs, access to distribution channels, cost disadvantages independent of scale and government policy. Implicitly he uses a broad definition for barriers to entry in order to encompass the barriers that result from strategic behaviour. He provides a kind of typology of barriers to entry that firms should take into account when their competitive strategy is developed. Porter's specification also shows that structural and strategic barriers are related. The barrier may be rooted in the market structure, but this will not discourage firms from reacting strategically to this characteristic. The upshot is that most structural barriers have a strategic component too. For example, advertising can be considered as a structural phenomenon in the automobile industry, however, each actor may develop its own advertising strategy (brand) that affects new competitors.

DEFINITION OF CONCEPTS AND DATA COLLECTION

In line with the broad perspective of this research we used the following definition of barriers to entry: 'all advantages of established sellers in an industry over potential entrant sellers, as perceived by firms which seek to enter a new market'. The focus is on the perception of firms and on entry to a new market. We prefer the concept 'market' to 'industry'. According to Ferguson (1992, p. 32) markets group together firms producing close substitutes from the buyer's point of view, while an industry groups together close substitutes from the supplier's point of view. These are usually broader groupings than markets. The advantage of the market concept is that it has a clearer meaning for the interviewed firm. Small firms operating in a specific niche are not always informed about the potential new competitors in the industry but they have a good overview of potential new competitors in the market in which they are active.

A large number of structural and strategic barriers to entry were presented in the questionnaire (Table 3.1). However, not all the barriers identified in the literature study (Blees et al., 2003) were addressed. Most important were time limitations. On the basis of previous experience we decided that the telephone interview should not take more than 15 minutes. Some issues were difficult to describe in an unambiguous question (for example, causal ambiguity). Other barriers to entry were covered by the answers on similar barriers (for example, brand name and customer loyalty are part of advertising; experience advantages are related to cost advantages; government regulations are related to government licences).

Some aspects were covered by two separate questions in order to be able to make a distinction between the importance of structural characteristics and behavioural characteristics. For example, with regard to advertising we presented two statements:

1. Firms in the market have high expenditures for advertising and promotion (structural).
2. The products are heavily supported by advertisement and promotion in order to make entry to the market less attractive for new competitors (strategic).

We claim that the listed barriers to entry in Table 3.1 give an overview of the most important barriers discussed in the extant literature.

Incumbent companies were asked to indicate on a five-point Likert scale to what extent new competitors would encounter the barrier in question.[3] Ideally the survey should have addressed new and potential competitors.[4]

Table 3.1 Barriers to entry derived from the literature survey

Barrier to entry	Source	Constitutes a barrier mainly for SMEs	Constitutes a barrier mainly for LEs	Constitutes a barrier mainly for both
Access to distribution channels (distribution)	Porter 1980; Yip 1982; Karakaya & Stahl 1989; Han et al. 2001	*		
Access to knowledge/ patents	Yip 1982; Harrigan 1983; Karakaya & Stahl 1989; Shepherd 1997			*
Advertising	Spence 1980; Harrigan 1981; Yip 1982; Netter 1983; Schmalensee 1983; Karakaya & Stahl 1989	*		
Capital requirement	Bain 1956; Porter 1980; Harrigan 1981; Yip 1982; Karakaya & Stahl 1989; Shepherd 1997	*		
Collusion	Singh et al. 1998			*
Cost disadvantages (absolute cost advantages of incumbents)	Bain 1956; Scherer 1970; Yip 1982; Karakaya & Stahl 1989; Geroski et al. 1990; Han et al. 2001			*
Cost of capital/ special risks and uncertainties	Demsetz 1982; Shepherd 1997	*?		
Customer switching costs	Porter 1980; Klemperer 1987, 1992; Karakaya & Stahl 1989; Shepherd 1997; Shy 2002			
Differentiation	Bain 1956; Porter 1980; Schmalensee 1982; Karakaya & Stahl 1989; Shepherd 1997; Martin 2002	*		
Economies of scale	Bain 1956; Scherer 1970; Dixit 1980; Spence 1980; Harrigan 1981; Schmalensee 1981; Yip 1982; Geroski et al. 1990	*		
Excess capacity	Spence 1977; Dixit 1980; Harrigan 1983; Lieberman 1987; Bunch &		*	

Table 3.1 (continued)

Barrier to entry	Source	Constitutes a barrier mainly for SMEs	Constitutes a barrier mainly for LEs	Constitutes a barrier mainly for both
	Smiley 1992; Shepherd 1997; Singh et al. 1998			
Financial risk/ sunk costs	Bain 1956; Porter 1980; Baumol et al. 1982; Geroski et al. 1990; Sutton 1991; Shepherd 1997			*
Government regulations	Porter 1980; Dixit & Kyle 1985; Karakaya & Stahl 1989; Shepherd 1997			*
Limit pricing	Bain 1956; Milgrom & Roberts 1982; Geroski et al. 1990; Bunch & Smiley 1992; Singh et al. 1998		*	
Masking profit/gaps and asymmetric information	Milgrom & Roberts 1982; Geroski et al. 1990; Bunch & Smiley 1992			*
Retaliation	Scherer 1970; Yip 1982; Karakaya & Stahl 1989; Bunch & Smiley 1992; Gatignon et al. 1997; Shepherd 1997; Thomas 1999		*	
Sales volume	Yip 1982			*?
Securing input/control over strategic resources	Scherer 1970; Yip 1982; Karakaya & Stahl 1989; Shepherd 1997; Singh et al. 1998; Cabral 2000			*
Strategic behaviour advertising	Bunch & Smiley 1992; Singh et al. 1998		*?	
Strategic behaviour differentiation/ packing the product space	Schmalensee 1978; Bunch & Smiley 1992; Shepherd 1997; Cabral 2000	*		
Strategic behaviour distribution channels	Singh et al. 1998	*	*?	

Table 3.1 (continued)

Barrier to entry	Source	Constitutes a barrier mainly for SMEs	Constitutes a barrier mainly for LEs	Constitutes a barrier mainly for both
Strategic behaviour knowledge/pre-emptive patents	Bunch & Smiley 1992; Singh et al. 1998	*?		
Strategic behaviour R&D	Harrigan 1981; Yip 1982; Daems & Douma 1985; Bunch & Smiley 1992; Singh et al. 1998	*?		

Notes:
* Strong confirmation is given in the cited literature that the barrier is relevant for the indicated group of firms.
*? An indication is given in the cited literature that the barrier may be relevant for the specific group of firms.
LEs = large enterprises.

However, potential newcomers are difficult to identify and, therefore, we decided to interview incumbents. As we are interested in barriers (potential) entrants may face and not the behaviour of the specific incumbents *per se*, the questions were directed at practices in the market rather than the firm's specific behaviour. In general, the incumbents were asked to indicate how important a specific barrier is if a comparable company (same size) wants to enter the major product market in which the incumbent is operational. As barriers to entry are related to product markets and most firms manage multi-product operations, we explicitly referred to the most important product market. The advantage of this format for the question is that all companies have experience with the market and, therefore, are able to value the importance of the specific barrier.

As the concepts involved are sometimes difficult to circumscribe in unambiguous questions a pilot study was carried out in November 2004, in which 40 students participated. The students tested the survey and were asked to write about 100 case studies of the companies they interviewed. The case studies have allowed us to understand the functioning of the perceived barriers to entry in the different industries under study and, therefore, have facilitated the interpretation of the results of the questionnaire. Moreover, some questions were refined to avoid ambiguous interpretations. The final questionnaire was pre-tested by telephone with potential respondents.

The sample consists of 1164 Dutch firms in six industries, that is, furniture, employment agencies, chemicals, ICT (information and communications technology), food (production of bread) and retail (clothing and shoes).[5] The aim was to collect data for approximately 175–200 firms per sector divided over three size categories (<10 employees, 10–49 employees, and 50+ employees). Per size category, the firms were selected at random from the Direct Marketing CD-database of MarketSelect.[6] In the 50+ size category in particular, in some sectors, all existing firms were contacted because of the limited number of firms with over 50 employees.

In total, 3562 firms were contacted for the telephone survey. This resulted in 1068 completed responses: a response rate of 30 per cent. Of the contacted firms, 33 per cent refused to cooperate. Another 24 per cent of the contacted firms could not be reached because of an answering machine, no answer, number engaged or more than six attempts with no response. Finally, an appointment was made with 13 per cent of the contacted firms, but the questionnaire was not completed because the targeted sample had been reached. The other 96 respondents were interviewed by our students in the pilot phase.[7]

The MarketSelect database was used to test for non-response bias. Smaller firms were more willing than large firms to participate in the research. This holds for the total sample as well as for the furniture, employment agencies, chemicals and ICT sectors. No significant differences related to size were found for the food industry and retail. In the food industry, firms were less willing to participate in the research compared to the other sectors, probably because of the Christmas rush.

Information about real entry was provided by starter ratios for the six industries (*s*) mentioned above. In total 12 provinces (*p*) were distinguished. In line with the entry/exit literature initiated by Mansfield (1962) and Orr (1974), the entry rates are explained by barriers and incentives. The survey discussed 23 barriers (*i*) with the firms and 10 variables were used to express the attractiveness of the market (*j*). The general model is as follows:

$$S.Ratio_{p,s} = \alpha + \beta_i Barrier_{i,p,s} + \beta_j Attract_{j,p,s}. \tag{3.1}$$

The following variables were used to indicate market attractiveness (*Attract*):

1. Failure rate: the number of firms in the sector declaring bankruptcy in the last quarter of 2004.
2. Growth: an average value expressing realized growth of 2003 and 2004 and expected annual growth for the coming 3 years.

3. Margin: an average of the realized margin in 2003 and 2004 and the expected annual margin for the coming 3 years. In order to control for sector differences the computation is based on deviations (%) from sector averages.
4. Dynamics: an average value of three items expressing the technological and non-technological dynamics in the market.
5. Capacity: expressing available excess capacity during the last year.
6. Concentration: expressing the market share of the 4 largest suppliers in the market.
7. B2B: dummy = 1 if B2B turnover is ≥ 75%.
8. B2C: dummy = 1 if B2C turnover is ≥ 75%.
9. Market coverage: dummy = 1 if the firm's market has a national or international coverage.
10. Size: full-time workforce, three classes are distinguished: <10 (class 1), 10–49 (class 2) and 50+ (class 3).

The market attractiveness variables were part of the survey on perceived entry barriers. The starter and failure ratios are derived from datasets available at the Chamber of Commerce and Statistics Netherlands (CBS).[8] Some variables in the model are multi-item scales (Growth, Margin, Dynamics). After a factor analysis to test for unidimensionality, the items of the variables are averaged.

FINDINGS: PERCEIVED ENTRY BARRIERS

In Table 3.2 the number of observations per industry and per size class are presented. Most observations are in the class of <10 employees, or micro firms. In the retail sector, we have only five observations of firms with 50 employees or more. As the sample was drawn from a database including subsidiaries and branches of larger firms, and responses were provided by

Table 3.2 Industry and size (full-time employees)

	Furniture	Employment agencies	Chemicals	ICT	Food	Retail	Total
<10 employees	109	128	79	95	82	170	663
10–49employees	73	41	57	77	37	18	303
50+ employees	27	35	38	43	38	5	186
Unknown	3	1	4	1	3	0	12
Total	212	205	178	216	160	193	1164

local managers, the questions concern employment figures of the selected subsidiary. About 40 per cent of the interviewed establishments are related to a larger company.

In Table 3.3 the perceived barriers are presented. Overall, securing input, collusion, knowledge, retaliation and strategic knowledge protection are the least important barriers. According to the interviewed firms, most barriers concern less important constraints (value lower than 3).[9] This can be interpreted as a good sign for the Dutch economy as competitive forces do not seem to be constrained by most entry barriers. Remarkably, some of the interviewed manager-owners raised the question why we were bothering about these issues, as solving these problems was considered to be their key competency. However, it is noted that only incumbents were interviewed, which may lead to a certain bias as these firms have surmounted existing barriers. Knowing how to solve a problem makes the problem trivial. To counter this argument it may be stated that only incumbents should be interviewed, as only the opinion of viable firms has to be taken into account.

In general the ranking of the importance of specific barriers to entry is consistent between the sectors: securing input and collusion are of minor importance for all but two sectors (respectively, retail and employment agencies), while sales volume and capital are most important for all sectors. However, for all barriers some significant sectoral differences are observed at the 5 per cent level, except for sales volume, which is significant at the 10 per cent level. For instance, securing input is relatively important in the retail sector and knowledge is relatively important in the chemicals industry. In the last column of Table 3.3 the significant differences are presented.

The most important barrier is the procurement of a viable sales volume. The average value attached to this barrier is significantly higher than the average value for other barriers. It may be argued that this high value results from the cumulative effect of all kinds of other (strategic) barriers (collusion, retaliation, limit pricing, switching costs). However, the values given to these specific entry barriers were significantly lower than the importance given to sales volume. This indicates that the problem is more related to the operation of normal competitive processes and, subsequently, that the requirements for successful entry (and survival) are not easy to meet.

Other important barriers are cost disadvantages, strategic behaviour related to differentiation and financial risk. Two sectors, employment agencies and ICT, have relatively low scores, whereas the food industry shows the highest scores on these barriers. Overall, the firms value only a few barriers as important constraints. Finance and sales volume are key issues in all sectors. The ICT and furniture industries are sectors with relatively low barriers, and the chemicals, retail and food industries show relatively high values for the barriers under consideration.

Table 3.3 Perceived barriers to entry (differences per sector)

Barrier	Furniture (*f*)	Employment agency (*e*)	Chemicals (*c*)	ICT (*i*)	Food (*b*)	Retail (*r*)	Total	Sign. differences
Securing input	1.54	1.13	1.92	1.36	1.77	2.81	1.74	$f, b > e; f, e, i < c, r; c, b < r; i < b$
Collusion	1.45	2.37	1.50	1.62	1.82	1.89	1.78	$f < e, b, r; e > f, c, i, b, r; c < r$
Knowledge	1.75	1.46	2.70	2.03	1.94	1.71	1.92	$f, e, i, b, r < c; e < i, b$
Retaliation	1.71	2.17	2.24	1.84	2.35	2.07	2.04	$f < e, c, b; c, b > i$
Behaviour knowledge	2.03	1.94	2.70	1.99	2.16	2.06	2.13	$f, e, i, b, r < c$
Limit pricing	2.15	2.53	2.27	2.05	2.51	2.02	2.25	$e, b > i, r$
Switching costs	2.00	2.04	2.57	2.93	2.13	1.91	2.27	$f, e, b, r < c, i;$
Masking profit	1.97	2.44	2.28	2.21	2.47	2.37	2.28	$f < e, b, r$
Behaviour R&D	2.05	1.90	3.06	2.65	2.31	2.01	2.32	$f, e, r < c, i; e < b; c > i, b$
Behaviour advertising	2.21	2.52	2.27	2.17	2.46	2.77	2.39	$f, c, i < r; e > i$
Behaviour distribution channel	1.88	3.00	2.58	2.34	2.52	2.25	2.42	$f < e, c, i, b; e > f, c, i, b, r$
Government regulations	2.42	2.47	3.35	1.69	3.53	2.06	2.53	$f, e < c, b; f, e, c, b > i; e, c, b > r;$
Distribution	2.60	2.89	2.99	2.60	3.06	2.55	2.76	$f, i, r < b; c > r$
Advertising	2.72	2.90	2.68	2.53	2.77	3.24	2.80	$f, c, i, b < r; e > i$
Excess capacity	2.79	2.95	2.84	2.71	3.25	2.75	2.87	$f, i, r < b$
Differentiation	2.76	2.65	3.17	3.22	3.21	3.25	3.03	$f, e < c, i, b, r$
Economies of scale	3.35	2.96	3.27	2.89	3.58	2.93	3.15	$f > e, i, r; e, i, r < b; c > i$
Costs of capital	3.18	3.21	3.04	2.83	3.66	3.56	3.23	$f, c, i < b, r; e < b$

Table 3.3 (continued)

Barrier	Furniture (*f*)	Employment agency (*e*)	Chemicals (*c*)	ICT (*i*)	Food (*b*)	Retail (*r*)	Total	Sign. differences
Cost disadvantage	3.23	2.93	3.31	2.96	3.74	3.44	3.24	$f, e, c, i < b; e < c, r; i < r$
Behaviour differentiation	3.24	3.11	3.40	3.22	3.63	3.44	3.32	$e, i < b$
Financial risk	3.40	3.38	3.53	3.10	3.84	3.88	3.50	$f, e, i < b, r; c < r; c > i$
Capital	3.55	3.29	3.59	3.03	3.99	3.89	3.53	$f, c, b, r > i$; $f, e, c, < b; e < r$
Sales volume	3.80	3.72	3.90	3.79	4.03	3.83	3.84	$e < b$ ($p < 0.10$)
Mean score all barriers	2.31	2.52	2.64	2.43	2.68	2.64	2.52	$f < e, c, b, r$ $i < c, b, r$

Note: Significant at $p < 0.05$ unless otherwise indicated. The reply options were: 1 = not at all, 2 = barely, 3 = somewhat, 4 = to a large extent, 5 = to a very large extent.

FINDINGS: RELATIONSHIP BETWEEN BARRIERS AND REAL ENTRY

All barriers discussed in the previous section and all variables expressing the attractiveness of the market are integrated in the general model equation (3.1). This model has been estimated and in order to identify the major drivers the least significant variables have been eliminated in a stepwise process (backward regression).[10] This process was complete as soon as all retained variables were significant at the 5 per cent level. We preferred the general to specific over the specific to general procedure as it starts the identification process on the basis of all information available. However, we checked the reliability of the outcome by running the stepwise specific to general model (forward regression) and we observed that it leads to only minor deviations with regard to the coefficients. The same variables are identified and the coefficients obtain the same signs and significance levels.

Table 3.4 presents the results of the specific model. Several barriers and attractiveness variables do indeed affect the starter ratio. However, the margin, size, excess capacity and market coverage are not retained in the

*Table 3.4 Starter ratio, market attractiveness and perceived entry barriers**

Variables	Perception barriers (Table 3.2)**	Unstandardized coefficients β	Std error	*t*	Sig.
Constant		5.223	0.474	11.028	0.000
Failure rate	*Attract.*	2.689	0.582	4.617	0.000
Capital	3.53	−0.194	0.074	−2.693	0.007
Economies of scale	3.15	−0.202	0.067	−2.997	0.003
Govt regulation	2.53	−0.633	0.058	−10.906	0.000
Switching costs	2.27	0.300	0.063	4.788	0.000
Retaliation	2.04	−0.174	0.068	−2.574	0.010
Behaviour R&D	2.32	−0.241	0.066	−3.665	0.000
Securing input	1.74	−0.205	0.073	−2.797	0.005
Concentration	*Attract.*	−0.156	0.074	−2.109	0.035
B2B	*Attract.*	0.647	0.182	3.559	0.000
Dynamics	*Attract.*	0.873	0.095	9.153	0.000
Growth	*Attract.*	0.013	0.003	3.831	0.000

Notes:

* The model is derived from general to specific (stepwise procedure, all variables significant at 5% were retained). For the presented model in this table we obtained an R-square = 0.302 and an Adjusted R-square = 0.293.

** For each entry barrier the average value presented in Table 3.2 is given. *Attract.* indicates that the variable expresses an element of market attractiveness.

specific model. Market growth has the expected positive sign and concentration the expected negative sign. Dynamics in the market and the failure rate are positively related to the starter ratio, which indicates that turbulence in the market, despite some negative consequences, has a positive overall effect on entry. Firms that are more business-to-business (B2B) orientated (in our sample especially employment agencies and ICT) have a higher entry rate. This is in line with the findings of Karakaya and Stahl (1989) that entry barriers in B2B markets are (on average) less severe.

A striking result is that several of the perceived 'most important' entry barriers do not show up in Table 3.4. Sales volume, financial risks, cost disadvantages, costs of capital and behaviour with regard to differentiation were expected to affect real entry. Of the most important perceived entry barriers, only capital and economies of scale are retained in the model presented in Table 3.4. Remarkably, the 'least important' entry barrier, securing input, also influences the starter ratio.

Most signs are negative and reflect the expected influence on real entry. The effect of switching costs is somewhat unexpected. It seems that the direct negative impact is overruled by the positive consequences that may apply after successful market entry. The results also confirm that both structural barriers (capital, economies of scale, government regulation) and strategic barriers (switching costs, retaliation, behaviour R&D and securing input) influence the starter ratio.

CONCLUSIONS

The question raised by Singh et al. (1998) regarding the need for empirical evidence for the importance of entry barriers is highly relevant. Some issues seem to be based purely on theory, while other barriers play a role in the real business world and need the proper attention of policy makers. In contrast to most literature that addresses the relationship between entry barriers and profits, this chapter examines the direct relationship between barriers and real entry.

The 'most important' perceived barriers are rooted in characteristics of the market structure: sales volume, capital, financial risks, cost disadvantages, costs of capital and economies of scale. Only one of the major barriers stems from strategic behaviour: behaviour with regard to differentiation. Although some differences between sectors are observed, the ranking of the importance of specific barriers to entry is consistent between sectors.

In general the results confirm the expected relationship between entry barriers and real entry. However, some barriers seem to influence the starter ratio more strongly. Remarkably, several of the 'most important' perceived barriers do not restrict real entry rates (for example, sales volume, financial risk and behaviour differentiation) while the 'least important' barrier (securing input) influences the starter ratio significantly. Interestingly, the results confirm that both structural and strategic barriers influence starter ratios. In the debate on entry barriers, several researchers stress the importance of one of the two strands. The results presented in Table 3.4 show that both types of barrier may hamper competition.

The results contain an interesting lesson for policy makers who regulate competition in market economies. They should not address important barriers *per se*, but scrutinize the effects of barriers that seem to restrict real entry. For example, government regulations are not perceived as one of the most important entry barriers. Nevertheless, this barrier has a strong impact on starter ratios. This result justifies why policy makers in the Netherlands reappraise the relevance of existing regulations. It is noted that these results also show a need for further research. This study involved only a few Dutch industries and it would be interesting to verify whether the results are confirmed in other sectors and countries.

NOTES

1. At the time of writing this chapter, Ron Kemp worked for EIM Business and Policy Research. These are the views of the authors and need not reflect those of EIM or the Netherlands Competition Authority. We would like to thank all students who participated in the fieldwork and the course 'Small Business Economics'. Their reports, enthusiasm and critical comments were highly appreciated.
2. Bain's emphasis on market structure has been criticized within the discipline of industrial organization. By the late 1970s these views became known as the the 'new industrial organization' (Geroski et al., 1990). They stressed the importance of behaviour as a determinant for market performance and market structure (in the long run). The approach comes close to the tradition of strategic management as behavioural aspects are considered to be key. However, in line with the tradition of industrial organization, the unit of analysis is the industry.
3. The reply options were: not at all, barely, somewhat, to a large extent, to a very large extent (or alternatively: strongly disagree, disagree, not agree/not disagree, agree, strongly agree).
4. Even the group of new and potential competitors can be considered as too broad. For the research information from the 'marginal entrant' is needed. This marginal firm is indeed difficult to identify.
5. The SBI-code of the Chamber of Commerce for the industries were 361 (furniture), 74501 (employment agencies), 24 excluding 241 (chemical industry), 721 and 722 (ICT), 158 (food, production of bread) and 5242 and 5243 (retail, clothing and shoes).
6. The database is based on information on business registrations by the Chamber of Commerce, address information by TPG Post and checks by MarketSelect.
7. For most barriers, no significant differences were found between the data from the telephone interview and the students' interviews. Therefore, pooling the data is admissible.
8. We obtained the number of firms active in the industry at 1 January 2005 from Statistics Netherlands (CBS). This number is rounded to fives by the CBS itself. For the chemical

industry (242, 243, 244, 245, 246, 247) and retail (52421, 52422, 52423, 52424, 52425, 52426, 52427, 52431, 52432) this can be more inaccurate due to rounding of each sub-industry.

9. The scores have the same range as previous research, see, for example, Smiley (1988) and Karakaya (2002).
10. Tests demonstrate that multicollinearity is not a problem in the analysis.

REFERENCES

Audretsch, D.B. and R. Thurik (2001), 'What's new about the new economy? Sources of growth in the managed and entrepreneurial economies', *Industrial and Corporate Change*, **10** (1), 267–315.

Bain, J.S. (1956), *Barriers to New Competition*, Cambridge, MA: Harvard University Press.

Barney, J.B. (1991), 'Firm resources and sustained competitive advantage', *Journal of Management*, March, 99–120.

Baumol, W.J., J. Panzar and R.D. Willig (1982), *Contestable Markets and the Theory of Industry Structure*, New York: Harcourt Brace Jovanovich.

Blees, J., R.G.M. Kemp, J. Maas and M. Mosselman (2003), *Barriers to Entry: Differences in Barriers to Entry for SMEs and Large Enterprises*, EIM Research Report H200301, Zoetermeer, The Netherlands.

Bunch, D.S. and R. Smiley (1992), 'Who deters entry? Evidence on the use of strategic entry deterrents', *Review of Economics and Statistics*, **74** (3), 509–21.

Cabral, L.M.B. (2000), *Introduction to Industrial Organisation*, Cambridge, MA and London: MIT Press.

Daems, H. and S.W. Douma (1985), *Concurrentie: Analyse en strategie*, Deventer: Kluwer.

Demsetz, H. (1982), 'Barriers to entry', *American Economic Review*, **72** (1), 47–57.

Dixit, A. (1980), 'The role of investment in entry-deterrence', *Economic Journal*, **90** (357), 95–106.

Dixit, A.K. and A.S. Kyle (1985), 'The use of protection and subsidies for entry promotion and deterrence', *American Economic Review*, **75** (1), 139–52.

Ferguson, R.P. (1992), *Industrial Economics: Issues and Perspectives*, London: Macmillan.

Gatignon, H., T.S. Robertson and A.J. Fein (1997), 'Incumbent defence strategies against new product entry', *International Journal of Research in Marketing*, **14**, 163–76.

Geroski, P., R.J. Gilbert and A. Jacquemin (1990), *Barriers to Entry and Strategic Competition: Fundamentals of Pure and Applied Economics 41*, Chur: Harwood Academic Publishers GmbH.

Han, J.K., N. Kim and H.B. Kim (2001), 'Entry barriers: a dull-, one- or two-edged sword for incumbents? Unravelling the paradox from a contingency perspective', *Journal of Marketing*, **65** (1), 1–14.

Harrigan, K.R. (1981), 'Barriers to entry and competitive strategies', *Strategic Management Journal*, **2** (4), 395–412.

Harrigan, K.R. (1983), 'Entry barriers in mature manufacturing industries', *Advances in Strategic Management*, **2** (1), 67–97.

Karakaya, F. (2002), 'Barriers to entry in industrial markets', *Journal of Business and Industrial Marketing*, **17** (5), 379–88.

Karakaya, F. and M.J. Stahl (1989), 'Barriers to entry and market entry decisions in consumer and industrial goods markets', *Journal of Marketing*, **53**, 80–91.
Klemperer, P. (1987), 'Entry deterrence in markets with consumer-switching costs', *Economic Journal*, **97**, 99–117.
Klemperer, P. (1992), 'Competition when consumers have switching costs: an overview', CEPR Discussion Paper Series 704, Centre for Economic Policy Research, London.
Lieberman, M.B. (1987), 'Excess capacity as a barrier to entry: an empirical appraisal', *Journal of Industrial Economics*, **4**, 607–27.
Mansfield, E. (1962), 'Entry, Gibrat's law, innovation, and the growth of firms', *American Economic Review*, **52**, 87–103.
Martin, S. (2002), *Advanced Industrial Economics*, Malden, MA: Blackwell.
Milgrom, P. and J. Roberts (1982), 'Limit-pricing and entry under incomplete information: an equilibrium analysis', *Econometrica*, **50** (2), 443–60.
Netter, J.M. (1983), 'Political competition and advertising as a barrier to entry', *Southern Economic Journal*, **50** (October), 510–20.
Orr, D. (1974), 'The determinants of entry: a study of the Canadian manufacturing industries', *Review of Economics and Statistics*, **56**, 58–66.
Porter, M.E. (1980), *Competitive Strategy*, New York: Free Press.
Porter, M.E. (1985), *Competitive Advantage: Creating and Sustaining Superior Performance*, New York: Free Press.
Rangone, A. (1999), 'A resource-based approach to strategy analysis in small-medium sized enterprises', *Small Business Economics*, **12**, 233–48.
Robinson, K.C., P. Philips McDougall (2001), 'Entry barriers and new venture performance: a comparison of universal and contingency approaches', *Strategic Management Journal*, **22**, 659–85.
Scherer, F.M. (1970), *Industrial Pricing: Theory and Evidence*, Chicago, IL: Rand McNally.
Scherer, F.M. (1988), 'Review of the economics of market dominance', *International Journal of Industrial Organization*, **6**, 517–19.
Schmalensee, R. (1978), 'Entry deterrence in the ready-to-eat breakfast cereal industry', *Bell Journal of Economics*, **9** (2), 305–27.
Schmalensee, R. (1981), 'Economies of scale and barriers to entry', *Journal of Political Economy*, **89** (6), 1228–38.
Schmalensee, R. (1982), 'Product differentiation advantages of pioneering brands', *American Economic Review*, **72** (3), 350–71.
Schmalensee, R. (1983), 'Advertising and entry deterrence: an exploratory model', *Journal of Political Economy*, **91** (4), 636–53.
Shepherd, W.G. (1997), *The Economics of Industrial Organisation*, Upper Saddle River, NJ: Prentice-Hall International.
Shy, O. (2002), 'A quick-and-easy method for estimating switching costs', *International Journal of Industrial Organization*, **20**, 71–87.
Singh, S., M. Utton and M. Waterson (1998), 'Strategic behaviour of incumbent firms in the UK', *International Journal of Industrial Organization*, **16**, 229–51.
Smiley, R. (1988), 'Empirical evidence on strategic entry deterrence', *International Journal of Industrial Organization*, **6**, 167–80.
Spence, A.M. (1977), 'Entry, capacity, investment and oligopolistic pricing', *Bell Journal of Economics*, **8** (2), 534–44.
Spence, A.M. (1980), 'Notes on advertising, economies of scale and entry barriers', *Quarterly Journal of Economics* (November), 493–507.

Stigler, G. (1968), *The Organization of Industry*, Chicago, IL: University of Chicago Press.

Sutton, J. (1991), *Sunk Costs and Market Structure: Price Competition, Advertising, and the Evolution of Concentration*, Cambridge, MA: MIT Press.

Thomas, L.A. (1999), 'Incumbent firms', response to entry: price, advertising and new product introduction', *International Journal of Industrial Organization*, **17**, 527–55.

Von Weizsaecker, C.C. (1980), 'A welfare analysis of barriers to entry', *Bell Journal of Economics*, **11** (2), 399–420.

Yip, G.S. (1982), *Barriers to Entry: A Corporate Perspective*, Lexicon, MA: Lexicon Books.

4. Traits versus attitudes in predicting future entrepreneurship

Rudolf Dömötör and Christopher Hader

INTRODUCTION

The prediction of entrepreneurial behaviour has received a lot of attention in entrepreneurship research. It is argued that identifying the characteristics of entrepreneurs would enable policy makers and educators to influence future behaviour with regard to the foundation of new businesses. Without proper knowledge of key entrepreneurial factors or processes, however, this interaction is not possible.

Over the years, a number of different theoretical and methodological approaches to the prediction of entrepreneurship have been developed, but studies which compare these approaches are rare. One of the most common approaches has been the use of personality theory with an emphasis on personal dispositions or traits. Based on their criticism of the entrepreneurial traits approach, Robinson et al. (1991) proposed the use of attitude theory to distinguish entrepreneurs from non-entrepreneurs.

The aim of this study is to compare traditional entrepreneurial traits and entrepreneurial attitudes with regard to their ability to predict future entrepreneurial behaviour. The practical benefit of such a comparison would be the ability to use these instruments more effectively in predicting future entrepreneurship and in training future entrepreneurs.

In the next section, we give an overview of the two theoretical approaches which form the basis for our study. The third section provides a critical summary and comparison of the two models, as well as deriving hypotheses. The fourth section presents the method applied in the empirical study, after which we summarize the results in the fifth section. Finally, we draw a number of conclusions based on our findings and point out directions for further research.

THEORETICAL MODELS FOR THE PREDICTION OF ENTREPRENEURSHIP

A number of theoretical approaches have been used in researching the propensity to become an entrepreneur. These include personality models as well as socio-cultural (demographic), economic and attitude models. In this chapter, we refrain from introducing all sorts of theoretical approaches. Instead, we focus on the traits and the attitude approaches, since our work centres around a comparison of the two.

Entrepreneurial Traits

The entrepreneurial traits approach is based on the assumption that entrepreneurs can be distinguished from non-entrepreneurs using a number of personality characteristics. This approach is based on personality theory and uses psychological personality tests to assess these characteristics.

Cole (1942) was the first to address the need to define the individual personality characteristics of entrepreneurs. McClelland (1961) followed this approach and developed a model which suggests that entrepreneurs show higher values than non-entrepreneurs in a characteristic which he called 'need for achievement', meaning that they feel personally responsible for solving problems, setting goals and reaching those goals (Brockhaus, 1982). McClelland found a relationship between the need for achievement and entrepreneurial thinking. In support of his theory, McClelland (1965) defined a specific achievement training programme and conducted several longitudinal studies which served to confirm his model.

Following McClelland, many other concepts regarding entrepreneurial traits were developed. One of the first was Rotter's concept of a 'locus of control' (Rotter, 1966), in which he distinguishes between an internal and an external locus of control. People with an external locus tend to attribute their outcomes (wins or losses) to external events, while people with an internal locus assign their outcomes to their personal skills.

Palmer (1971) and Liles (1974) drew attention to the entrepreneur's risk-taking propensity, arguing that entrepreneurs are willing to take higher risks than non-entrepreneurs. Brockhaus (1980) tried to confirm this assumption, but ultimately failed in his attempt. In his study, he found no evidence that entrepreneurs can be distinguished from managers (nor from the general public) on the basis of the risk-taking personality trait.

Crandall (1973) examined the concept of self-esteem, which deals specifically with self-confidence. In two studies, Chen et al. (1998) found that self-efficacy (a construct related to self-esteem) distinguishes entrepreneurs from non-entrepreneurs.

Preference for innovation was another trait used in this field of study. People who score higher in this characteristic generally prefer to be innovative. For example, Stewart (1996) compared eight studies measuring the innovativeness of entrepreneurs. Although research on the innovativeness trait is limited in quantity compared to studies on the need for achievement, for example, the relevant literature does suggest that innovativeness is a key predictor of entrepreneurial behaviour. Two other personality concepts used to predict entrepreneurship are also worth mentioning here: proactivity and tolerance for ambiguity (Knight, 1921; Kirzner, 1997).

Entrepreneurial traits are the single most important approach to predicting entrepreneurship, and they are frequently cited in the literature (for example, Brockhaus, 1982; Carland et al., 1984, 1988; Brockhaus and Horwitz, 1986; Gartner, 1988, 1989; Hisrich and Peters, 1992). As mentioned above, the entrepreneurial traits approach attempts to predict entrepreneurship by measuring personality traits. However, three problems have been identified in this approach. First, personality traits are very broad dispositions. As a result, it is rather difficult to develop personality scales specifically for predicting entrepreneurship – if statements are overly specific, they will tend to measure attitude instead of personality. Nevertheless, some researchers have tried to develop such scales (Wortman, 1986), but according to Hull et al. (1980) none has been successful in these endeavours.

Robinson et al. (1991a) mention the second point of criticism: many scales have been developed, but most of them correlate poorly. The third problem – which is also addressed by Robinson et al. – is that personality traits are usually employed to measure general tendencies. If they are used in a specific context, they may lose their predictive validity (Fishbein and Ajzen, 1975). A highly detailed critique of the entrepreneurial trait approach in general and on specific personality traits can be found in Chell et al. (1991).

Attitude Theory

An attitude is defined as a learned predisposition to respond in a consistently favourable or unfavourable manner with respect to a given object (Fishbein and Ajzen, 1975; see also Herkner, 2001). A conceptual distinction has been drawn between two major approaches. One approach, originally defined by Allport (1935), separates the attitude towards an object into three types of reaction: 'affect' (that is, positive or negative feelings towards the attitude object), 'cognition' (that is, beliefs and thoughts about an attitude object) and 'conation' (that is, behavioural intentions towards the object). On the other hand, the one-dimensional approach developed by Fishbein and Ajzen (1975) draws no distinctions between these reactions. It has been shown repeatedly that there is no difference between Allport's three-dimensional approach and Ajzen and Fishbein's one-dimensional approach (for example, Chaiken and Stangor, 1987).

There are two major differences between personality and attitude: first, while personality is assumed to remain stable throughout one's adult life, an attitude can change over time; and second, an attitude can be more distinct regarding a specific object than a personality (Oppenheim, 1992). Personality refers to a very broad disposition (for example, a person might have a risk-averse personality). However, one must be careful in this context – there are indeed very broad attitudes (for example, if a person has a risk-averse personality, s/he is likely to have a generally risk-averse attitude) and very distinct attitudes (for example, some may be risk averse in the sports context but enjoy taking risks in the financial context).

Gartner (1989) was the first to propose the use of attitudes to distinguish entrepreneurs from non-entrepreneurs. Robinson et al. (1991b) then developed and validated a scale for the prediction of entrepreneurship using attitudes: the Entrepreneurial Attitude Orientation (EAO). The EAO consists of four subscales: achievement in business, innovation in business, perceived personal control of business outcomes, and perceived self-esteem in business. These four subscales cover areas similar to the corresponding personality traits (need for achievement, innovativeness, locus of control and self-esteem), but are expressed as attitudes. This means that each statement is designed to be closely related to business situations.

The close relation of the statements to the business context should lead to better predictive results. McCline et al. (2000) reported higher EAO scores for entrepreneurs in the health-care industry compared to non-entrepreneurs in the same industry. Robinson et al. (1991b) conducted a study in which they compared two groups: (i) businessmen and students who had actually started a business within the last five years, and (ii) white-collar workers and psychology students who had never started a business. They found that over 90 per cent of the variance between the two groups could be explained by the EAO measures. Van Wyk and Boshoff (2004) were able to verify these findings only for the innovation subscale.

COMPARISON

Theoretical Comparison

Having presented each of the two concepts on its own, we shall now attempt to compare them on a theoretical basis. When developing the EAO, Robinson et al. (1991b) argued that attitudes usually explain 0.40 to

0.70 of the variance in actual behaviour (Ajzen, 1982), while personality traits explain only 0.10 to 0.30 (Epstein, 1984). However, Ajzen also argued that there is no superiority of attitudes over traits *per se*: instead, each research field has to find out for itself which of the concepts better suits its requirements.

These studies are not closely linked to the business context, but there is a business field of study which uses attitudes and personality for behaviour prediction. The concept of 'organizational citizenship behavior' (OCB) was developed in 1983 (Bateman and Organ, 1983; Smith et al., 1983) and deals with the informal behaviour of business organization members, how it can be influenced, and the factors on which it depends. An impressive number of studies have been conducted since the publication of the first two articles. Organ and Ryan (1995) carried out a meta-analysis of 55 studies in an attempt to predict OCB using attitudes, personality traits and several other variables. They found that most of the attitude measures were very sound predictors of OCB, while the personality measures correlated very poorly with it.

There is yet another facet to the hypothesis that attitudes are better suited for predicting entrepreneurship. The concepts of self-esteem and self-efficacy (see Bandura, 1977 for information on self-efficacy) have already been mentioned above. While self-esteem is by definition a very general term, self-efficacy is used in the entrepreneurial context as a belief construct (Boyd and Vozikis, 1994) which is indeed more closely related to attitudes than to personality. A comparison of these two approaches led us to the hypotheses presented below.

Hypotheses

- H1: Attitudes towards achievement in business will show higher correlation with intentions to become an entrepreneur than the 'need for achievement' personality trait.
- H2: Attitudes towards internal locus of control in business will show higher correlation with intentions to become an entrepreneur than the 'locus of control' personality trait.
- H3: Attitudes towards risk taking in business will show higher correlation with intentions to become an entrepreneur than the 'risk-taking propensity' personality trait.
- H4: Attitudes towards self-esteem in business will show higher correlation with intentions to become an entrepreneur than the 'self-esteem' personality trait.
- H5: Attitudes towards proactivity in business will show higher correlation with intentions to become an entrepreneur than the 'proactivity' personality trait.

H6: Attitudes towards innovation in business will show higher correlation with intentions to become an entrepreneur than the 'innovativeness' personality trait.

H7: Attitudes towards ambiguity in business will show higher correlation with intentions to become an entrepreneur than the 'tolerance for ambiguity' personality trait.

In order to test these hypotheses by empirical means, we conducted the study described in the section below.

METHOD

We developed two tests to compare entrepreneurial traits and attitudes in the entrepreneurial context. The first one consisted of seven common trait subscales derived from various tests, while the second consisted of seven attitude subscales, of which four were derived from the EAO and three were developed by the authors. In both tests, one subscale was employed for each of the above hypotheses. We tested the hypotheses on two subject groups, with one group responding to the trait scales and the other responding to the attitude scales.

Measures

We used four of the subscales of the F-DUP (*Fragebogen zur Diagnose unternehmerischer Potenziale*; Mueller, 2004), which is a German version of the entrepreneurial potential questionnaire (King, 1985). Although the F-DUP is designed for the entrepreneurial context, it is a common traits test and can thus also be used to measure personality in broader terms. The F-DUP presents three specific answers for each item. We used four subscales to measure the following personality traits: need for achievement, risk-taking propensity, tolerance for ambiguity and locus of control (36 items in total). In the F-DUP test manual, Mueller lists alphas ranging from 0.59 to 0.78 for these scales.

The self-esteem personality trait was assessed using the Rosenberg self-esteem (RSE) scale (Rosenberg, 1965). For the RSE, reliabilities of 0.80 to 0.90 have been reported in numerous studies (for example, Rosenberg, 1965; Silbert and Tippett, 1965; Hudson et al., 2000). The proactivity scale developed by Bateman and Crant was used to measure this personality trait. Cronbach's alpha for this scale was specified between 0.85 and 0.88 (Crant, 1996). Moreover, we used a subscale from the Jackson Personality Inventory (Jackson, 1983), a highly detailed and commonly accepted personality test in the entrepreneurship context (Sexton and Bowman, 1983, 1984; Robbins, 1987; Carland et al., 1988), to measure innovativeness. Jackson conducted various studies to test the reliability of his JPI-R and reports alpha coefficients ranging from 0.82 to 0.87 for the innovativeness scale. In our study, we used a six-point Likert scale ranging from 1 (strongly agree) to 6 (strongly disagree) to measure self-esteem, proactivity and innovativeness. All three scales were translated into German.

As mentioned above, we used the four scales from the EAO to measure need for achievement, innovativeness, locus of control and self-esteem. We translated all of the statements into German and then developed three new scales to measure attitudes in an entrepreneurial context: risk-taking propensity, tolerance for ambiguity and proactivity. Twenty statements were generated for each of these scales. We then asked members of our department to rate which statements would best fit the requirements of the scale. For each scale, 10 statements were selected on the basis of these ratings. All seven scales were measured on a six-point Likert scale. Robinson et al. (1991b) give alphas ranging from 0.73 to 0.90 for their four scales. In addition, we asked for minor demographic data in both tests.

Description of Sample

We conducted our study during nine summer courses at the Vienna University of Economics and Business Administration in September 2005. The students in these courses (which do not deal specifically with entrepreneurship) were asked to fill out the questionnaires at the beginning or at the end of a course session. Five groups filled out the attitude test (n=143), and four filled out the traits test (n= 143).

As the definition of an entrepreneur has frequently been a subject of discussion (see Carland et al., 1984; Gartner, 1988) and no single accepted definition of an entrepreneur exists, we refrained from differentiating entrepreneurs based on external variables such as past work experience. Instead, we used four items measuring the entrepreneurial intentions of the subjects as a dependent variable in both tests. We regard the intention to start one's own business as a suitable proxy for actual entrepreneurial behaviour in our sample. Below we provide English translations of the items used in German:

- Interest item: 'How interested would you be in starting your own business?'
- Probability item: 'How probable is it that you will start a business in the course of your working life?'
- Period item: 'If you ever founded your own business, when would you expect to do so?'

- Planning item: 'How concrete are your plans to found your own business?'

The interest and probability items were measured on a six-point Likert scale, while the period and planning items used five concrete options. We assumed that at least one of the above items would be a sound predictor of future entrepreneurship and should therefore correlate with the traits or attitudes linked with entrepreneurs.

RESULTS

We used Cronbach's alpha to measure the internal consistency of each subscale. The interest item demonstrated the highest correlations with most of the subscales, the probability item had slightly lower correlations, and the period and planning items showed almost no correlations with the subscales. As a result, the analysis below is based solely on the interest item.

Traits Tests

Table 4.1 shows the Cronbach's alphas for each of the seven subscales. We were not able to improve these values by eliminating individual items. As the table reveals, the four F-DUP scales returned low alpha values, while the other three scales yielded sound alpha results.

Table 4.2 lists the correlations of the seven trait subscales, gender and age with the interest item. Since gender had a significant influence on the interest item, we also conducted a partial correlation test to control for gender. Only the scores for 'need for achievement' and 'proactivity' correlated significantly with the interest item. The need for achievement score showed a negative correlation, which was a rather unexpected result.

Table 4.1 Cronbach's alphas of the trait subscales

	Cronbach's alpha	Number of items
Need for achievement	0.53	9
Self-esteem	0.91	10
Locus of control	0.42	9
Innovativeness	0.82	20
Tolerance for ambiguity	0.51	9
Risk-taking propensity	0.31	9
Proactivity	0.87	15

Attitude Tests

Table 4.3 provides an overview of the Cronbach's alphas for the attitude subscales. For five of the scales, we were able to improve the alpha value by deleting certain items. Table 4.3 also lists the number of deleted items. The alpha values for all subscales were within an acceptable range.

In the attitude test, we calculated correlations and – because gender again had a significant influence – we also ran a partial correlation test to control for gender. The results can be found in Table 4.4. The partial correlation test shows slightly different values and increases the significance of all correlations. Five of the seven subscales show a strong influence on the respondents' interest in becoming an entrepreneur at the 0.001 level, one

Table 4.2 Correlations of the trait subscales, gender and age

	Correlations with interest item		Partial correlations with interest item controlling for gender	
	R	Significance	*R*	Significance
Need for achievement	−0.170*	0.043	−0.193*	0.022
Self-esteem	0.087	0.300	0.113	0.184
Locus of control	−0.090	0.286	−0.071	0.401
Innovativeness	0.101	0.231	0.111	0.191
Tolerance for ambiguity	−0.010	0.905	−0.040	0.640
Risk-taking propensity	0.061	0.469	0.018	0.829
Proactivity	0.318***	0.0001	0.283***	0.001
Gender	0.310***	0.0002		
Age	0.420	0.625		

Note: * Significant at the 0.05 level, ** significant at the 0.01 level, *** significant at the 0.001 level.

Table 4.3 Cronbach's alphas of the attitude subscales

	Cronbach's alpha	Number of items (deleted)
Need for achievement	0.790	23 (0)
Self-esteem	0.579	7 (7)
Locus of control	0.659	7 (5)
Innovativeness	0.779	22 (4)
Tolerance for ambiguity	0.726	8 (2)
Risk-taking propensity	0.780	10 (0)
Proactivity	0.680	9 (1)

Table 4.4 Correlations of the attitude subscales, gender and age

	Correlations with interest item		Partial correlations with interest item (controlling for gender)	
	R	Significance	*R*	Significance
Need for achievement	0.215**	0.010	0.243**	0.004
Self-esteem	−0.014	0.865	−0.021	0.801
Locus of control	0.210*	0.012	0.267***	0.001
Innovativeness	0.358***	0.00001	0.383***	0.000003
Tolerance for ambiguity	0.317***	0.0001	0.312***	0.0002
Risk-taking propensity	0.356***	0.00001	0.291***	0.0005
Proactivity	0.257**	0.002	0.290***	0.0005
Gender	0.321***	0.0001		
Age	0.083	0.325		

Note: * Significant at the 0.05 level, ** significant at the 0.01 level, *** significant at the 0.001 level.

item also has a relatively strong influence at the 0.01 level, while self-esteem shows no correlation whatsoever.

Comparison of the Results

To compare the results, we conducted a Fisher z-transformation on all partial correlation coefficients and then compared the coefficients for each corresponding pair of subscales. The results are given in Table 4.5.

Five attitude subscales demonstrated significantly higher correlation (all of them at least at the 0.01 level) than their corresponding trait subscales. Therefore, we did not reject Hypotheses 1, 2, 3, 6 and 7. For the self-esteem subscale, we found no significant difference – neither the trait subscale nor the attitude subscale showed a significant correlation with the intention to start a business (Hypothesis 4 rejected). As regards proactivity, both the attitude and the trait subscale exhibited a significant correlation with the interest item, but neither had a significantly higher correlation than the other (Hypothesis 5 rejected).

CONCLUSION

We proposed that attitudes represent better predictors of entrepreneurial intent than entrepreneurial traits. In order to test this proposition, we

Table 4.5 Comparison of the correlations by Fisher z*-transformation*

	z-value	Significance
Need for achievement	−3.71***	0.0001
Self-esteem	1.13	0.918
Locus of control	−2.88**	0.002
Innovativeness	−2.44**	0.007
Tolerance for ambiguity	−3.04***	0.001
Risk-taking propensity	−2.36**	0.009
Proactivity	−0.06	0.476

Note: * Significant at the 0.05 level, ** significant at the 0.01 level, *** significant at the 0.001 level.

conducted a survey among 286 business students at the Vienna University of Economics and Business Administration. Half of the respondents filled out the attitude questionnaire, while the other half filled out the traits questionnaire. Both of these questionnaires included seven subscales measuring need for achievement, self-esteem, locus of control, innovativeness, tolerance for ambiguity, risk-taking propensity and proactivity.

Five of the seven attitude scales (need for achievement, locus of control, innovativeness, tolerance for ambiguity and risk-taking propensity) show significantly higher correlations with the intention of starting a business than the corresponding trait scales.

Our results have implications for entrepreneurial education programmes: we would suggest using attitude scales to evaluate the outcomes of entrepreneurship programmes and/or courses. Attitudes are subject to change over time and can be influenced by educators, thus they are better suited for evaluating the success of training activities.

A further step in our research would be to analyse the differences between attitudes and traits in a sample of real entrepreneurs and non-entrepreneurs. As mentioned above, we regard entrepreneurial intent as a suitable proxy for actual entrepreneurial behaviour in our sample of students. A study among real entrepreneurs, however, would shed more light on the 'traits versus attitudes' discussion in entrepreneurship research. Another issue which should be addressed in future research is an in-depth investigation of the direction of causality: did the students in our sample have the attitudes we measured because they wanted to become entrepreneurs, or did they want to become entrepreneurs because of their attitudes?

REFERENCES

Ajzen, I. (1982), 'On behaving in accordance with one's attitude', in M.P. Zanna, E.T. Higgins and C.P. Herman (eds), *Consistency in Social Behaviour: The Ontario Symposium*, Hillsdale, NJ: Lawrence Erlbaum Associates, pp. 3–15.

Allport, G.W. (1935), 'Attitudes', in C. Murchinson (ed.), *Handbook of Social Psychology*, Worcester, MA: Clark University, pp. 798–884.

Bandura, A. (1977), *Social Learning Theory*, Englewood Cliffs, NJ: Prentice-Hall.

Bateman, T.S. and D.W. Organ (1983), 'Job satisfaction and the good soldier: the relationship between affect and employee "citizenship"', *Academy of Management Journal*, **26** (4), 587–95.

Boyd, N.G. and G.S. Vozikis (1994), 'The influence of self-efficacy on the development of entrepreneurial intentions and actions', *Entrepreneurship Theory and Practice*, **18** (4), 63–77.

Brockhaus, R.H. (1980), 'Risk taking propensity of entrepreneurs', *Academy of Management Journal*, **23** (3), 509–20.

Brockhaus, R.H. (1982), 'The psychology of the entrepreneur', in C.A. Kent, D.L. Sexton and K.H. Vesper (eds), *Encyclopaedia of Entrepreneurship*, Englewood Cliffs, NJ: Prentice-Hall, pp. 39–71.

Brockhaus, R.H. and P.S. Horwitz (1986), 'The psychology of the entrepreneur', in D.L. Sexton and R.W. Smilor (eds), *The Art and Science of Entrepreneurship*, Cambridge, MA: Ballinger, pp. 25–48.

Carland, J.W., J.A. Carland, F. Hoy and W.R. Boulton (1988), 'Distinctions between entrepreneurial and small business ventures', *International Journal of Management*, **5** (1), 98–103.

Carland, J.W., F. Hoy, W.R. Boulton and J.A. Carland (1984), 'Differentiating entrepreneurs from small business owners: a conceptualization', *Academy of Management Review*, **9** (2), 354–9.

Chaiken, S. and C. Stangor (1987), 'Attitudes and attitude change', *Annual Review of Psychology*, **38**, 575–630.

Chell, E., J. Haworth and S. Brearley (1991), *The Entrepreneurial Personality: Concepts, Cases, and Categories*, London: Routledge.

Chen, C.C., P.G. Greene and A. Crick (1998), 'Does entrepreneurial self-efficacy distinguish entrepreneurs from managers?', *Journal of Business Venturing*, **13** (4), 295–316.

Cole, A.H. (1942), 'Entrepreneurship as an area of research', *The Task of Economic History* (supplement to *Journal of Economic History*), pp. 118–26.

Crandall, R. (1973), 'The measurement of self-esteem and related constructs', in J. Robinson and P. Shaver (eds), *Measures of Psychological Attitudes*, Ann Arbor, MI: Institute for Social Research, pp. 80–82.

Crant, M.J. (1996), 'The proactive personality scale as a predictor of entrepreneurial intentions', *Journal of Small Business Management*, **34** (3), 42–9.

Epstain, S. (1984), 'A procedural note on the measurement of broad dispositions', *Journal of Personality*, **52**, 318–25.

Fishbein, M. and I. Ajzen (1975), *Belief, Attitude, Intention and Behaviour*, Reading, MA: Addison-Wesley.

Gartner, W.B. (1988), '"Who is an entrepreneur?" is the wrong question', *American Journal of Small Business*, **12** (4), 11–32.

Gartner, W.B. (1989), 'Some suggestions for research on entrepreneurial traits and characteristics', *Entrepreneurship: Theory and Practice*, **14** (1), 27–37.

Herkner, W. (2001), *Lehrbuch Sozialpsychologie*, Bern: Verlag Hans Huber.
Hisrich, R.D. and M.P. Peters (1992), *Entrepreneurship: Starting, Developing, and Managing a New Enterprise*, Homewood, IL: Irwin.
Hudson, D.B., S.M. Elek and C. Campbell-Grossman (2000), 'Depression, self-esteem, loneliness, and social support among adolescent mothers participating in the New Parents Project', *Adolescence*, **35** (139), 444–53.
Hull, D.L., J.J. Bosley and G.G. Udell (1980), 'Renewing the hunt for the heffalump: identifying potential entrepreneurs by personality characteristics', *Journal of Small Business Management*, **18** (1), 11–18.
Jackson, D.N. (1983), *Jackson Personality Inventory – Revised* (Manual), Port Huron, MI: Sigma Assessment Systems.
King, A.S. (1985), 'Self-analysis and assessment of entrepreneurial potential', *Simulation and Games*, **16**, 399–416.
Kirzner, I.M. (1997), 'Entrepreneurial discovery and the competitive market process', *Journal of Economic Literature*, **35** (1), 60–85.
Knight, F. (1921), *Risk, Uncertainty and Profit*, Cambridge, MA: Houghton Mifflin.
Liles, P.R. (1974), *New Business Ventures and the Entrepreneur*, Homewood, IL: Richard D. Irwin.
McClelland, D.C. (1961), *The Achieving Society*, New York: Van Nostrand.
McClelland, D.C. (1965), 'Achievement motivation can be developed', *Harvard Business Review*, **43** (6), 6–178.
McCline, R.L., S. Bhat and P. Baj (2000), 'Opportunity recognition: an exploratory investigation of a component of the entrepreneurial process in the context of the health care industry', *Entrepreneurship Theory and Practice*, **25** (2), 81–94.
Mueller, G.F. (2004), *Fragebogen zur Diagnose unternehmerischer Potenziale (F-DUP)*, Koblenz-Landau: Campus Landau.
Oppenheim, A.N. (1992), *Questionnaire Design, Interviewing and Attitude Measurement*, New York: Continuum.
Organ, D.W. and K.R. Ryan (1995), 'A meta-analytic review of attitudinal and dispositional predictors of organizational citizenship behavior', *Personnel Psychology*, **48** (4), 775–802.
Palmer, M. (1971), 'The application of psychological testing to entrepreneurial potential', *California Management Review*, **13** (3), 32–8.
Robbins, N.E. (1987), 'Entrepreneurial assessment: characteristics which differentiate entrepreneurs, intrapreneurs, and managers', doctoral dissertation, University of Minnesota, Minneapolis, MN, Dissertation Abstracts International, 47, 5083B.
Robinson, P.B., J.C. Huefner and H.K. Hunt (1991a), 'Entrepreneurial research on student subjects does not generalize to real world entrepreneurs', *Journal of Small Business Management*, **29** (2), 42–50.
Robinson, P.B., D.V. Stimpson, J.C. Huefner and H.K. Hunt (1991b), 'An attitude approach to the prediction of entrepreneurship', *Entrepreneurship Theory and Practice*, **14** (4), 13–31.
Rosenberg, M. (1965), *Society and the Adolescent Self-image*, Princeton, NJ: Princeton University Press.
Rotter, J.B. (1966), 'Generalized expectancies for internal versus external control of reinforcement', *Psychological Monographs*, **80** (1), 1–28.
Sexton, D.L. and N.B. Bowman (1983), 'Comparative entrepreneurship characteristics of students: preliminary results', in J. Hornaday, J. Timmons and K. Vesper (eds), *Frontiers of Entrepreneurship Research*, Wellesley, MA: Babson College, pp. 18–25.

Sexton, D.L. and N.B. Bowman (1984), 'Personality inventory for potential entrepreneurs: evaluation of a modified JPI/PRF-E test instrument', in *Proceedings of the Babson Entrepreneurship Conference*, 513–28.

Silbert, E. and J.S. Tippett (1965), 'Self-esteem: clinical assessment and measurement validation', *Psychological Reports*, **16**, 1017–71.

Smith, C.A., D.W. Organ and J.P. Near (1983), 'Organizational citizenship behavior: its nature and antecedents', *Journal of Applied Psychology*, **68** (4), 653–63.

Stewart, W.H. Jr (1996), *Psychological Correlates of Entrepreneurship*, New York and London: Garland.

Van Wyk, R. and A.B. Boshoff (2004), 'Entrepreneurial attitudes', *South African Journal of Business Management*, **35** (2), 33–8.

Wortman, M.S. (1986), 'A unified framework, research typologies, and research prospectuses for the interface between entrepreneurship and small business', in D.L. Sexton and R.W. Smilor (eds), *The Art and Science of Entrepreneurship*, Cambridge, MA: Ballinger, pp. 273–332.

5. Prediction or control? Exploring the influence of career experience and career motives on entrepreneurial decision making

Jonas Gabrielsson and Diamanto Politis

INTRODUCTION

Literature and research on entrepreneurship increasingly emphasize the discovery of opportunities and the decision to exploit them as the essence of entrepreneurial activity (Shane and Venkataraman, 2000; Shane, 2003). Considering that entrepreneurs often deal with new and ill-defined business concepts whose commercial applications are not yet fully explored, the new venture creation process can be considered as exploratory in nature and associated with high scarcity of available resources (Sarasvathy, 2001a). This implies that new venture creation activities require frequent decisions about what opportunities are worth pursuing and, among the various solutions available, which are worth exploring (Simon et al., 2000). These decisions are in turn complicated by the uncertainty that surrounds the commercial return of most entrepreneurial initiatives.

In a recent study, Sarasvathy (2001a) describes two kinds of decision-making modes in business settings: causation and effectuation. Causation is described as the use of techniques of analysis and estimation to explore and exploit existing and latent markets. Causal reasoning focuses on what ought to be done given predetermined goals and possible means, implying a process that rests on the logic of *prediction*. Effectuation, on the other hand, calls for the use of synthesis and imagination to create new markets that do not already exist. Effectual reasoning emphasizes the question of what can be done given possible means and imagined ends, implying a process that rests on the logic of *control*.

Sarasvathy's (2001a) theory of effectuation has been the first attempt to develop a baseline of entrepreneurial decision making based on how entrepreneurs perceive, process and use market information, or information relating to the creation of new markets. The underlying assumption is that individuals may have different perceptions to what extent they consider the future as predictable and controllable, something which in turn will influence their decision making (ibid.; Wiltbank et al., 2006). The specific context where entrepreneurs operate is central in this argument as it will influence their perception of what is preferable and effective. Causation, for example, is extremely valuable, and thus also more likely to be seen, in situations where there is a market which is existent and measurable. Effectuation on the other hand does not assume pre-existent markets and is particularly useful and effective, and thus also more likely to be seen, in domains where new markets are created. A conclusion that can be drawn is consequently that the specific context where entrepreneurs operate very much matter for explaining entrepreneurial decision making. The same entrepreneur can use both causal and effectual reasoning but at different times depending on what circumstances call for.

However, even if it seems reasonable to assume that entrepreneurial decision making very much depends on the specific context, there may be other factors that will influence whether individuals would prefer relying on causation or effectuation as their predominant decision-making logic. Based on previous research, two factors can be identified as likely to have an influence on entrepreneurial decision making. The first factor is the *career experience* of the entrepreneur. Previous research suggests that individuals tend to focus their attention and activities on what has been working well in the past, meaning that prior experience serves as a guideline for future actions and decision making (Minniti and Bygrave, 2001; Mullins and Forlani, 2005; Politis, 2005). Hence, it can be argued that experienced business founders develop a unique 'knowledge corridor' through which they interpret the outside world as a basis for decision making (Ronstadt, 1988; Venkataraman, 1997). This line of reasoning can be related back to Cyert and March (1963) who assert that goals and procedures primarily are a function of an individual's prior experience. The other factor is the *career motives* of the entrepreneur. For example, it is well known that the career motives of individuals both guide and constrain decision making (Schein, 1987). The basic premise of this argument is that most individuals develop diverse concepts of what a career means to them, which greatly influence their choice of career path and experience at work (Brousseau et al., 1996). Entrepreneurs with different career motives can hence be expected to seek different types of entrepreneurial events and learning situations (Politis, 2005), which in turn can influence their preferred decision-making logic in entrepreneurial settings. These arguments consequently suggest that entrepreneurial decision making should be seen as a result of not only the specific context where entrepreneurs operate, but also what they bring with them (their career experience) and what they aim for in their careers (their career motives). Studies of how entrepreneurs' career experience and career motives influence their preference for relying on causal or effectual decision-making modes in the new venture creation process are, however, surprisingly scarce.

Based on the discussion above, the aim of the study is to examine the influence of prior career experience and career motives on entrepreneurs' preferred mode of decision making. By doing this the study contributes to existing theory and research on entrepreneurial decision making in several ways. First, it develops theory-driven hypotheses and empirically tests them on a sample of entrepreneurs in order to develop our understanding of causal and effectual decision making in entrepreneurial settings. Research on entrepreneurial decision making has, with a few exceptions, primarily been conceptual in nature, or been conducted in highly experimental settings (for example, Forlani and Mullins, 2000; Simon et al., 2000; Gustafsson, 2004; Lévesque and Schade, 2005; Mullins and Forlani, 2005). In this respect the study will empirically test propositions derived from previous literature and research on a sample of surveyed 'average' entrepreneurs. Second, in order to empirically test our propositions we have developed exploratory measures to assess the extent to which entrepreneurs are involved in causal and effectual modes of decision making. The measures are based on the theoretical work of Sarasvathy (2001a). To our knowledge no existing operationalizations have so far been presented, something which makes our study interesting for continued research in this area. Third, the study integrates concepts and models from career theory (Schein, 1987; Brousseau et al., 1996) into the entrepreneurship field. Extant research has shown that entrepreneurs are a heterogeneous group of individuals that differ in terms of characteristics, behaviours and career motivations (for example, Katz, 1994; Westhead and Wright, 1998). By acknowledging this difference we aim to add to our knowledge of how different career motives of entrepreneurs may guide and constrain their future decision making.

The rest of the chapter proceeds as follows. The next section presents a literature review of research into entrepreneurial decision making, career experience and career motives. The hypotheses to be tested are developed in this section. Thereafter follows the method section with a description of the sample and variables used in the empirical study, followed by the analysis with a presentation and discussion of the results. The study ends with a concluding section where the study's implications are summarized.

LITERATURE REVIEW AND HYPOTHESES

Entrepreneurial Decision Making

Decision making lies at the very heart of the entrepreneurial process. Entrepreneurs have to make a plethora of different decisions on a daily basis, for example concerning refinements of the business idea, creating or identifying a market niche, solving technical problems, acquiring resources, recruiting key personnel and so on (Davidsson and Klofsten, 2003). Many of these decisions can have longlasting consequences, and critical decisions taken at early stages may have unforeseeable impacts upon the entire future success and performance of the new venture (Reuber and Fischer, 1999; Vohora et al., 2004). Studying entrepreneurial decision making, therefore, is important for a better understanding of the process whereby individuals create and exploit new venture opportunities.

Sarasvathy (2001a) has identified two modes of reasoning that individuals may apply when making decisions in business settings: *causation* and *effectuation*. Causal reasoning is a problem-solving decision model that rests on the logic of prediction (Sarasvathy, 2001a; Wiltbank et al., 2006). The choice of means is driven by the entrepreneur's knowledge of possible means, as well as the characteristics of the effects the entrepreneur wants to create. The market is assumed to exist independently of the entrepreneur and the main task is to grasp as much of that market as possible. This is done by being involved in planning and gathering necessary information to see how strategies materialize according to plan and to identify possible reasons why plan and outcome differ.

Effectual reasoning on the other hand is a problem-solving decision model that rests on the logic of control where the entrepreneur focuses on the question of what can be done given possible means and imagined ends (Sarasvathy, 2001a; Wiltbank et al., 2006). The logic of using effectuation processes can best be described as follows: 'to the extent that we can control the future, we do not need to predict it' (Sarasvathy, 2001a: 252). This means that effectual thinkers believe in a yet-to-be-made future that can be shaped and hence controlled by human action. Based on this view, the decision makers themselves are considered to influence the environment through their decisions and actions in conjunction with pre-committed stakeholders and customer-partners (Sarasvathy, 2001a). Effectual reasoning thus calls for synthesis and imagination to create new markets, where the centre of attention is on exploiting contingencies to explore new environments. In Table 5.1, causation and effectuation are contrasted against each other.

As can be seen in Table 5.1, causation and effectuation represent two fundamentally different logics of decision making in business settings.

Table 5.1 Causation and effectuation logic contrasted

Causation	Effectuation
Focusing on predictable aspects of an uncertain future	Focusing on controllable aspects of an unpredictable future
Using techniques of analysis and estimation to explore and exploit existing and latent markets	Using synthesis and imagination to create new markets that do not already exist
Seeking to identify the optimal alternative to achieve the given goal	Allowing goals to emerge contingently over time
Avoiding uncertain situations to the greatest possible extent	Seeking uncertain situations in the hope of being able to use them
Strategic and goal-orientated relationships with stakeholders	Accidental and informal relationships with stakeholders
Pre-calculated and detailed competitive analyses for investigating the need for or interest in a product or service	Informal methods for investigating the need for or interest in a product or service

Source: Sarasvathy (2001a).

However, despite the differences, both causation and effectuation are integral parts of human reasoning and can occur simultaneously, overlapping and intertwining over different contexts of decisions and actions (ibid.; Dew and Sarasvathy, 2002). Entrepreneurs can hence use effectual and causal reasoning at different times depending on both circumstances and individual preferences.

The underlying assumption guiding our study is that entrepreneurs' decision-making preference may vary and change in response to certain career experiences and career motives. Thus, although we acknowledge that such preference to a large degree may vary in response to the unique situational context (for example, Sarasvathy, 2001a; Bergendahl, 2005; Douglas, 2005), in this chapter we are particularly interested in whether individual experiences and preferences may make them more in favour of one decision-making logic than another. The rest of the section will review the literature and research to develop hypotheses of the expected influence of individuals' prior career experience and career motives on their preferred mode of decision making in entrepreneurial settings. In the next subsection we shall discuss the influence of prior career experience. Thereafter follows a discussion on the influence of career motives.

Career Experience

One particular aspect that can be expected to have a potential impact on entrepreneurial decision making is the career experience of the entrepreneur. A career can be defined as 'any social strand of any person's course through life' (Goffman, 1961: 127), which means that a career not only includes what an individual does in a particular occupation but rather consists of the total experience of an individual's working life. Previous studies have suggested that individuals tend to focus their attention and activities on what has been working well in the entrepreneur's past career. Minniti and Bygrave (2001) argue, for example, that many entrepreneurs tend to choose actions that replicate, or are closely related to the ones they have already taken, thereby exploiting their pre-existing knowledge (see also similar arguments in Starr and Bygrave, 1992; McGrath, 1999; Politis, 2005). This implies that experienced business founders develop a knowledge corridor through which they interpret the outside world as a basis for their future decision making (Ronstadt, 1988; Venkataraman, 1997). The insights gained from prior career experience can thus be expected to create a perceived 'path' for future business venturing where the entrepreneur has moved from his/her specific observations to make broader generalizations and theories of how to achieve success in the new venture.

This line of reasoning can be related back to Cyert and March (1963), who assert that decision making is primarily a function of prior experience. Problems are dealt with by applying problem-solving heuristics and memorized routines to reduce the complexity of decision making. For instance, when an entrepreneur discovers a solution to a problem by searching in a particular way, he/she will be more likely to base future decisions for problems of the same type on the same solution. On the other hand, when an entrepreneur fails to find a solution, it will be less likely that he/she will base future decisions in that way in future problems of the same type. It can hence be argued that individuals over time develop, stabilize and follow certain patterns of decision-making behaviour. Moreover, these experientially acquired patterns, or routines, are fairly difficult to change since they function as carriers of knowledge and experience (ibid.).

Can we expect any consistent patterns between entrepreneurs' prior career experience and their preferred decision-making logic? Literature and research suggest three types of experience that may have an influence on entrepreneurial decision making: 'start-up experience', 'small business management experience', and 'large business management experience'. Previous studies indicate, for example, that prior start-up experience provides the entrepreneur with tacit knowledge that facilitates decision making about entrepreneurial opportunities under uncertainty and time pressure

(Johannisson et al., 1998; McGrath, 1999; Sarasvathy, 2001a). By continually being involved in new venture creation processes, entrepreneurs can learn to value uncertain situations in the hope of capitalizing on these occurrences. Moreover, research on habitual entrepreneurship has shown that entrepreneurs with multiple start-up experience are often highly explorative and alert, taking a broad intuitive perspective that incorporates many different inputs at once without necessarily having one predetermined goal in mind (Westhead and Wright, 1998; Westhead et al., 2005). Thus, it can be expected that experienced entrepreneurs have developed a cognitive mindset that makes them more alert in acting on entrepreneurial opportunities that arise around them (ibid.). Sarasvathy (2001b) also points out that experienced entrepreneurs are used to starting with the means that are closest at hand, and moving almost directly into action without elaborate planning which speaks in favour of an effectual decision-making logic (see also Johannisson, 2000 for similar arguments). Hence, it seems reasonable to assume that entrepreneurs with prior start-up experience are likely to prefer effectual over causal reasoning in the new venture creation process. Based on this argument, the following hypothesis is proposed:

H1: Prior start-up experience is positively associated with effectual decision-making logic.

A similar preference for effectual reasoning may be the case when an individual has prior small-business management experience. Small-business managers generally have narrow decision windows and a short time span in terms of opportunity commitment (O'Gorman, 2000). Moreover, they are often pressured by the need to be innovative and proactive while constrained by a lack of in-house resources. Competitiveness is hence largely driven by an orientation towards action, combined with a large degree of flexibility and adaptiveness. This situation, in turn, may open up for experimental actions and creative problem solving when small-business managers seek alternative ways of meeting or reducing their need of resources (Winborg and Landström, 2001). This may in turn force them to rely on fluid short-term goals that emerge continuously over time, based on the imagination and diverse aspirations of the small-business managers and the people they interact with (Sarasvathy, 2001b). Based on this argument, the following hypothesis is proposed:

H2: Prior small-business management experience is positively associated with effectual decision-making logic.

On the other hand, the case of having large-business experience may instead speak in favour of a more causal mode of reasoning. Large established companies are driven by formal administrative principles and rigid planning cycles to administer the resources under their control (Bower, 1986). Strategies come to life through careful planning and subsequent execution. Authority, responsibility and reward systems are clearly defined. Failure to meet financial targets is often worse than neglecting to pursue opportunities (Stevenson and Gumpert, 1985). Individuals with prior large-business management experience can hence be expected to prefer efficient competitive strategies targeted at existing markets, rather than making decisions in the absence of pre-existent goals. The discussion above leads us to propose the following hypothesis:

H3: Prior large-business management experience is positively associated with causal decision-making logic.

Career Motives

While decision making can be seen as a function of entrepreneurs' prior experience we may also have to consider that their intentions, in terms of what they aim for and where they want to go in the future, can influence their decision making as well (Krueger, 2003). In this study we are particularly interested in entrepreneurs' career motives as it is widely acknowledged that the career motives of individuals can both guide and constrain future actions and decision behaviours (Schein, 1987; Brosseau et al., 1996). The basic premise underlying this argument is that most individuals develop diverse concepts of what a career means to them, which in turn greatly influence their choice of career path and experience at work (ibid.). Most studies of careers in the entrepreneurship domain have, however, focused on the decision to start a venture and become an entrepreneur (see, for example, Starr and Fondas, 1992; Harvey and Evans, 1995; Simon et al., 2000). What is less known is how entrepreneurs' career motives may influence future actions and decision behaviours (Katz, 1994; Shane et al., 2003; Politis, 2005). This implies that the majority of entrepreneurship scholars have put much emphasis on understanding the factors that influence someone to start a new venture, while neglecting the issue of how their preferred career paths and underlying motives can explain entrepreneurial decision making in the new venture creation process.

A theoretical model that may be helpful for our purpose is the career concept model (Driver, 1979, 1988; Brousseau et al., 1996). This model is based on observed differences in the underlying work and career-related motives of individuals, and it differentiates between four basic career motives; linear, expert, spiral and transitory. The four career concepts are based on distinctly different sets of career motives. The differences are based on the terms of direction (career movement or change) and frequency of movement within and across different kinds of work over time (durability in a given field of work). This means that individuals who differ in their particular career motives also differ predictably in their underlying work- and career-related orientations (ibid.). Based on this argument, it seems reasonable to assume that entrepreneurs with different kinds of career motives can be expected to seek different types of entrepreneurial events and learning situations, which in turn can influence their preferred decision-making logic in entrepreneurial settings.

A 'linear' career motive is characterized by the preference for a progressive series of steps upward in a hierarchy (such as a managerial hierarchy) with infrequent changes in career fields (ibid.). Upward promotions to positions of increasing authority and responsibility are desired as frequently as possible and power and achievement become key motives behind their career choices. Efficiency, competitiveness and leadership are important competencies. The (managerial) emphasis on stability and prediction means that the focus is much directed towards finding optimal solutions, given predetermined goals and possible means to explore and exploit existing and latent markets (Sarasvathy, 2001a). Individuals driven by a linear career motive can hence be expected to prefer causal decision making. On the other hand, an 'expert' career motive is characterized by the preference for lifelong commitment to a specific occupation (Brousseau et al., 1996). The individual strives for further development and refinement within a certain niche or specialty, and important competencies are quality, commitment and specialization. The expert career motive closely resembles the professional small-business 'craftsmen' described in Smith (1967) who develop their praxis and skills in terms of genuine, often tacit knowledge within their specific professions (see also Schön, 1983). For individuals with an expert career motive, carrying on the traditions of the trade is generally important, which speaks in favour of causal decision-making logic. A main task becomes to achieve skill mastery and develop the reputation to grasp as much of the existing (niche) market as possible. As with the linear career motive, individuals driven by an expert career motive can be expected to prefer causal decision making as they mainly strive to refine their pre-existent knowledge and to stay within their professions and existing specializations. Based on these arguments, the following hypotheses are proposed:

H4: A linear career motive is positively associated with causal decision-making logic.

H5: An expert career motive is positively associated with causal decision-making logic.

While the two career motives discussed above mainly emphasize stability and prediction, the two following ones are more inclined towards seeking variety and change. A 'spiral' career motive is characterized by a preference for major moves across occupational areas, specialties, or disciplines that are closely related to previous ones (Brousseau et al., 1996). Their new field draws on knowledge developed in the previous field and at the same time provides opportunities to develop an entirely new set of knowledge. This implies that creativity, teamwork and skill diversity are important competencies, where their set of means and their set of possible effects can change and become reconfigured through their actions. On the other hand, a 'transitory' career motive is characterized by the preference for highly project-orientated and episodic jobs, where adaptiveness, speed and networking become important competencies (ibid.). Individuals with a transitory career motive rarely consider themselves as actually having a career. Instead they are likely to have a fascinating smorgasbord of work experiences as a result of their continuous search for variety and independence in an unpredictable future. Both the 'spiral' and 'transitory' career motives show similarities to the 'opportunists' in Smith (1967), who he describes as energetic individuals with an overriding need to create new businesses and a constant striving for new challenges. Exploration of new possibilities often requires making decisions in the absence of pre-existent goals (Sarasvathy, 2001a). Individuals with these career motives can in this respect be expected to thrive on opportunities that emerge by using means that they can imagine and implementing possible effects that can be created. Hence, it seems fair to argue that individuals driven by either a spiral or a transitory career motive prefer relying on an effectual mode of decision making rather than conventional causation models. This discussion above leads us to propose the following two hypotheses:

- H6: A spiral career motive is positively associated with effectual decision-making logic.
- H7: A transitory career motive is positively associated with effectual decision-making logic.

METHOD AND DATA

Sample and Design

To answer the research question and test the hypotheses developed in the literature review, we designed the empirical study as a questionnaire survey. The mail questionnaire was sent out to a randomly selected group of

1000 individuals who started a new independent firm registered during 1998–2002. The sampling frame consisted of new independent firms across all industries according to SNI2002 (the Swedish Industry Trade Index). Contact addresses were administrated by SCB's (Statistics Sweden) register of firms. The questionnaires were addressed to the CEO and/or the managing director of the targeted firms. A control question was included in the questionnaire to verify that the person that answered the questionnaire had experience of starting up a new firm. Fifteen questionnaires were returned due to business closures, ownership changes and unknown addresses, and were hence excluded from the sample. This led to an initial sample of 985 entrepreneurs. After two reminders we received 291 responses (a response rate of approximately 30 per cent).

We conducted a series of chi-square and *t*-tests to assess whether the results from the sample can be generalized to the initial population. These tests revealed no statistically significant differences between respondents and non-respondents with regard to industry, geographical location, firm size, or the age of their current business. Moreover, we conducted tests to examine whether there were any differences between respondents who answered the mail questionnaire after the first mailing round (approximately 70 per cent of total responses) and those who answered the second time (approximately 30 per cent of total responses) with respect to the same variables. We could not find any significant differences between the early and late responses in any of the following variables: industry, geographical location, firm size and firm age. Moreover, we found no significant differences between early and late respondents with regard to the variables used in the study (see the subsection below). Hence, we have no reason to suspect that there are any significant response biases in the sample.

Variables and Measures

In line with our frame of reference, decision-making logic was divided into two dimensions: *effectuation* and *causation*. A Likert-type scale consisting of 10 items was developed to gauge the entrepreneurs' preference for an effectual or causal reasoning. These items were based on the theoretical work of Sarasvathy (2001a). A factor analysis using varimax rotation was conducted to validate the two scales. The results from the factor analysis led to us dropping one item that loaded with an absolute value less than 0.50. The rest of the constituent items loaded significantly on the expected factors with eigenvalues exceeding 1.0, and together these two factors explained 40.0 per cent of the variance. This procedure resulted in effectuation being measured as the mean of four items ($\alpha = 0.53$), and

Table 5.2 Factor analysis of causation and effectuation measures

Items[1]	Causation[2]	Effectuation[2]
The market exists independently of me and my firm, and the task is to grasp as much of that market as possible	**0.54**	0.27
I prefer to have predetermined goals and to strive to achieve these goals	**0.67**	0.05
I try to avoid uncertain situations to the greatest possible extent	**0.52**	−0.20
I prefer to use pre-calculated and detailed competitive analyses when investigating the need for, or the interest in my product/service	**0.50**	−0.09
I prefer to have strategic, long-term and goal-orientated relationships with my stakeholders	**0.65**	−0.16
I prefer accidental and informal relationships with my stakeholders	0.13	**0.57**
I prefer to have flexible goals and to be able to change direction in the business depending on outcomes	0.00	**0.72**
I welcome uncertain situations in the hope of capitalizing on these occurrences	−0.20	**0.70**
I prefer to use more informal methods when investigating the need for, or interest in my product/service (for example, by asking people among my acquaintances, making own observations in my surroundings etc.)	0.13	**0.57**
Eigenvalue	2.12	1.49
% of variance explained	20.69	19.41
Cronbach's α	0.53	0.53

Notes:
1. Items follow a 5-point scale (1 = very low emphasis vs. 5 = very high emphasis).
2. Absolute loadings of 0.50 or higher are significant.

causation as the mean of five items ($\alpha = 0.53$). A detailed report of the factor analysis can be found in Table 5.2.

The research model involves two main groups of predictors. The first group consists of three career experience variables. In line with Reuber and Fischer (1999) we measured entrepreneurs' accumulated stock of experience at the time when we conducted the study. 'Start-up experience' was measured as the total number of new venture start-ups that the entrepreneur had been involved in. 'Small-business management (SBM) experience' was measured as the total number of years that the entrepreneur has had a management position in a small firm. 'Large-business management (LBM) experience' was measured as the total number of years that the entrepreneur has had a management position in a large firm. We followed the EU definition of small and large firms (small firm = firm with fewer than 50 employees, large firm = firm with more than 249 employees).

The second group of predictors consists of four variables related to the entrepreneurs' career motives. A Likert-type scale consisting of 18 items was used to gauge the four different career motives. The items were extracted from the conceptual foundations of the career concept model which has been extensively researched (Brousseau et al., 1996; Larsson et al., 2001). The questions capture the respondents' career preferences in terms of durability, direction and change in occupational contents. Based on these questions, the career motives were measured as the mean of 3–6 items with Cronbach's alphas as follows: expert career motive ($\alpha = 0.48$), linear career motive ($\alpha = 0.63$), spiral career motive ($\alpha = 0.61$), transitory career motive ($\alpha = 0.47$).

Even if individuals may prefer certain decision models before others it should be noted that decision making is also situational and contingent upon the environment in which an individual operates (Tversky and Simonson, 1993). Effectual reasoning, for example, is expected to be favoured in dynamic and fast-changing environments where predictability and pre-existent goals are not available to the decision maker (Sarasvathy, 2001a). Based on this argument, we included two variables in the research model to control for their experience of starting up and/or managing businesses in industries characterized by dynamic and fast-changing environments. The first control variable included in our model is the perceived degree of 'technological change' in the industry. The second is the degree of 'competitiveness' in the industry. Studies have indicated that the environment can be highly heterogeneous both within and across industries (Keats and Hitt, 1988; Zahra, 1993). Therefore we chose to measure the individuals' perception of the degree of technological change and competitiveness in the industry rather than classifying specific industries that we thought could be considered dynamic and fast changing. We measured both variables on a Likert-type scale (1 = minor degree, 5 = major degree).

It should be noted that several of the measures developed for this study can be considered as highly exploratory. Cronbach's alpha is generally expected to exceed 0.7 for a scale to be deemed reliable (Hair et al., 1998). However, in exploratory research it can be acceptable for the scale to be as low as 0.5 (Nunnally, 1978). Scale developments, replications and larger sample sizes may hence be needed to confirm the findings from this research.

Common method variance is a potential problem when using self-reported data from a single source as it could inflate the strength of correlations between variables (Podsakoff et al., 2003). In order to assess whether common method variance may pose a serious problem in our data we ran Harman's one-factor test (Podsakoff and Organ, 1986). The test produced multiple factors with no single factor featuring significant loadings for all items (if common method variance is a problem, one dominant factor should emerge). In addition, some of the variables included in the analysis are reports of factual data, for example the actual number of years of experience, which are not really susceptible to common method variance, thus further strengthening the belief that common method variance is not likely to be any problem in the present study (ibid.).

RESULTS AND DISCUSSION

In this study we examine the influence of prior career experience and career motives on entrepreneurs' preferred mode of decision making. The empirical data was analysed by multiple regression analyses in SPSS (Statistical Package for the Social Sciences). Table 5.3 contains descriptive statistics and correlations for all variables used in the study.

We checked for multicollinearity by examining the bivariate correlation coefficients as well as the variance inflation factors (VIFs) for each explanatory variable used in the regression analysis. As can be seen in Table 5.3, all correlations coefficients are less than $r = 0.70$, which is the standard threshold used to determine high correlation (Nunnally, 1978). All explanatory variables in the regression analysis had low VIF values (ranging between 1.01 and 1.36), which led us to conclude that no problems of multicollinearity exist in the empirical data (Hair et al., 1998). The regression analyses are presented in Table 5.4.

Career Experience and Entrepreneurial Decision Making

Contrary to Hypothesis 1, there was no association between start-up experience and effectual reasoning. The results consequently suggest that prior start-up experience has no particular influence on entrepreneurial decision making. However, before jumping to conclusions there are some things that we should bear in mind. When studying the bivariate correlations in Table 5.3 it can be observed that prior start-up experience is significantly associated with effectual reasoning (0.05-level), while this association disappears in the linear regression analyses in Table 5.4 when other factors are accounted for. It may hence be possible that the positive influence that occurs due to an individual's start-up experience is not fully linear. To investigate this issue we first divided the sample into two groups,

Table 5.3 Descriptive statistics and correlations

	Variables	Mean	Std dev.	1	2	3	4	5	6	7	8	9	10
1.	Causation	3.36	0.64	1.00									
2.	Effectuation	2.91	0.73	−0.18**	1.00								
3.	Technological change	2.85	1.31	−0.02	0.18**	1.00							
4.	Competitiveness	3.76	3.06	0.06	0.18**	0.16**	1.00						
5.	Start-up experience	2.51	1.90	−0.00	0.16**	0.16**	0.05	1.00					
6.	SBM experience	9.61	8.54	0.17**	−0.02	0.08	0.11	0.29**	1.00				
7.	LBM experience	1.26	4.01	−0.07	0.24**	0.05	0.01	0.14*	−0.15**	1.00			
8.	Linear career motive	3.36	0.80	0.23**	0.09	0.03	−0.01	−0.17**	0.03	−0.10	1.00		
9.	Expert career motive	3.56	0.79	0.25**	−0.06	0.01	0.10	0.05	0.06	0.05	0.29**	1.00	
10.	Spiral career motive	3.77	0.76	0.11	0.27**	0.13*	0.04	0.16**	0.04	0.07	0.59**	0.28**	1.00
11.	Transitory career motive	3.86	0.85	0.03	0.34**	0.14*	0.08	0.17**	0.03	0.01	0.38**	0.13*	0.49**

Note: * $p<0.05$; ** $p<0.01$.

Table 5.4 Regression analysis

Independent variables	Causation	Effectuation
Technological change (control)	−0.02	0.10
Competitiveness (control)	0.03	0.15*
Start-up experience	0.01	0.04
SBM experience	0.13*	−0.03
LBM experience	−0.05	0.12*
Linear career motive	0.21**	−0.15*
Expert career motive	0.20**	−0.09
Spiral career motive	−0.07	0.21**
Transitory career motive	−0.07	0.28**
R^2	0.11	0.22
Adj R^2	0.08	0.19
F (sign)	3.42**	7.44**

Note: The table reports β (partial standardized coefficients), R^2, adjusted R^2, and significance level * $p<0.05$, and ** $p<0.01$.

one with novices (first-time entrepreneurs, 31.3 per cent) and one with habitual entrepreneurs (those with prior start-up experience, 69.7 per cent), and conducted a *t*-test to compare the two groups. The results from the *t*-test show no support for the notion that entrepreneurs with prior start-up experience were in favour of effectual reasoning. Then we divided the sample of entrepreneurs into two other groups – one with novices and less-experienced habitual entrepreneurs (1–3 start-ups, 81.2 per cent) and one with more-experienced habitual entrepreneurs (four or more start-ups, 18.8 per cent) – and conducted an additional *t*-test to compare the two groups. Interestingly, the results from the *t*-test now show that the experienced habitual entrepreneurs to a larger extent favour effectual reasoning compared to novices and less-experienced habitual entrepreneurs (0.00 level). The results suggest that the influence from having prior start-up experience on entrepreneurs' decision-making logic is very small, or even insignificant, at the beginning of the entrepreneurial career. On the other hand, highly experienced entrepreneurs, in terms of start-ups, may be more inclined to use a higher degree of effectual decision making, which is in line with the reasoning of Sarasvathy (2001a). However, these speculations are beyond the scope of this study and require further empirical investigation. Consequently, while we found no association between prior start-up experience and entrepreneurs' decision-making logic in the present study there are several avenues to explore the nature of this non-linear relationship in future research.

Similarly, the results for testing Hypothesis 2 show no association between SBM experience and decision-making logic. Instead, and much to our surprise, SBM experience was positively associated with causal decision-making logic. An explanation for this may be that many entrepreneurs with SBM experience in the sample have experience from relatively stable and mature industries with relatively modest potential for unexpected or rapid technological changes. The correlation matrix in Table 5.3 supports this assumption: SBM experience shows no significant association with experience of a high degree of technological change, environments that generally are in favour of more effectual reasoning (ibid.). The entrepreneurs may in this respect prefer to repeat actions and decision patterns that have worked well in the past as it stimulates confidence and persistence as well as provides a secure and stable base for the launching of new business activities. Some recent studies have pointed in this direction. For example, in a study of the nascent venturing process, Samuelsson (2004) found that most new business opportunities are incremental improvements or replications of already existing business opportunities rather than groundbreaking innovations. Contrasted against the findings in Hills et al. (1999) where 50–90 per cent of start-up ideas is predicted to come from prior work experience, this could suggest that individuals with prior SBM experience may try to maximize their gain by focusing on the effect they want to create based on their pre-existent knowledge of possible means. Decision routines can be encoded deeply in memory and are likely to be recalled and enacted in problem situations that are perceived as similar. It may consequently be reasonable to suggest that entrepreneurs with SBM experience are more likely to be driven by their knowledge of possible means and choose actions that replicate or are closely related to the ones they have already taken, thereby repeating old certainties (Minniti and Bygrave, 2001). However, it should be pointed out that this potential explanation is highly tentative and in need of much further empirical investigation.

As can be seen in Table 5.4, the unexpected pattern of the career experience variables was also true for Hypothesis 3. No association was found between LBM experience and causal decision-making logic, while LBM experience instead was positively and significantly associated with effectual reasoning (0.01 level). Although surprising at first sight, the finding may point towards the need to rephrase the question and instead ask what characterizes those individuals with prior LBM experience who choose to start a new venture. Studies have found, for example, that a previous career as manager in various types of businesses may serve as a valuable personal resource for subsequent new business venturing, providing individuals with the opportunity to utilize their skills and knowledge in new projects as well as developing new knowledge in the entrepreneurial ventures they become involved with (Politis and Landström, 2002). The ability to successfully launch and manage new ventures can hence be seen as the result of distinctive personal resources developed over time through a wide range and variety of experiences acquired throughout their career (Lazear, 2005). We conducted some additional analyses to explore this issue a bit further and found that LBM experience is positively and significantly associated with varied management experience, that is, management experience from different-sized firms. This distinguishes them significantly from the entrepreneurs in the sample that have prior SBM experience (discussed above) as they typically have no experience with managing different-sized firms. Entrepreneurs with LBM experience should hence be seen as individuals who have a rich and varied career background, something that may influence their preferred decision-making mode in entrepreneurial settings. Some studies have suggested that varied work experience may be beneficial for individuals who are involved in new venturing activities. Individuals with experience from working in various kinds of firms are, for example, generally used to dealing with large numbers of people and this may also help in bringing valuable knowledge about a wider set of potential customers and reliable suppliers, as well as valuable social contacts with important stakeholders (Baucus and Human, 1994). Management experience from different firm contexts can also expose individuals to opportunities for learning from a wider variety of situations and problems (Reuber, 1997). This argument is similar to the jack-of-all-trades view on entrepreneurship where varied work and educational backgrounds are favourable for pursuing a successful entrepreneurial career (Lazear, 2005). In sum, although we can provide only tentative speculations at this stage, the findings suggest that entrepreneurs with management experience from various situations and contexts – in this study captured by the LBM experience variable – may lead to a greater inclination towards effectual reasoning. The influence that LBM experience (and/or varied management experience) may have on entrepreneurial decision making is consequently largely unexplored, which calls for further study of this issue.

Career Motives and Entrepreneurial Decision Making

The data in Table 5.4 support Hypothesis 4, showing that a linear career motive is positively and significantly (0.01 level) associated with causal decision-making logic. This finding is in line with the arguments that individuals with a linear career motive have a preference for stability and efficiency (Brousseau et al., 1996). Hence, the findings suggest that entrepreneurs who are motivated by the prospect of rising in position and power in their career seem to prefer a causal mode of decision making, thus focusing on efficient ways to achieve their predetermined goals. Further, consistent with Hypothesis 5, Table 5.4 shows a positive and significant (0.01 level) association between the expert career motive and causal decision-making logic. The underlying key motive of individuals is to refine their pre-existent knowledge to become experts within their specific professions and domains (Schön, 1983). The lifelong commitment to an occupational field or specialty seems in this respect to make them more inclined to rely on a causal mode of decision making, where a distinct focus on professional goals may help them to achieve the specialist knowledge they so highly desire. These results consequently support the general arguments for Hypotheses 4 and 5.

The findings also support Hypothesis 6. As Table 5.4 shows, there is a positive significant (0.01 level) association between a spiral career motive and effectual decision-making logic. Individuals with a spiral career motive are generally described as having a preference for periodic major moves across occupational areas, specialties or disciplines that are closely related to previous ones (Brousseau et al., 1996) which seems to speak in favour of a preference for exploiting contingencies around them. Hence, the findings suggest that entrepreneurs with a spiral career motive to a large extent use effectuation as a coping strategy for dealing with uncertainty.

Similarly, Table 5.4 shows a positive and significant association (0.01 level) between a transitory career motive and effectual decision-making logic. The underlying key motives of individuals with a transitory career motive are the search for variety and independence, with a preference for frequent changes of organization and job to very different or completely unrelated fields or areas (ibid.). These individuals favour adaptiveness and networking, where plans are continuously made, revised and recast through actions and interactions with others, thus allowing goals to emerge contingently over time. As expected, the results imply that entrepreneurs with a transitory career motive favour effectual decision-making logic. Hypothesis 7 was consequently supported.

Additionally, our regression analysis in Table 5.4 also shows an interesting pattern regarding the association between entrepreneurs' career motive and their preferred mode of entrepreneurial decision making, something which echoes suggestions from previous research that the four career motives should be seen on a continuum (ibid.). At the one end of the continuum we have the linear career motive, which in the analyses is positively and significantly associated with a causal mode of decision making (0.21, $p<0.01$), while negatively and significantly associated with an effectual mode of decision making (-0.15, $p<0.05$). Then follows the expert career motive, which in the analysis shows a positive and significant association with a causal mode of decision making (0.20, $p < 0.01$). Thereafter we have the spiral career motive, which in the analysis is positively and significantly associated with an effectual mode of decision making (0.21, $p < 0.01$). Finally, there is the transitory career motive, which is positively and significantly associated with an effectual mode of decision making (0.28, $p < 0.01$). These findings imply that the linear career motive is associated most strongly with a causal mode of decision making, while the other career motives follow in order where the positive association becomes a little less weak for the expert career, and then insignificant for the spiral and transitory career motive. Similarly, the transitory career motive is associated most strongly with an effectual mode of decision making, while the following career motivations follow in an order where the positive association becomes somewhat weaker for the spiral career, then negative association for the expert career, and then finally there is a negative but significant association between the linear career and a causal mode of decision making. The pattern of associations in the regression analysis between the four career motives and entrepreneurial decision making consequently supports the notion that the four career motives can be seen as a continuum (ibid.), something which provides several interesting avenues for further research.

CONCLUSION AND IMPLICATIONS

Recent research has argued for the need to better understand how human minds solve problems and make decisions in entrepreneurial settings (for example, Gustafsson, 2004; Douglas, 2005; Forbes, 2005; Lévesque and Schade, 2005; Mullins and Forlani, 2005). The motivating factor for this study has been an attempt to gain further insight into underlying factors influencing entrepreneurial decision making. Hence, although we acknowledge that entrepreneurs' decision-making preference to a large degree may vary in response to the unique situational context, we have been particularly interested in whether career experiences and career motives may make them more in favour of one decision-making logic than another. Taking Sarasvathy's theory of effectuation as the point of departure, we provide evidence indicating that entrepreneurs' career experience and career motives influence entrepreneurial decision making. The empirical findings suggest that entrepreneurs with prior SBM experience, and with a linear or expert career motive, have a higher preference for a more causal mode of decision making. Entrepreneurs with prior managerial experience from large firms, and with a spiral or transitory career motive, have on the other hand a higher preference for a more effectual mode of decision making. No association was found between prior start-up experience and entrepreneurs' decision-making logic. Instead, there were indications of a non-linear relationship between start-up experience and effectual decision making. Overall, although some associations did not fall out as predicted, our findings give ample support for the argument that entrepreneurs' career experience and career motives have a significant influence on entrepreneurial decision making.

Conceptually, an important implication of this study is the linkage between entrepreneurs' career experience and career motives, and their preferred decision-making logic. As such, we acknowledge that entrepreneurs cope with uncertainty and complexity reduction in decision-making situations by routinely simplifying and structuring information through their perceptual filters and pre-existent knowledge structures. The reliance on experientially acquired routines may facilitate action by presenting entrepreneurs with readily available solutions and preferences for typical problems that may arise (Minniti and Bygrave, 2001). In addition, the intention of entrepreneurs can also influence their decision behaviours, given that the behaviour is feasible and desirable (Krueger, 2003). Entrepreneurs' career experience (routines) and career motives (their intended directions) can in this respect help them to simplify complex situations and cope with problem situations in the new venture creation process. Thus, although entrepreneurial decision making may change in response to the unique situational context (Douglas, 2005) our findings suggest that entrepreneurs also seem to have some stable preferences that make them favour one decision-making logic over another. Hence, even if it may be more effective to rely on causal or effectual reasoning, depending on the specific circumstance entrepreneurs are facing they may, based on their routines and intended directions, have a preference for causal or effectual reasoning. In short, what is effective is one thing and what is preferred another.

As discussed in the previous sections, the empirical results contribute to a more detailed understanding of the antecedents of causal and effectual modes of reasoning. The findings suggest that future research into entrepreneurial decision making should include career experience and career motives as contingency variables. Furthermore, the chapter provides an attempt to operationalize entrepreneurs' preference for causal and effectual modes of reasoning. To our knowledge no such operationalization exists, which makes the developed constructs interesting for further research in this area. Based on these contributions, we believe that our study is an important step in research that seeks to examine decision making in entrepreneurial settings.

REFERENCES

Baucus, D.A. and S.E. Human (1994), 'Second-career entrepreneurs: a multiple case study of entrepreneurial processes and antecedent variables', *Entrepreneurship Theory and Practice*, **19** (2), 41–71.

Bergendahl, J. (2005), 'Exploring the complexity of the venture creation process – Insights into founders' diary notes in real time, paper presented at the RENT XIX conference in Naples, 16–18 November.

Bower, J.L. (1986), *Managing the Resource Allocation Process: A Study of Corporate Planning and Investment*, Boston, MA: Harvard Business School Press.

Brousseau, K.R., M.J. Driver, K. Eneroth and R. Larsson (1996), 'Career pandemonium: realigning organizations and individuals', *Academy of Management Executive*, **10** (4), 52–66.

Cyert, R.M. and J.G. March (1963), *A Behavioral Theory of the Firm*, Englewood Cliffs, NJ: Prentice-Hall.

Davidsson, P. and M. Klofsten (2003), 'The business platform: developing an instrument to gauge and to assist the development of young firms', *Journal of Small Business Management*, **41** (1), 1–26.

Dew, N. and S.D. Sarasvathy (2002), 'What effectuation is not: further development of an alternative to rational choice', paper presented at the Academy of Management Conference in Denver, USA, August.

Douglas, D. (2005), 'The human complexities of entrepreneurial decision making: a grounded case considered', *International Journal of Entrepreneurial Behaviour and Research*, **11** (6), 422–35.

Driver, M.J. (1979), 'Career concepts and career management in organizations', in C. Cooper (ed.), *Behavioral Problems in Organizations*, Englewood Cliffs, NJ: Prentice-Hall, pp. 79–139.

Driver, M.J. (1988), 'Careers: a review of personal and organizational research', in C. Cooper and I.T. Robertson (eds), *International Review of Industrial and Organizational Psychology*, Chichester: Wiley, pp. 245–77.

Forbes, D.P. (2005), 'The effects of strategic decision making on entrepreneurial self-efficacy', *Entrepreneurship Theory and Practice*, **29** (5), 599–626.

Forlani, D. and J.M. Mullins (2000), 'Perceived risks and choices in entrepreneurs' new venture decisions', *Journal of Business Venturing*, **15** (4), 305–22.

Goffman, E. (1961), 'The moral career of the mental patient', in Goffman (ed.), *Asylums: Essays on the Social Situation of Mental Patients and Other Inmates*, New York: Anchor Books, pp. 125–69.

Gustafsson, V. (2004), 'Entrepreneurial decision-making: individual, tasks and cognition', Doctoral dissertation, No. 022. Jönköping International Business School, Jönköping.

Hair, J.F., R.E. Anderson, R.L. Tatham and W.C. Black (1998), *Multivariate Data Analysis*, 5th edn, Englewood Cliffs, NJ: Prentice Hall.

Harvey, M. and R. Evans (1995), 'Strategic windows in the entrepreneurial process', *Journal of Business Venturing*, **10** (5), 331–47.

Hills, G.E., R.C. Shrader and G.T. Lumpkin (1999), 'Opportunity recognition as a creative process', in P. Reynolds, W. Bygrave, S. Manigart, C. Mason, G.D. Meyer, H. Sapienza and K.G. Shaver (eds), *Frontiers of Entrepreneurship Research*, Wellesley, MA: Babson College, pp. 216–27.

Johannisson, B. (2000), 'Networking and entrepreneurial growth', in D.L. Sexton and H. Landström (eds), *Handbook of Entrepreneurship*, Oxford: Blackwell Business, pp. 368–86.
Johannisson, B., H. Landström, and J. Rosenberg (1998), 'University training for entrepreneurship – an action frame of reference', *European Journal of Engineering Education*, **23** (4), 477–96.
Katz, J.A. (1994), 'Modeling entrepreneurial career progressions: concepts and considerations', *Entrepreneurship Theory and Practice*, **19** (2), 23–39.
Keats, B. and M. Hitt (1988), 'A causal model of linkages among environmental dimensions, macro organizational characteristics, and performance', *Academy of Management Journal*, **31,** 570–98.
Krueger, N.F. Jr (2003), 'The cognitive psychology of the entrepreneur', in Z.J. Acs and D.B. Audretsch (eds), *Handbook of Entrepreneurship Research*, Dordrecht: Kluwer Academic, pp. 105–40.
Larsson, R., M. Driver, M. Holmqvist and P. Sweet (2001), 'Career dis-integration and re-integration in mergers and acquisitions: managing competence and motivational intangibles', *European Management Journal*, **19** (6), 609–18.
Lazear, E.P. (2005), 'Entrepreneurship', *Journal of Labor Economics*, **23** (4), 649–80.
Lévesque, M. and C. Schade (2005), 'Intuitive optimizing: experimental findings on time allocation decisions within newly formed ventures', *Journal of Business Venturing*, **20** (3), 313–42.
McGrath, R.G. (1999), 'Falling forward: real options reasoning and entrepreneurial failure', *Academy of Management Review*, **24** (1), 13–30.
Minniti, M. and W. Bygrave (2001), 'A dynamic model of entrepreneurial learning', *Entrepreneurship Theory and Practice*, **25** (3), 5–16.
Mullins, J.M. and D. Forlani (2005), 'Missing the boat or sinking the boat: a study of new venture decision making', *Journal of Business Venturing*, **20** (1), 47–69.
Nunnally, J.C. (1978), *Psychometric Theory*, New York: McGraw-Hill.
O'Gorman, C. (2000), 'Strategy and the small firm', in S. Carter and D. Jones-Evans (eds), *Enterprise and Small Business: Principles, Practice and Policy*, Harlow: Financial Times, pp. 283–99.
Podsakoff, P.M., S.B. MacKenzie, J.Y. Lee and N.P. Podsakoff (2003), 'Common method biases in behavioural research: a critical review of the literature and recommended remedies', *Journal of Applied Psychology*, **88**, 879–903.
Podsakoff, P.M. and D.W. Organ (1986), 'Self-reports in organizational research: problems and prospects', *Journal of Management*, **12** (4), 531–44.
Politis, D. (2005), 'The process of entrepreneurial learning: a conceptual framework', *Entrepreneurship Theory and Practice*, **29** (4), 399–424.
Politis, D. and H. Landström (2002), 'Informal investors as entrepreneurs – the development of an entrepreneurial career', *Venture Capital*, **4** (2), 78–101.
Reuber, R.A. (1997), 'Management experience and management expertise', *Decision Support Systems*, **21**, 51–60.
Reuber, R. and E. Fischer (1999), 'Understanding the consequences of founders' experience', *Journal of Small Business Management*, **37** (2), 30–45.
Ronstadt, R. (1988), 'The corridor principle', *Journal of Business Venturing*, **3** (1), 31–40.
Samuelsson, M. (2004), 'Creating new ventures: a longitudinal investigation of the nascent venturing process', Doctoral dissertation, No. 020, Jönköping International Business School, Jönköping.

Sarasvathy, S.D. (2001a), 'Causation and effectuation: toward a theoretical shift from economic inevitability to entrepreneurial contingency', *Academy of Management Review*, **26** (2), 243–88.
Sarasvathy, S.D. (2001b), 'What makes entrepreneurs entrepreneurial?', unpublished working paper, www.effectuation.org/ftp/effectua.pdf.
Schein, E.H. (1987), 'Individuals and careers', in J.W. Lorsch (ed.), *Handbook of Organizational Behaviour*, Englewood Cliffs, NJ: Prentice-Hall, pp. 155–71.
Schön, D. (1983), *The Reflective Practitioner*, New York: Basic Books.
Shane, S. (2003), *A General Theory of Entrepreneurship: The Individual–Opportunity Nexus*, Cheltenham, UK and Northampton, MA, USA: Edward Elgar.
Shane, S., E.A. Locke and C.J. Collins (2003), 'Entrepreneurial motivation', *Human Resource Management Review*, **13**, 257–79.
Shane, S. and S. Venkataraman (2000), 'The promise of entrepreneurship as a field of research', *Academy of Management Review*, **25** (1), 217–26.
Simon, M., S.M. Houghton and K. Aquino (2000), 'Cognitive biases, risk perception, and venture formation: how individuals decide to start companies', *Journal of Business Venturing*, **15** (2), 113–34.
Smith, N.R. (1967), *The Entrepreneur and His Firm: The Relationship between Type of Man and Type of Company*, East Lansing, MI: Michigan State University.
Starr, J.A. and W.D. Bygrave (1992), 'The second time around: the outcomes, assets, and liabilities of prior start-up experience', in S. Birley and I.C. MacMillan (eds), *International Perspectives on Entrepreneurship Research 1991: Proceedings of the First Annual Global Conference on Entrepreneurship Research*, Amsterdam: Elsevier, pp. 340–63.
Starr, J.A. and N. Fondas (1992), 'A model of entrepreneurial socialization', *Entrepreneurship Theory and Practice*, **17** (1), 67–76.
Stevenson, H.H. and D. Gumpert (1985), 'The heart of entrepreneurship', *Harvard Business Review*, **85** (2), 85–94.
Tversky, A. and I. Simonson (1993), 'Context-dependent preferences', *Management Science*, **10**, 1179–89.
Venkataraman, S. (1997), 'The distinctive domain of entrepreneurship research', in J.A. Katz (ed.), *Advances in Entrepreneurship, Firm Emergence, and Growth*, Greenwich, CT: JAI Press, pp. 119–38.
Vohora, A., M. Wright and A. Lockett (2004), 'Critical junctures in the development of university high-tech spin-out companies', *Research Policy*, **33**, 147–75.
Westhead, P., D. Ucbasaran and M. Wright (2005), 'Decisions, actions and performance: do novice, serial and portfolio entrepreneurs differ?', *Journal of Small Business Management*, **23** (1), 72–98.
Westhead, P. and M. Wright (1998), 'Novice, portfolio, and serial founders: are they different?', *Journal of Business Venturing*, **13** (3), 173–204.
Wiltbank, R., N. Dew, S. Read and S. Sarasvathy (2006), 'What to do next? The case for non-predictive strategy', *Strategic Management Journal*, **27** (10), 981–98.
Winborg, J. and H. Landström (2001), 'Financial bootstrapping in small businesses examining small business managers' recourse acquisition behaviours', *Journal of Business Venturing*, **16** (3), 235–54.
Zahra, S. (1993), 'Environment, corporate entrepreneurship, and financial performance: a taxonomic approach', *Journal of Business Venturing*, **8** (4), 319–40.

6. Start-ups in the Netherlands: a longitudinal study on the factors for growth

Petra Gibcus, Pauline de Jong-'t Hart and Ron Kemp

INTRODUCTION

The dynamics and growth of firms are considered to be important for enhancing economic growth, and growth is an issue at all times. Growing firms are a stimulus for the economic development of nations (Audretsch et al., 2004). Not surprisingly, the growth of firms and growth patterns have received much attention from researchers during the last two decades (Bruno et al., 1992; Welbourne et al., 1998; Brown et al., 2001; Delmar et al., 2003; Bosma et al., 2004, Garnsey et al., 2006). Bangma and Verhoeven (2000) found four different types of growth patterns in the Netherlands: fast-growing firms, those growing at a normal rate, stable firms and shrinking businesses. This classification of firms in a growth pattern is not stable over time. Fast-growing companies do not go on growing rapidly for years. Even over a short time horizon the dynamics are considerable. Fast-growing firms accounted for almost 44 per cent of employment creation between 1998 and 2002 (Bangma et al., 2005). More importantly Bangma and Verhoeven (2000) note that start-ups in particular show (fast) growth.

From an organizational point of view, growth is an important issue as well. Growth is often seen as an important performance measure that gives insight into the vitality and competitiveness of the company. For start-ups, growth in the first years is often a prerequisite for survival. On a general level, organizations can benefit from growth in many ways, including greater efficiency through economies of scale, increased power, the ability to withstand environmental change, increased profits and increased prestige for organizational members (Philipsen and Kemp, 2003).

Given the importance of growth and growing firms and start-ups, we need to obtain a better understanding of the growth development of start-ups. To date, most studies focus on a relatively small number of explanatory variables, use a small number of case studies, use cross-sectional data or use initial conditions to explain growth (for example, Romanelli, 1989; Cooper et al., 1994; Bamford et al., 1999; Bosma et al., 2004). In the present study we map the development of start-ups in terms of growth and explain the growth using a large panel dataset of firms that were founded in 1994. In this panel we have the availability of a large amount of (annually collected) information over a period of 10 years. Therefore the dataset contains not only information about the initial founding conditions, but also variables (and changes therein) over the lifetime (up to 10 years) of the company. The longitudinal data are very valuable. This research is the first initiative towards more comprehensive longitudinal research. It is almost impossible to capture all the variables at one time and also perform an exhaustive number of analyses. However, we are aware that the start-up panel offers us many possibilities for profound research. In the present exploratory study we take a closer look at the determinants available in the panel and the way in which they should be constructed for useful analysis. We perform correlation and regression analyses to investigate whether the potential determinants and growth relate to each other. In particular, the growth in the first five years can be explained. Important factors are, among others, unfulfilled needs in the market, a partner with an own firm, previous management and sector experience, a growth objective and networking.

START-UPS IN THE NETHERLANDS

In the Netherlands more than 99 per cent of all firms are small and medium-sized enterprises (SMEs) (fewer than 100 employees). Therefore it is not surprising that SMEs contribute enormously to the total level of employment. In 2004, SMEs accounted for approximately 55 per cent of total employment with five million jobs (EIM, 2005). The creation of jobs by new firms is often considered to be a solution to the unemployment problem. Persson (2004) argues that in the short run, job creation by new firms and job destruction when companies close are of minor importance, compared to the contribution made by firms already in existence. She reveals that job creation at new firms in Sweden was on average 3.5 per cent of total employment each year, while the creation of jobs at already existing, expanding firms was 7.7 per cent. Van Stel and Storey (2004), in an empirical study for Great Britain, found no significant relationship between start-ups and employment creation in the 1980s. In this section we shall take a closer look at the number of start-ups in the Netherlands, the employment they create and their survival rates.

Table 6.1 Number of start-ups and start-up rate, 1994–2004

Year	Number of start-ups	Number of firms	Start-up rate (%)
1994	39 100	583 200	6.7
1995	41 500	604 800	6.9
1996	39 600	626 500	6.3
1997	40 100	647 100	6.2
1998	42 000	667 000	6.3
1999	47 200	689 600	6.8
2000	53 800	717 700	7.5
2001	47 300	734 700	6.4
2002	42 600	744 900	5.7
2003	40 600	748 100	5.4
2004	48 300	760 900	6.3

The number of start-ups increased gradually until 2000 and reached its peak in that year, approximately 54 000 start-ups (see Table 6.1). After 2000, the number of start-ups decreased, mainly as a reaction to the economic recession. However, in 2004 the number of start-ups increased again. Usually pull factors, such as new market opportunities, are responsible for positive tendencies in the number of start-ups. However, this was not the case for 2004: push factors, such as (possible) unemployment, resulted in more start-ups. Even in the retail and catering industries the number of start-ups increased although these industries are strongly influenced by the stagnating consumer expenditures.

The number of start-ups as a percentage of the number of firms is called the 'start-up rate'. In 2000 the start-up rate reached its peak: 7.5 per cent. From that year on, the rate decreased until 2004 when it increased again, the result of the large rise in the number of start-ups.

It is hard to place the Dutch figures in an international context. Each country has its own definition of a start-up. Some countries count the number of enterprises whereas others count the number of establishments. Using a standardization procedure, start-up data are collected for 11 countries: Belgium, Denmark, Finland, France, Germany, Ireland, Italy, Japan, the Netherlands, the United Kingdom and the United States. The start-up rate is defined as the number of entries as a percentage of the total number of enterprises. In 2004 the start-up rate in the Netherlands was 8.8 per cent, which lies somewhere in the middle. Japan scores the lowest rate with 5.4 per cent and Ireland the highest with 13.3 per cent. In the last five years the start-up rate in the Netherlands decreased from 11.1 to 8.8 per cent. A reduction was also visible in Ireland. In the majority of other countries this development has been more stable (De Jong-'t Hart and Verhoeven, 2006).

Another way of looking at the international context is to compare the Total Early-stage Entrepreneurial Activity (TEA) index. The TEA is a combination of nascent entrepreneurs (people currently involved in concrete activities to set up a new business) and owners of young businesses (people currently owning a business that is less than 42 months old). In 2004 the TEA in the Netherlands was 5.1 per cent. For the EU-15 countries the TEA was also 5.1 per cent and for the OECD countries it was 6.8 per cent (Hessels et al., 2005). Again the position of the Netherlands is somewhere in the middle.

Start-ups create many jobs, but what is their contribution to total employment? In 2000 approximately 54 000 firms were started, creating 78 000 new jobs. The employment creation by start-ups in 2004 was 66 700 jobs. On average, each start-up created employment for 1.6 persons in 1997 and for 1.3 persons in 2004, thus the average start-up size decreased over the years. Of the total employment creation, on average 53 per cent of this employment creation between 1994 and 2004 was due to start-ups.

The net change in employment is a result of job creation by new firms, job destruction the consequence of exits and growth and shrinkage of existing firms. Table 6.2 depicts the contribution of each of these groups to the net employment growth as a percentage of total employment (in average annual rates between 1994 and 2004). The table shows that total job creation in the Netherlands was on average 2.7 per cent each year. Job creation by incumbent firms was 1.5 per cent. Small start-ups are responsible for the highest rate (4.7 per cent) in net employment growth. Employment creation is fairly constant over time.

Table 6.2 Net employment growth and its components in the Netherlands, 1994–2004, average annual rates as a percentage of total employment

	Small firms (0–9 employees)	Medium-sized firms (10–99 employees)	Large firms (≥ 100 employees)	Total
Employment creation rate	7.3	1.3	0.0	2.7
Start-ups (entry)	4.7	0.1	0.0	1.6
New subsidiary companies	2.7	1.1	0.0	1.0
Employment destruction rate	4.5	1.5	0.5	2.0
Employment change existing firms	−0.4	2.6	2.0	1.5
Net employment change	2.4	2.3	1.5	2.2

Although many entrepreneurs are eager to start up their own business, many of these will not survive. The first few years, in particular, are extremely difficult. In Figure 6.1, we look at the survival rates of all firms that started their business in 1994.

A third of the start-ups exited the market within three years. The second year shows the highest number of exits. Almost 16 per cent of the start-ups quit in the second year. After 10 years approximately 63 per cent of the firms that entered the market in 1994 have exited the market.

Bangma et al. (2005) claim that the survival rates of Dutch firms are constant over time. This is quite remarkable. There seems to be no effect of the economic situation on the survival rate. Nor does there seem to be any effect of the law of large numbers, because some cohorts have more start-ups than others. The rate of the number of exits related to the number of start-ups is fairly constant. Large differences in survival rates are apparent across industries. Firms in the Netherlands that have the largest chance of survival are those in the chemicals industry and in banking and insurance. Start-ups in the retail, wholesale and the hotel and catering industry have the lowest chance of survival.

DETERMINANTS OF GROWTH

Important theories on the evolution and revolution in corporate development and on the growth of firms were developed more than 40 years ago (Gibrat, 1931; Penrose, 1959). Entrepreneurship researchers have indicated that growth is a crucial indicator of venture success, more crucial than other performance indicators (Covin and Slevin, 1997; Low and MacMillan, 1988). One group of researchers focus on concepts that explain growth, that is, what are the antecedents of organizational growth and what are the consequences for the company itself? In this section a short overview is presented of determinants for growth from literature on strategic management and entrepreneurship. Philipsen and Kemp (2003) present an overview of both theoretical and empirical studies on determinants for growth.

Concepts that proved to have an impact on the growth of SMEs can be classified into several groups of resources, such as human capital, the entrepreneur's social capital, financial capital, structure of the company and market variables (Davidsson, 1991; Man et al., 2002). Other authors of recent studies have proposed that a combination of individual, organizational and market dimensions provides a more comprehensive prediction of venture development and growth than each of the dimensions in isolation (Covin and Slevin, 1997; Almus and Nerlinger, 1999; Baum et al., 2001;

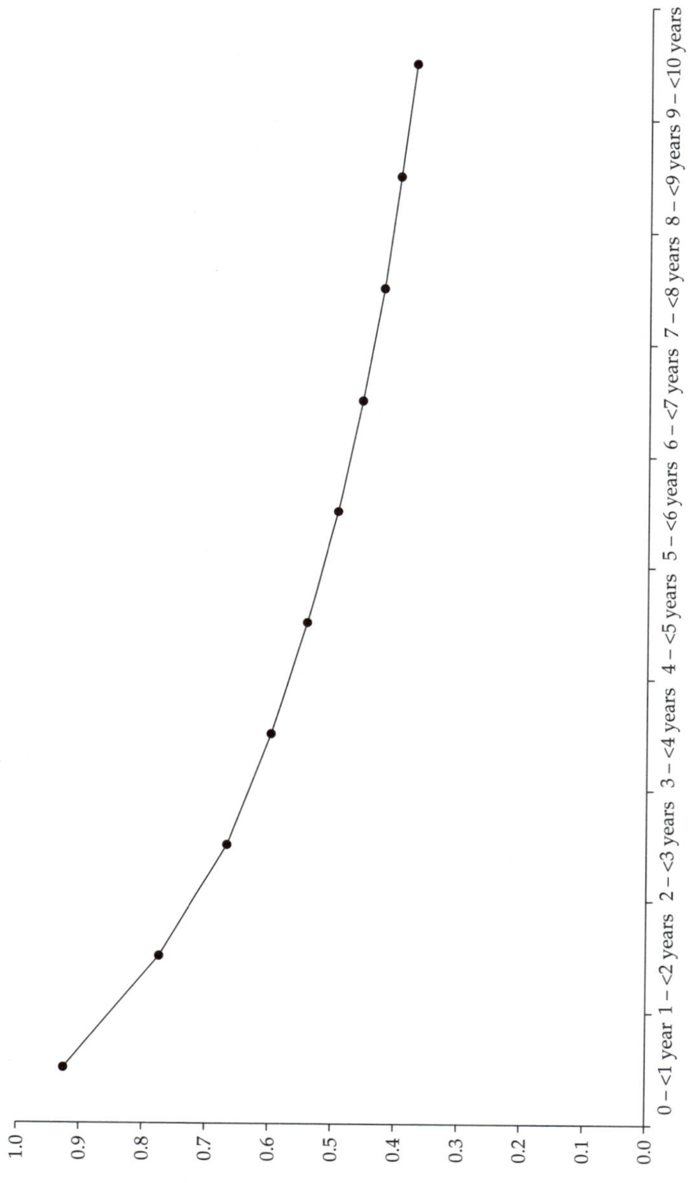

Figure 6.1 Survival rates of the start-up cohort 1994

Lumpkin and Dess, 2001). However, the examination of multi-dimensional models is limited. In this study, we shall build on these models including variables from the market/industry, the entrepreneurial/managerial and the firm-specific dimensions. The following subsections take a closer look at each of the three elements.

Market/Industry Dimension

The lack of market power and the turbulent nature of newly emerging markets often make SMEs more vulnerable than larger firms to external influences. Barringer et al. (1997) found that fast-growing entrepreneurial firms operate in more munificent environments than slower-growing firms, suggesting a positive influence of environmental opportunities. Other authors take a more proactive approach when considering the external factors. Slevin and Covin (1995), for example, suggest that continuous repositioning is needed if smaller new firms are to anticipate and respond to the action of (larger) competitors. The influence of the environment on a firm's growth cannot be ignored.

Baum et al. (2001) consider that the external factors are dynamism, munificence and complexity. Wijewardena and Cooray (1995) showed the importance of the type of industry and the nature of the competition. Pelham (1999) argued that external factors that influence growth are industry growth, market concentration, value added per employee and the market segment. Lau and Busenitz (2001) emphasized the influence of difficulty in market conditions on firm growth. Difficulties can be caused by problems such as borrowing, operational facilities, competition, policy change and labour. Wiklund (1999) found that environmental dynamism, capital availability and type of industry are relevant for growth in terms of sales and employment.

Entrepreneurial/Managerial Dimension

The process of achieving growth is strongly influenced by entrepreneurs or managers. The task of creating organizational capabilities and competencies is seen as one of the functions of the entrepreneur (Gartner and Starr, 1993). De Koning and Muzyka (1998) found that opportunity orientation is an important factor in explaining growth. Eggers et al. (1994) showed that leadership style differs in different stages of organizational growth. According to Davidsson (1991), growth is influenced by the entrepreneur's need for achievement, ability, opportunity and growth motivation. Lau and Busenitz (2001) examined growth intentions of entrepreneurs and found that an entrepreneur's commitment, need for achievement, and social environment are important, but that a cognitive understanding of the environment also has a deep impact on growth intensions.

Baum et al. (2001) identified three different research domains which focus on the entrepreneur: personal traits and general motives, personal competencies, and situational-specific motivations. Personal traits and general motives are age, education, ambition and ambiguity of the entrepreneur. Ambiguity allows the entrepreneur more latitude to interpret and influence an environment that is not yet settled (Mintzberg, 1973). Individual competencies are the knowledge and capabilities required to perform a specific job (for example, skills specific for the industry, and opportunity recognition). Situational-specific motivations refer to strategic vision, business goals and self-efficacy. Specific challenging goals lead to higher performance. Also Rauch et al. (2005) found strong support for the relationship between human capital of the business owners and employment growth.

Firm-specific Dimensions

The resource-based view of the firm shows that the internal factors of the firm are important for its performance. Rangone's study (1999) points out the importance of innovation, production and market-management capabilities. Lee et al. (2001) found that technological capabilities and financial resources were important predictors of a venture's growth. Furthermore, Baum et al. (2001) reported that a new venture's internal capabilities are the primary determinants of the venture's performance. Firm characteristics identified by the authors are age and size of the firm; endogenous internal factors here are strategy, available resources, financial situation, products, working methods, cooperation, profitability and innovative behaviour. Entrepreneurial processes put forward by Lumpkin and Dess (2001) are innovation, risk taking, proactiveness and aggressiveness.

Almus and Nerlinger (1999) introduced five factors of firm-specific characteristics that influence growth: age, size, liability, networks and diversification of products. Research by Wijewardena and Cooray (1995) again draws attention to age and the size of the firm. The authors further examined the influence of capital intensity, export orientation, advertisement expenditure, research and development (R&D) expenditure and the number of skilled workers relative to the total number of employees. Autio et al. (2000) found that learning new capabilities helps firms to compete effectively, and to survive and grow. The accumulation of knowledge through learning constitutes a driving force in the development and growth of young firms (Penrose, 1959; Spender and Grant, 1996).

MEASUREMENT OF GROWTH

As we have seen in the previous sections, growth is multidimensional in nature, allowing different attributes (for example, sales, personnel value and capital) of the firm to change during growth. Many different measurements for growth are used. In this section we take a closer look at this topic.

According to Penrose (1959) the size of a firm should be measured according to the present value of the resources (including personnel) used for its own productive purposes. This proved almost impossible in practice. Garnsey et al. (2006) argued that Penrose was somewhat sceptical of measuring firm attributes that are unique to individual firms. These attributes may not be reducible to any common denominator and are therefore unsuitable for quantitative treatment. But Penrose recognized the need to measure the growth performance of fixed assets.

Garnsey et al. stated that a firm's growth can be measured in terms of inputs (investment funds, employees), the value of the firm (assets, market capitalization, economic value added) or outputs (sales revenues). They argued that many new studies on new venture growth cite funds invested at various stages, but these track the 'burn rate' of investment funds rather than the growth of productive resources. Sales figures (turnover) have to be adjusted for inflation, and are affected by vertical integration (how much of final sales is produced internally or brought in). Profits are expressed in various ways and are often influenced by tax and accounting systems. This creates comparison problems. Valuation of the firm's assets is a composite indicator of growth. This includes tangible assets, for example production equipment and buildings, and a valuation of intangible assets, the firm's expertise and reputation. The valuation of intangible assets is particularly difficult.

In empirical literature the possible indicators for measuring growth are: assets, employment, market share, physical output, profit and sales (Delmar, 1997; Ardichvili et al., 1998). The most commonly used growth indicators according to Delmar's study are employment and sales. Employment figures are used because they offer standardized, comparable data about the rate and direction in which a firm has been expanding. In Bennett and Robson (1999), for example, the relative employee and turnover growth measures are investigated. Almus and Nerlinger (1999) look at the growth in the number of employees between 1989 and 1997. Baum et al. (2001) measure growth in terms of employees, but also in annual sales and profit. Davidsson (1991) uses growth of employees and sales as the dependent variable in his analysis. Beal (2000) focuses on the growth of sales and profits only. Chandler and Hanks (1994) examine the growth of market share, cash flow and sales. In our study, we focus on employment growth. This measure is suitable for comparing firms of different industries, is not influenced by inflation and so on. Furthermore, it builds on a large stream of previous empirical research on firm growth (Delmar, 1997).

DATA

Many empirical research studies on new firms have a retrospective character. Entrepreneurs are asked about their activities and the firm performance some years after the start of their firm. According to Schutjens and Stam (2003) this leads to two problems. First, the reasons for the closure or migration of the new firms that did not survive can no longer be ascertained, since by definition the research population will consist only of those entrepreneurs that did survive. The second problem is that memory problems can be quite substantial, especially when the firms are some years old. It may be hard to remember the exact reasons for specific firm strategies after a few years. The 'Start-up panel: cohort 1994' was founded by EIM Business and Policy Research (hereafter EIM) to avoid these problems and to analyse the major changes in the early life stages of start-ups. We use this panel for our empirical analyses. The population in this panel consists of firms in the Netherlands that started their business in 1994. First, we give a description of the start-up panel and then we present the relevant variables.

The Start-up Panel

Data was collected in the 'Start-up panel: cohort 1994'. In 1994 EIM started to work with a representative panel of firms that were registered as independent start-ups in 1994. Almost 2000 firms, started in the first part of 1994, were interviewed on various aspects concerning the start of their business, and the start-ups have been followed since then. The main themes have remained the same over the years and cover subjects such as characteristics of the firm and entrepreneur, finance and investment, bottlenecks, strategy and goals, market and environment, realization versus expectation. Now we have 10 years of valuable information at our disposal.

Approximately 12000 addresses were selected in 1994. The business owners were called and asked whether they would like to participate in a research project on start-ups. Almost 3000 owners were interested. They all received a questionnaire by mail. A total of 1938 completed questionnaires were returned. A year later, in 1995, the participants were approached again. In 1995 almost 1750 business owners expressed their interest in participating in the research and 1007 completed questionnaires were returned. This procedure was used until 1999 and since then computer assisted telephone interviewing (CATI) has been used to gather information. In 2000 current but also previous participants who could be traced were phoned, resulting in 670 completed interviews. Figure 6.2 shows the number of participants in the panel between 1994 and 2004. In 2004, 10 years later, there were still 435 participants in the panel.

Throughout the years only 23 per cent of our panel participants survived. It is necessary to take into account the fact that some firms refused to participate in the panel in later years and that other firms were hard to trace because they stopped their economic activities, went bankrupt or simply moved. In the end the first problem mentioned by Schutjens and Stam (2003) could not be avoided entirely in this panel. Stam et al. (2005) used the start-up panel: cohort 1994, but also included cohorts 1998, 1999 and 2000 in their study on renascent entrepreneurship, entrepreneurs that have a stated or revealed preference for starting a new firm after firm exit. They traced the firms that did not survive within one year subsequent to the closure of the business and a number of characteristics were recorded in a survey. At the end of 2004 they had contacted 510 ex-entrepreneurs who had closed their business in a previous decade. Ultimately they collected data from 240 respondents on several variables reflecting entrepreneurial experience, current occupations and entrepreneurial intentions. Their non-response analysis revealed that there are no significant differences between the non-respondents and respondents, with the exception of age: respondents tend to be older than non-respondents, which suggests that renascent entrepreneurs (as these tend to be relatively young) were undersampled. Stam et al. attribute this response bias to the higher mobility of younger people, which makes it harder to trace them via telephone surveys. Fifty-seven per cent of the interviewed entrepreneurs were renascent entrepreneurs. The other 43 per cent were considered to be one-night stands: ex-entrepreneurs who have not stated or revealed a preference for starting a new firm.

Sample Characteristics

On average the entrepreneurs in our panel were 38 years old in 1994. The youngest was 19 and the oldest 61. There are more male participants in the panel than females, almost 75 per cent of them are men. Approximately 27 per cent of the participants have a bachelor's or master's degree.

The distribution of start-ups across industries in the panel is as follows: manufacturing and construction (15 per cent), wholesale (9 per cent),

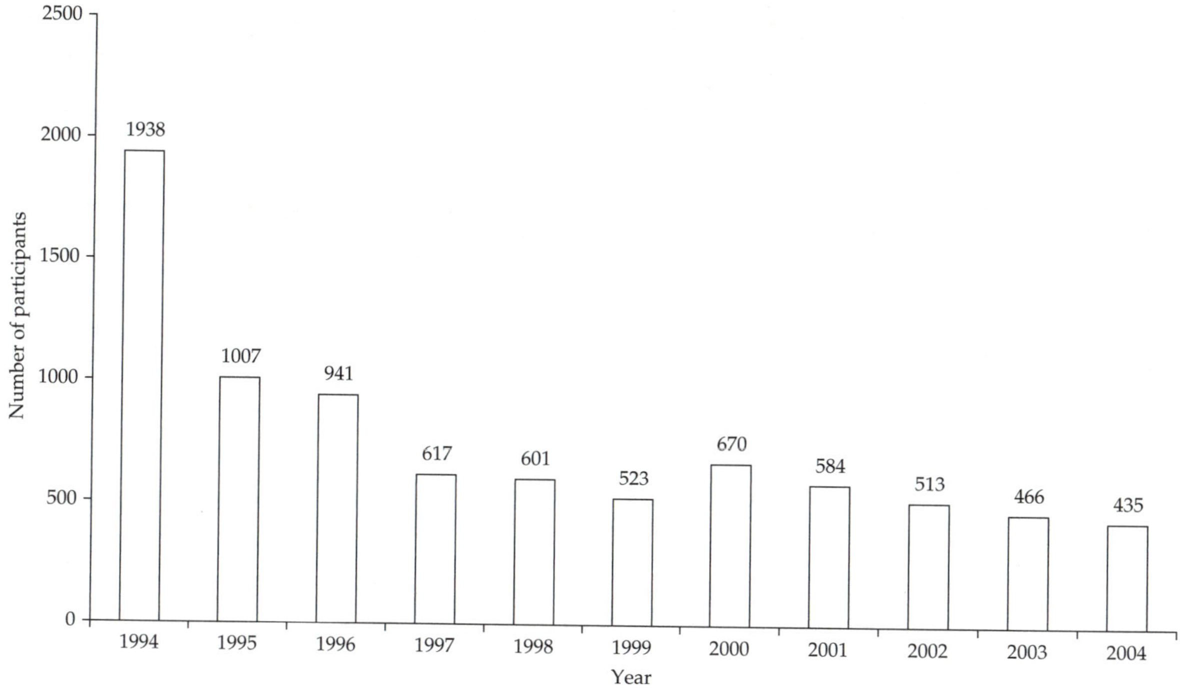

Figure 6.2 *Number of participating firms in the 'Start-up panel: cohort 1994', 1994–2004*

Table 6.3 Growth patterns of participants in the start-up panel (%)

	1995–1999	2000–2004
Fast-growing firms (growth rate ≥ 1.5)	13.7	4.0
Firms growing at the normal rate (0.05 ≤growth rate <1.5)	20.5	17.6
Stable firms (−0.05 <growth rate <0.05)	66.1	58.4
Shrinking firms (growth rate ≤−0.05)	6.5	20.0

Note: EIM growth rate is: $|empl_t - empl_{t\text{-}4}|^{0.25} \times (empl_t - empl_{t\text{-}4})/empl_{t\text{-}4}$.

retail (18 per cent), catering and transport (11 per cent), business services (21 per cent) and other services (27 per cent). It should be noted that our data are not a representative sample of start-ups of the business population in 1994 in the Netherlands as a whole.

The average firm size in 2004 was 3.8 persons. In 1994 the average employment creation of a start-up in the panel was 1.6 persons. According to the Dutch definition of SMEs, all firms should have fewer than 100 employees. None of the firms in the panel has grown so rapidly since 1994 that it has become a large firm. In fact 60 per cent of the panel participants did not have any employees at all in 2004. We also looked at the growth patterns identified by Bangma and Verhoeven (2000). Table 6.3 presents the growth patterns of the firms in the panel for the 1995–99 and 2000–04 periods.

More firms grew between 1995 and 1999 than between 2000 and 2004: 34.2 versus 21.6 per cent. The start-ups in the panel are more eager to grow in their early years and for some firms it is also necessary to grow to gain sufficient scale economies.

Variables

The start-up panel contains approximately 2500 individual items. Growth is measured by the number of employees. We look at the growth in two periods: 1995 to 1999 and 2000 to 2004. We define growth as:

$$G_{1995\text{–}1999} = \ln(1999) - \ln(1995), \tag{6.1}$$

$$G_{2000\text{–}2004} = \ln(2004) - \ln(2000). \tag{6.2}$$

We also computed the EIM growth rate developed by Bangma and Verhoeven (2000), who use a combination of absolute and relative growth in employment. This growth rate is related to the Birch growth rate. However, the EIM growth rate reduces the impact of absolute growth compared to the Birch growth rate. The EIM growth rate was also computed for the 1995–99 and 2000–04 periods. Therefore we have:

$$GR_{1995\text{–}1999} = |empl_{12\text{-}31\text{-}1999} - empl_{01\text{-}01\text{-}1995}|^{0.25} \times (empl_{12\text{-}31\text{-}1999} - empl_{01\text{-}01\text{-}1995}) / empl_{01\text{-}01\text{-}1995} \quad (6.3)$$

$$GR_{2000\text{–}2004} = |empl_{12\text{-}31\text{-}2004} - empl_{01\text{-}01\text{-}2000}|^{0.25} \times (empl_{12\text{-}31\text{-}2004} - empl_{01\text{-}01\text{-}2000}) / empl_{01\text{-}01\text{-}2000}. \quad (6.4)$$

Not all individual items in the database are important for this research and it was necessary to select the relevant variables for our purpose. For instance, as all business owners started their business in 1994, tenure is not a relevant variable in our study. Earlier we described three main determinants of growth – market/industry, entrepreneurial/managerial and firm specific – and we looked for these determinants in the panel. It should be noted that our analysis is ad hoc. As a result, not all specific items that belong to a determinant can be found in the panel.

Although we made use of a longitudinal dataset, some questions were asked only once. In 1994, for example, the entrepreneurs were asked about their previous sector experience. Other questions were available for a period of some years or for the whole period of 10 years. We constructed new single variables for these multi-year questions. For example, when covering a period of years, entrepreneurs were asked whether they had joined an association of entrepreneurs. If the entrepreneur had joined such an association we assigned the value one to the entrepreneur, otherwise we assigned the value zero. There were other variables for which we counted the number of years in which a certain activity was carried out. We know exactly how many years the company exported or performed R&D activities and we used the number of years of export and of R&D activities for our analyses. We are aware that the method used has some limitations, which are discussed in the section on future research. The reason for constructing the variables was to be able to keep our analysis as simple as possible and to get a first glimpse of the determinants of growth. The database has so many data points that it is impossible to capture all data and analysis at one time. Eventually we had 113 (constructed) variables at our disposal.

The (constructed) variables were standardized and a factor analysis was performed to reduce the number of variables, which resulted in 36 determinants. The relevant variables are presented in Tables 6.4, 6.5 and 6.6. Market/industry determinants are captured by four variables (Table 6.4). These variables describe the type of industry, competition, unfulfilled

Table 6.4 Variables in the analysis: market/industry determinants

Variable	Type
Type of industry	Dummies
Competition	Continuous (factor scores)
Unfulfilled needs	Continuous (factor scores)
Growth potential	Continuous (factor scores)

Table 6.5 Variables in the analysis: entrepreneurial/managerial determinants

Variable	Type
Gender	Boolean
Education (university degree)	Boolean
Family with business experience	Boolean
Partner has an own company	Boolean
Age of the entrepreneur	Continuous
Previous management experience	Continuous (factor scores)
Previous experience in entrepreneurship	Continuous (factor scores)
Previous sector experience	Continuous (factor scores)
Openness for change	Continuous (factor scores)
Openness for experience	Continuous (factor scores)
Risk attitude	Continuous (factor scores)
Leadership abilities	Continuous (factor scores)
Customer orientation	Continuous (factor scores)
Start-up motives: pull (opportunity)	Continuous (factor scores)
Start-up motives: push (unemployment/bad income)	Continuous (factor scores)

needs and growth potential. There are 15 variables available in the panel as entrepreneurial/managerial determinants of growth (Table 6.5). And finally, 23 variables focus on the firm determinants of growth (Table 6.6).

RESULTS

In this section we analyse which determinants actually have an effect on the growth of start-ups. First we performed a correlation analysis and then we performed regression analysis.

Table 6.6 Variables in the analysis: firm-specific determinants

Variable	Type
Growth objective	Continuous (factor scores)
Ambition: improvement	Continuous (factor scores)
Firm autonomy	Continuous (factor scores)
Ambition: fewer employees	Continuous (factor scores)
Ambition: cut back	Continuous (factor scores)
Perceived growth barriers	Continuous (factor scores)
R&D	Continuous (factor scores)
Networking	Continuous (factor scores)
Export	Continuous (factor scores)
Own financial resources	Continuous (factor scores)
Market orientation: external	Continuous (factor scores)
Customer orientation: price stunts	Continuous (factor scores)
Formalization: business plan before start-up	Continuous (factor scores)
Formalization: business plan after start-up	Continuous (factor scores)
Strategy: service and quality	Continuous (factor scores)
Strategy: high prices	Continuous (factor scores)
Knowledge acquisition: buyers and suppliers	Continuous (factor scores)
Knowledge acquisition: employees	Continuous (factor scores)
Knowledge acquisition: trade fairs	Continuous (factor scores)
Knowledge acquisition: other firms	Continuous (factor scores)
Information search: literature and experts	Continuous (factor scores)
Information search: customers/suppliers	Continuous (factor scores)
Information search: research institutes	Continuous (factor scores)

Correlation Analysis

A correlation analysis was performed to find which determinants influence growth. Correlation analysis is the statistical tool that we can use to describe the degree to which one variable is linearly related to another. Correlation analysis is frequently used in conjunction with regression analysis to measure how well the least squares line fits the data. Correlation analysis can also be used on its own, however, to measure the degree of association between two variables. Only the significant correlations (on 1 and 5 per cent levels) are presented in Table 6.7.

There are several determinants that have a positive relation with growth in the 1995–99 period. One market/industry determinant appears to have a significant correlation with growth between 1995 and 1999: unfulfilled needs. This is not unexpected at all. Entrepreneurs starting their business in a market where needs are unfulfilled have more space to expand their business. Three entrepreneurial/managerial determinants show positive

Table 6.7 Correlations between growth and its determinants

Determinant	$G_{1995–1999}$	$GR_{1995–1999}$	$G_{2000–2004}$	$GR_{2000–2004}$
Market/industry determinants				
Unfulfilled needs	0.124**	0.129**	–	–
Entrepreneurial/managerial determinants				
Previous management experience	0.102*	–	–	–
Previous sector experience	0.137**	0.111*	–	–
Openness for change	–	–	−0.184**	−0.101*
Risk attitude	0.114*	–	–	–
Firm-specific determinants				
Growth objective	0.296**	0.187**	–	–
Firm autonomy	–	0.099*	–	–
Perceived growth barriers	0.130*	0.095*	–	–
Formalization: business plan before start-up	–	–	–	0.106*
Strategy: high prices	–	–	−0.101*	–
Knowledge acquisition: buyers and suppliers	−0.110*	−0.116*	–	–
Knowledge acquisition: employees	0.158*	0.198**	–	0.116*

Note: * Significant at the 0.05 level; ** significant at the 0.01 level.

correlation with growth in the 1995–99 period. Businesses of entrepreneurs with previous management and sector experience are more likely to grow than those where entrepreneurs lack experience. Experience has a positive relation with the early stage growth. Entrepreneurs willing to accept higher risks show higher growth rates in their first years after start-up. Four firm-specific determinants correlate with growth in the 1995–99 period. First, the highest positive correlation occurs between growth and the ambition to expand the business. This phenomenon is in line with our expectations. Firms that clearly aim to expand their business are more likely to grow than other firms. If an entrepreneur perceives growth barriers, this has a positive effect on firm growth. Apparently the entrepreneur puts more effort into survival and growth should he/she perceive the existence of growth barriers. Organizational learning is also an important aspect. A firm realizes higher growth if it is informed by its own employees, but business relations have a negative impact on growth. The correlations on the growth rate show similar results to growth. The only differences are that previous management experience and risk attitude do not correlate with the growth rate, but self-control does show a significant correlation.

When we examine the determinants of growth for the 2000–04 period, we find only two significant correlation coefficients. During this period, being open to change has a negative effect on growth. Also a strategy of high prices negatively influences growth. It is not surprising that only two determinants correlate with growth, because we have already seen that fewer firms grew between 2000 and 2004. Openness to change also correlates with the growth rate for the 2000–04 period. It appears that entrepreneurs benefited if they had set up a business plan before start-up. Knowledge acquisition by employees correlates significantly with the growth rate.

Regression Analysis

Next a regression analysis, which depicts the relation of the effect, was performed. Tests show that multicollinearity is not an issue in our regression analysis. Because we have 43 independent variables at our disposal we show only the significant coefficients at 5 and 10 per cent levels. The results of the regression analysis of growth and the growth rate in the 1995–99 period are presented in Table 6.8. The *R*-square for growth equals 0.314 and for the growth rate it equals 0.241. Both regression models are significant.

Linear regression with growth over the 1995–99 period as a dependent variable, resulted in 13 significantly related determinants. Remarkably, educational level has a negative coefficient. This means that firms with highly educated entrepreneurs tend to grow on average more slowly. It is possible that these entrepreneurs are self-employed and have no ambition to expand. Should the entrepreneur's partner own a firm this has a positive influence on the growth of the firm. Moreover, this variable shows the highest coefficient. This potentially has to do with a role modelling function and/or experiences that can be shared. Entrepreneurial determinants with positive coefficients are previous management experience, previous sector experience and risk attitude. Firm-specific determinants influencing growth in a positive way are the ambition to expand, perceived growth barriers, challenge as a start-up motive, networking and knowledge acquisition through employees. On the other hand, knowledge acquisition via buyers and suppliers and other firms has a negative coefficient. It seems that a lot is known about running a business, but market knowledge is lacking.

Table 6.9 also shows the results of the regression analysis when the growth rate is used as the dependent variable. Again educational level has a negative coefficient. But it is not the only variable that relates negatively to the growth rate. Family with business experience, the ambition of

Table 6.8 Results of regression analysis for growth and growth rate, 1995–1999

Determinant	$G_{1995-1999}$ ($R^2 = 0.314$)		$GR_{1995-1999}$ ($R^2 = 0.241$)	
	Coefficient	Significance level	Coefficient	Significance level
Market/industry determinants				
Competition	–	–	0.200	0.064
Unfulfilled needs	0.078	0.001	0.346	0.001
Entrepreneurial/managerial determinants				
Education level	−0.127	0.046	−0.559	0.059
Family with business experience	–	–	−0.641	0.018
Partner with own firm	0.287	0.024	1.124	0.057
Previous management experience	0.056	0.017	–	–
Previous sector experience	0.062	0.007	0.223	0.039
Risk attitude	0.051	0.028	–	–
Firm-specific determinants				
Growth objective	0.149	0.000	0.430	0.000
Ambition: improvement	–	–	−0.206	0.051
Firm autonomy	–	–	0.195	0.061
Perceived growth barriers	0.067	0.002	0.241	0.019
Start-up motives: pull (opportunity)	0.044	0.049	–	–
Networking	0.046	0.038	0.199	0.056
Export	–	–	0.176	0.096
Strategy: high prices	–	–	0.175	0.088
Knowledge acquisition: buyers and suppliers	−0.045	0.040	−0.206	0.044
Knowledge acquisition: employees	0.081	0.000	0.446	0.000
Knowledge acquisition: trade fairs	−0.045	0.042	–	–

improvement and knowledge acquisition via buyers and suppliers have negative coefficients.

A few years later, when the start-ups have matured there will possibly be other determinants that influence growth. Therefore, we also performed regression analysis for growth and the growth rate between 2000 and 2004. The regression analyses were found to be insignificant. The *R*-squares are also low. The results in Table 6.9 should be interpreted very carefully.

Table 6.9 Results of regression analysis for growth and growth rate, 2000–2004

Determinant	$G_{2000-2004}$ ($R^2=0.134$)		$GR_{2000-2004}$ ($R^2=0.127$)	
	Coefficient	Significance level	Coefficient	Significance level
Age	−0.296	0.041	−1.143	0.097
Openness for change	−0.088	0.000	−0.209	0.050
Ambition: improvement	–	–	0.175	0.091
Formalization: business plan before start-up	–	–	0.231	0.023
Strategy high prices	−0.048	0.022	–	–
Knowledge acquisition: employees	–	–	0.245	0.014

The results show that there are several determinants of growth, which differ over time. In other words, growth in the first five years after start-up is determined by other factors than is growth in a more mature phase of the life cycle.

CONCLUSION AND FUTURE RESEARCH

Conclusion

In this exploratory study we make a first attempt to explain the growth of start-ups based on a longitudinal dataset. In the previous sections we saw that our dataset contains a great deal of valuable information and allows us to distinguish several determinants of growth in all three dimensions: market/industry, entrepreneurial/managerial and firm specific. The results show that constructs from all three dimensions are important in the explanation of growth. The growth in the first five years can be explained more readily. Determinants that are important for the growth of start-ups are unfulfilled needs, previous management and sector experience, a partner with an own firm, a growth objective and networking. For later periods it is much harder to explain the growth – the firms might have changed a lot, and many characteristics have lost their explaining power.

Directions for Future Research

We made use of the start-up panel for our analyses. In this study we look only at the respondents who survived in the panel over a period of 10 years, from which we obtained a considerable amount of information. We also have additional information that has not been used in this study. We are aware that, during the past few years, although many of our respondents have withdrawn from the start-up panel, we have information for many of them covering five or eight years. In our future research we shall utilize this information. One aspect we wish to investigate is whether firms still in the panel differ from those that dropped out. A Cox survival analysis will be a useful tool.

Although the start-up panel contains a great deal of information it is quite possible that not all determinants of growth have been covered. Variables such as personal traits (for example, locus of control, ingenuity, affiliation need, tolerance for ambiguity or need for power) are not contained in our database. It may also be assumed that these personal traits influence some of the exogenous variables. The distinction between 'exogenous' and 'endogenous' variables in a model is a subtle and sometimes controversial complication (Greene, 1997). This subject is widely discussed in the literature, for example, Granger (1969), Zellner (1979) and Engle et al. (1983). When considering the growth of start-ups, as in our study, it is possible to argue that many explanatory variables are potentially endogenous. If this is the case then the ordinary least squares (OLS) method produces a biased and inconsistent estimator for the parameters in the model. In the present study we paid no attention to this phenomenon. In future research we should consider alternative estimation methods. All the consistent and efficient estimation methods in general use can be placed under the umbrella of instrumental variable estimators (Greene, 1997), for example two-stage least squares or general methods of moments.

Some questions on the panel questionnaire were asked only once, whereas others were repeated each year for several years. We constructed single variables. In this way, we had cross-sectional data at our disposal. It could be argued that this looks a lot like data mining and information is lost. Additionally we are not making optimum use of the longitudinal nature of our database. In econometrics, datasets like the start-up panel are called panel data. A panel dataset contains repeated observations about the same units (individuals, households, firms), collected over a number of periods (Verbeek, 2004). The availability of repeated observations allows us to specify and estimate more complicated and more realistic models than a single cross-section or a single time series would do. In other words, the fundamental advantage of a panel dataset over a cross-section is that it will allow the researcher far greater flexibility in modelling differences in behaviour across individuals (Greene, 1997). Panel data allow the identification of certain parameters or questions without the need to make restrictive assumptions. Several studies on panel data have been written in the last few years: Wansbeek (2001), Baltagi and Summey (2002), Woolridge (2002), Arellano (2003), Hsiao (2003), Frees (2004) and Baltagi (2005). We refer to these studies for an extensive review of panel data analysis. However, we give a brief discussion of some elements of panel data analysis when considering our start-up panel. Two types of effects can be considered from panel data: individual and time effects. There are two ways to deal with these effects: one way is to take them as fixed parameters to be estimated (the fixed-effects models) and the other way is to take them as random variables (the random-effects models). Whether to treat the individual effects as fixed or random is not an easy question to answer (Verbeek, 2004). A useful test was developed by Hausman (1978). In future research we should test whether fixed or random effects are more appropriate for our panel. Instrumental variables can also be added to panel data.

We measured growth for two periods: 1995–99 and 2000–04. In our further analysis we need to focus on growth in other periods too. About 60 per cent of all firms in the panel showed no growth at all. In our analysis we included growing and non-growing firms. It is quite possible that the determinants of growth of start-ups will differ if we consider growing firms only. It is possible to make this distinction by using a Tobit model and this is a useful tool when using panel data. One disadvantage of a Tobit model for our future research is that shrinking firms are not included in the analysis. A fixed- or random-effects model also allows us to include growing and shrinking firms.

In this study we measured growth by using the number of employees (business owner is included). We considered the relative growth by taking the difference of the natural logarithms of the number of employees in two periods and the EIM growth rate. In future research we intend to use more measures of growth. First, we want to measure growth in terms of turnover. When the firm starts many entrepreneurs do not work full time in their firm. Of the 435 participants in the start-up panel, 20 per cent of the entrepreneurs worked fewer than 10 hours, almost 34 per cent worked 10 to 40 hours at the time of the start-up and all the other entrepreneurs worked over 40 hours a week. A year later only 11 per cent worked fewer than 10 hours. Our suggestion is to use the number of hours worked by the entrepreneur(s) and their employees. We have to check whether such a measure is feasible. The respondent is asked about the number of hours worked every year, but there is a lack of information about the hours worked by business partners and employees.

It is our opinion that our future studies will prove to be very interesting for scientific research, but also for policy making. The variables applying to the environment of the firm will be most interesting for policy makers. The government can make policy only on environmental matters – it is impossible for the government to develop policy to change an entrepreneur's character and it is difficult to do anything about the internal organization of a firm. The results of the regression analysis indicate that the environmental variables have almost no effect on the growth of the firm. In our future research we intend to pay more attention to the possibilities for policy making.

REFERENCES

Almus, M. and E.A. Nerlinger (1999), 'Growth of new technology-based firms: which factors matter?', *Small Business Economics*, **13** (2), 141–54.

Ardichvili, A., S. Cardozo, S. Harmon and S. Vadakath (1998), 'Towards a theory of new venture growth', paper presented at the Babson Entrepreneurship Research Conference, Ghent, Belgium, 21–23 May.

Arellano, M. (2003), *Panel Data Econometrics*, Oxford: Oxford University Press.

Audretsch, D.B., L. Klomp, E. Santarelli and A.R. Thurik (2004), 'Gibrat's law: are the services different?', *Review of Industrial Organization*, **24** (3), 301–24.

Autio, E., H.J. Sapienza and J.G. Almeida (2000), 'Effects of age at entry, knowledge intensity and imitability on international growth', *Academy of Management Journal*, **43** (5), 909–24.

Baltagi, B.H. (2005), *Econometric Analysis of Panel Data*, 3rd edn, New York: John Wiley & Sons.

Baltagi, B.H. and G. Summey Jr (2002), *Recent Developments in Panel Data*, Cheltenham, UK and Northampton, MA, USA: Edward Elgar.

Bamford, C., T. Dean and P. McDougall (1999), 'An examination of the impact of founding conditions and decisions upon the performance of new banks start-ups', *Journal of Business Venturing*, **15** (3), 253–77.

Bangma, K.L., P. Gibcus and P.A. Van Eck-Van der Sluijs (2005), *Firm Dynamics and Employment* ('Bedrijvendynamiek en werkgelegenheid'), Zoetermeer: EIM.

Bangma, K.L. and W.H.J. Verhoeven (2000), *Growth Patterns of Dutch Firms* ('Groeipatronen van bedrijven'), Zoetermeer: EIM.

Barringer, B.R., F.F. Jone and P.S. Lewis (1997), 'A qualitative study of the management practices of rapid-growing entrepreneurial firms', *Journal of Entrepreneurship*, **9** (2), 21–35.

Baum, J.R., E.A. Locke and K.G. Smith (2001), 'A multidimensional model of venture growth', *Academy of Management Journal*, **44** (2), 292–303.

Beal, R.M. (2000), 'Competing effectively: environmental scanning, competitive strategy, and organizational performance in small manufacturing firms', *Journal of Small Business Management*, **38** (1), 27–47.

Bennett, R.J.T.J. and P.J.A. Robson (1999), 'The use of external business advice Britain', *Entrepreneurship and Regional Development*, **11** (2), 155–80.

Bosma, N.S., C.M. van Praag, A.R. Thurik and G. de Wit (2004), 'The value of human and social capital investments for the business performance of start-ups', *Small Business Economics*, **23** (3), 227–36.

Brown, T.E., P. Davidsson and J. Wiklund (2001), 'An operationalisation of Stevenson's conceptualisation of entrepreneurship as opportunity-based firm behaviour', *Strategic Management Journal*, **22** (10), 953–68.

Bruno, A.V., E.F. McQuarrie and C.G. Torgrimson (1992), 'The evolution of new technology ventures over 20 years: patterns of failure, merger, and survival', *Journal of Business Venturing*, **7** (4), 291–302.

Chandler, G.N. and S.H. Hanks (1994), 'Market attractiveness, resource-based capabilities, venture strategies, and venture performance', *Journal of Business Venturing*, **9**, 331–49.

Cooper, A.C., F.J. Gimeno-Gascon and C.Y. Woo (1994), 'Initial human and financial capital as predictors of new venture performance', *Journal of Business Venturing*, **9** (5), 371–95.

Covin, J.G. and D.P. Slevin (1997), 'High growth transitions: theoretical perspectives and suggested directions', in D.L. Sexton and R.W. Smilor (eds), *Entrepreneurship 2000*, Chicago, IL: Upstart, pp. 99–126.

Davidsson, P. (1991), 'Continued entrepreneurship: ability, need and opportunity as determinants for small firm growth', *Journal of Business Venturing*, **6**, 405–29.

De Jong-'t Hart, P.M. and W.H.J. Verhoeven (2006), *International Benchmark Entrepreneurship 2005* ('Internationale Benchmark 2005: benchmark ondernemerschap, bedrijvendynamiek en snelle groeiers'), Zoetermeer: EIM.

De Koning, A. and D.F. Muzyka (1998), 'Sustainable enterprises: creating growth in mid-sized companies', INSEAD Working Paper, 98/42/ENT, European Institute of Business Administration Fontainebleau, France.

Delmar, F. (1997), 'Measuring growth: methodological considerations and empirical results', in R. Donckels and A. Miettinen (eds), *Entrepreneurship and SME Research: On Its Way to the Next Millennium*, Aldershot and Brookfield, VA: Ashgate, pp. 190–216.

Delmar, F., P. Davidsson and W. Gartner (2003), 'Arriving at the high-growth firm', *Journal of Business Venturing*, **18** (2), 189–216.

Eggers, J.H., K.T. Leahy and N.C. Churchill (1994), 'Stages of small business growth revisited: insights into growth path and needed leadership/management skills in low and high growth companies', in W.D. Bygrave, S. Birley, N.C. Churchill, E. Gate Wood, F. Hey, R.H. Keeley and W.E. Wetzel Jr (eds), *Frontiers of Entrepreneurship Research*, Wellesley, MA: Babson College, pp. 131–44.

(EIM) (2005), *Small Scale Entrepreneurship 2005* ('Kleinschalig Ondernemen 2005'), Zoetermeer: EIM.

Engle, R.F., D.F. Hendry and J. F. Richard (1983), 'Exogeneity', *Econometrica*, **51** (2), 277–304.

Frees, E.W. (2004), *Longitudinal and Panel Data: Analysis and Applications in the Social Sciences*, Cambridge: Cambridge University Press.

Garnsey, E., E. Stam and P. Hefferman (2006), 'New firm growth: exploring processes and paths', *Industry and Innovation*, **13** (1), 1–24.

Gartner, W.B. and J.A. Starr (1993), 'The nature of entrepreneurial work', in S. Birley and I.C. MacMillan (eds), *Entrepreneurship Research: Global Perspectives*, Amsterdam: North-Holland, pp. 35–67.

Gibrat, R. (1931), *Les inégalités économiques; applications: aux inégalités des richesses, à la concentration des entreprises, aux populations des ville, aux statistiques des familles, etc., d'une loi nouvelle, la loi de l'effet proportionnel*, Paris: Librairie du Recueil Sirey.

Granger, C.W.J. (1969), 'Investigating causal relations by econometric models and cross-spectral methods', *Econometrica*, **37**, 424–38.

Greene, W.H. (1997), *Econometric Analysis*, Englewood Cliffs, NJ: Prentice-Hall.

Hausman, J. (1978), 'Specification tests in econometrics', *Econometrica*, **46** (6), 1251–71.
Hessels, S.J.A., N.S. Bosma and A.R.M. Wennekers (2005), *New Entrepreneurship Is Recovering* ('Nieuw ondernemerschap in herstel: Global Entrepreneurship Monitor 2004 the Netherlands'), Zoetermeer: EIM.
Hsiao, C. (2003), *Analysis of Panel Data*, 2nd edn, Cambridge: Cambridge University Press.
Lau, C.M. and L.W. Busenitz (2001), 'Growth intentions of entrepreneurs in a transitional economy: the People's Republic of China', *Entrepreneurship Theory and Practice*, **26** (1), 5–20.
Lee, C., K. Lee and J.M. Pennings (2001), 'Internal capabilities, external network and performance: a study on technology-based ventures', *Strategic Management Journal*, **22** (6–7), 615–40.
Low, M.B. and I.C. MacMillan (1988), 'Entrepreneurship: past research and future challenges', *Journal of Management*, **14** (2), 139–61.
Lumpkin, G.T. and G.G. Dess (2001), 'Linking two dimensions of entrepreneurial orientation to firm performance: the moderating role of environment and industry life cycle', *Journal of business Venturing*, **16** (5), 429–51.
Man, T.W.Y., T. Lau and K.F. Chan (2002), 'The competitiveness of small and medium enterprises: a conceptualization with focus on entrepreneurial competition', *Journal of Business Venturing*, **17** (2), 123–42.
Mintzberg, H. (1973), *The Nature of Managerial Work*, New York: Harper & Row.
Pelham, A.M. (1999), 'Influence of environment, strategy, and market orientation of performance in small manufacturing firms', *Journal of Business Research*, **45** (1), 33–46.
Penrose, E. (1959), *The Theory of Growth of the Firm*, New York: Wiley.
Persson, H. (2004), 'The survival and growth of new establishments in Sweden, 1987–1995', *Small Business Economics*, **23** (5), 423–40.
Philipsen, R.L.C. and R.G.M. Kemp (2003), *Capabilities for Growth: An Exploratory Study on Medium-sized Firms in Dutch ICT Services and Life Sciences*, Zoetermeer: EIM.
Rangone, A (1999), 'A resource-based approach to strategy analysis in small–medium sized enterprises', *Small Business Economics*, **12** (3), 233–48.
Rauch, A., M. Frese and A. Utsch (2005), 'Effects of human capital and long-term human resource development and utilization on employment growth of small scale business: a causal analysis', *Entrepreneurship Theory and Practice*, **29** (6), 681–98.
Romanelli, E. (1989), 'Environments and strategies at start-ups: effects on early survival', *Administrative Science Quarterly*, **34** (3), 369–87.
Schutjens, V. and E. Stam (2003), 'The evolution and nature of young firm networks: a longitudinal perspective', *Small Business Economics*, **21** (2), 115–34.
Slevin, D.P. and J.G. Covin (1995), 'New ventures and total competitiveness: a conceptual model, empirical results, and case studies examples', in W.D. Bygrave, B.J. Bird, S. Birley, N.C. Churchill, M.G. Hay, R.H. Keeley and W.E. Wetzel Jr (eds), *Frontiers of Entrepreneurial Research*, Wellesley, MA: Babson College, pp. 574–88.
Spender, J.C. and R.M. Grant (1996), 'Knowledge and the firm: overview', *Strategic Management Journal*, **17** (Winter special issue), 45–62.
Stam, E., D. Audretsch and J. Meijaard (2005), 'Renascent men or entrepreneurship as a one-night stand: entrepreneurial intentions subsequent to firm exit', paper presented at the Nascent Entrepreneurship: The Hidden Potential conference, Durham Business School, 21–23 September.

Van Stel, A.J. and D.J. Storey (2004), 'The link between firm births and job creation: is there a upas tree effect?', *Regional Studies*, **38** (8), 893–909.

Verbeek, M. (2004), *A Guide to Modern Econometrics*, 2nd edn, Chichester: John Wiley & Sons.

Wansbeek, T. (2001), 'GMM estimation in panel data models with measurement error', *Journal of Econometrics*, **104** (2), 259–68.

Welbourne, T.M., G.D. Meyer and H.M. Neck (1998), 'Getting past the "entrepreneurial growth ceiling": a longitudinal study of IPO firm growth through solution-driven strategies', paper presented at the Babson Entrepreneurship Research conference, Ghent, Belgium, 21–23 May.

Wijewardena, H. and S. Cooray (1995), 'Determinants of growth in small Japanese manufacturing firms: survey evidence from Kobe', *Journal of Small Business Management*, **33** (4), 87–91.

Wiklund, J. (1999), 'The sustainability of the entrepreneurial orientation–performance relationship', *Entrepreneurship Theory and Practice*, **24** (1), 37–48.

Wooldridge, J.M. (2002), *Econometric Analysis of Cross Section and Panel Data*, Cambridge, MA: MIT Press.

Zellner, A. (1979), 'Statistical analysis of econometric models', *Journal of the American Statistical Association*, **74**, 628–43.

7. A gender analysis of the supply of, and demand for, new venture finance in Ireland

Siri Terjesen and Colm O'Gorman

INTRODUCTION

The domain of entrepreneurship includes the 'study of how, by whom, and with what effects opportunities to create future goods and services are discovered, evaluated and exploited' (Shane and Venkataraman, 2000, p. 218). Following this reasoning, a key aspect of entrepreneurship scholarship includes the study of the set of individuals who pursue and fund new venture opportunities, including females. Many countries are not realizing their full entrepreneurial potential due to the lack of participation by females in new business activities. For example, in a 41 country study, females were found to comprise only 36 per cent of all entrepreneurs (Reynolds et al., 2004). A low level of female entrepreneurial activity may impact negatively on a nation's economic growth and development. In countries such as the US, there is evidence that the 10.6 million female-owned companies employing 19.1 million people and generating $2.5 trillion in sales play a major role in the growth of economy (Center for Women's Business Research, 2005). Despite this economic contribution, the participation of females in entrepreneurship has been neglected in academic studies (Baker et al., 1997).

Entrepreneurship theory suggests that to participate in new venture activity, nascent entrepreneurs need access to resources and, in particular, financial capital (Wetzel, 1981; Mason and Harrison, 1999). However, new ventures face significant 'liabilities of newness' that make them unattractive investment opportunities for providers of finance (Aldrich and Fiol, 1994; Bhide, 2000). Nascent entrepreneurs are therefore typically under-resourced during the new venture creation process, that is, entrepreneurs, irrespective of gender, face barriers in trying to access resources, including external finance (ibid.). New ventures are typically financed from the nascent entrepreneur's own resources, through accessing informal venture capital from friends, family and foolhardy investors, and bootstrapping strategies (ibid.; Harrison et al., 2004). Researchers have called for an increased focus on informal capital flows into emerging and recently formed new ventures (Bygrave et al., 2003; Bygrave, 2005) and in nations not previously studied (Mason and Harrison, 1999).

In parallel, there have been calls for entrepreneurship studies that take into account female perspectives (Brush, 1992; Bird and Brush, 2002), particularly concerning female involvement in the supply and demand of entrepreneurial finance (Carter et al., 2003; Amatucci and Sohl, 2004; Greene et al., 2004). A limited body of research explores entrepreneurship from both demand and supply perspectives (Thornton, 1999), including a gendered perspective (Greene et al., 2001; Brush et al., 2002). Extant research suggests that there are a number of gender-related differences in the domain of entrepreneurship. It is suggested that female entrepreneurs differ from male entrepreneurs in factors such as personality, background, motivations and sectors of activity (for example, Watkins and Watkins, 1986; Birley et al., 1987; Kalleberg and Leicht, 1991; Loscocco et al., 1991; Brush, 1992; Cowling and Taylor, 2001; Levesque and Minniti, 2006). Furthermore, past research indicates that female-owned firms are typically in service-orientated sectors (Kalleberg and Leicht, 1991; Loscocco et al., 1991) and that female entrepreneurs are less likely to possess relevant work experience (Watkins and Watkins, 1986). From the demand perspective, it is argued that access to finance is a key barrier to entrepreneurial activity by females (Fabowale et al., 1995; Carter and Rosa, 1998; Brush et al., 2002; Carter et al., 2003). However, others have argued that gender is not an important issue in entrepreneurship research (Ahl, 2004), and that gender does not explain differences in the financing of new ventures (Read, 1998). On the supply side, there is a paucity of research on informal investment (Mason and Harrison, 1999), especially taking into account the role of females (Greene et al., 2001; Brush et al., 2002).

In this chapter we explore female involvement in the supply of, and demand for, new venture finance in Ireland. We are interested in understanding whether there are differences in the financing of new ventures planned by female and male nascent entrepreneurs, and if so, do these differences explain why females have participated to a much lesser extent in the supply of, and demand for, entrepreneurial finance? Our approach is as follows. First, we seek to identify whether there are gender differences in the financing of the ventures planned by nascent entrepreneurs. We focus on the entrepreneurs' planned total capitalization of the new venture, planned personal investment, and sources of external funds. Second, we explore whether there are gender differences in the investments of informal investors in terms of the amounts invested and the relationship ties between the investor and the entrepreneur. Given the paucity of research on female entrepreneurship activity, we report the demographic profiles and aspects of personal context of the entrepreneurs and informal investors. Third, we seek to explain why it is that Irish females, as compared to Irish males, have a lower demand for entrepreneurial finance and are less involved in informal investment activity. We do this by comparing Irish females to Irish males in terms of aspects of personal context we expect to be associated with participation in entrepreneurial activity, either as an entrepreneur or as an informal investor. We focus on both female nascent entrepreneurs and female informal investors, as we believe these activities to be interrelated. Others have argued that entrepreneurs and informal investors are co-creators of new ventures, and as such informal investment is not merely a support to entrepreneurial activity but is in fact an intrinsic component of entrepreneurial activity (Landström, 1998; Sætre, 2003).

National Context: Ireland

We choose Ireland, the 'Celtic Tiger' economy, because overall rates of participation by females in both the supply and demand for entrepreneurial finance are low when compared to activity by males, yet Ireland appears to be an environment that is rich in entrepreneurial opportunity. Ireland has an underrepresentation of female entrepreneurs (OECD, 2001; Central Statistics Office, 2004). The ratio of female to male entrepreneurs in Ireland is 1 to 2.54, the lowest rate in Europe, one of the lowest in the developed world and the seventh lowest of 41 countries surveyed from 2000 to 2003 (Reynolds et al., 2004). Ireland's rapid economic growth, deregulation, and the inflow of foreign direct investment have led to increased entrepreneurial opportunity and increased entrepreneurial activity in what has been referred to as the 'Celtic Tiger' (Acs et al., 2007). Although Ireland has one of the higher rates of entrepreneurial activity of any European Union (EU) country in the Global Entrepreneurship Monitor (GEM) (Acs et al., 2005), it appears that the positive entrepreneurial environment has led, as far as it is possible to ascertain, to increased entrepreneurial activity among males rather than females (Fitzsimons and O'Gorman, 2005).

There has been limited examination of the financing of businesses in Ireland, particularly female entrepreneurs and investors. The extant research suggests important gender differences among Irish entrepreneurs, although it does not suggest that there are gender-based differences in the financing of new businesses. For example, in interviews with 20 established female entrepreneurs in Ireland and Northern Ireland, Henry and Kennedy (2003) found that 11 respondents mentioned difficulties accessing finance and managing cash flows. The Irish government's Gender Equality Unit reported that there are important gender differences between entrepreneurs in Ireland (Gender Equality Unit, 2003). However, in the area of finance there were few reported differences between males and females. For example, both female and male entrepreneurs identified finance as the biggest barrier to starting a new firm; both groups equally felt they had adequate 'financial credit' from their financial institute; and both groups equally reported that they provided personal savings as some of their seed capital (ibid., 2003). One area of difference reported in the study was that females received more of their funds from family than males did.

THE DEMAND FOR FINANCE: NASCENT ENTREPRENEURS AND NEW VENTURE FINANCE

Entrepreneurs face significant barriers in establishing new ventures, particularly in trying to access finance. Casson (1982) argues that access to personal wealth is a key barrier to entrepreneurial activity and that a lack of personal wealth typically restricts the scale of entrepreneurial activity engaged in by the individual. Furthermore, he suggests that educational qualifications are very important in reducing the constraints imposed by the lack of personal wealth. Higher education degree qualifications open access to employment opportunities, and are therefore a way of amassing personal wealth, enabling access to existing institutions and other people's capital.

Entrepreneurs typically start their new ventures using relatively small amounts of money. Research evidence from the US suggests that ventures' resource requirements at founding are very low. Typically most entrepreneurs start with little capital and with few, if any, employees (Aldrich, 1999). For example, Aldrich presents evidence suggesting that most new firms start with fewer than five employees and that the majority of entrepreneurs might need as little as $5000 (a 1987 survey) to start a new business. The capital required in the US is typically sourced from the entrepreneur's own resources, often personal savings. Bhidé (2000) suggests that new ventures are 'unremarkable in their origins', with the fastest-growing new ventures being characterized by significant capital constraints. Of the *Inc. 500* list of the fastest-growing companies in the United States, nearly 80 per cent started with less than $50 000 (ibid.). Based on a study of 34 countries, Bygrave (2005) reported that the average amount of start-up capital nascent entrepreneurs plan to use to start their business is $53 673 and that these entrepreneurs typically provide 65.8 per cent of the capital required.

The lack of legitimacy that entrepreneurs have with external stakeholders, particularly the providers of finance (Aldrich and Fiol, 1994), may reflect the entrepreneurs' relative inexperience. There are information asymmetries in expectations between the entrepreneur and external investors, and uncertainty inherent in the entrepreneur's judgement about the market opportunity (Bhidé, 2000). Therefore, the lack of personal capital and poor access to external finance results in new ventures being typically underresourced at start-up. Most entrepreneurs start with relatively small absolute amounts of funds, and rely on self-financing, access informal venture capital from family, friends, and 'fool-hardy' investors (Bygrave, 2005) and bootstrap their new ventures (Winborg and Landström, 2001).

Female Entrepreneurs: Demand for Start-up Capital

Research typically reports that females use less start-up capital than do males. For example, in a 2004 study across 34 countries, the absolute amount of start-up capital employed by female entrepreneurs is nearly half of the amount of start-up capital used by males (Minniti et al., 2005). Others have reported larger differences, with, for example, Carter and Rosa (1998) finding that males use three times the amount of start-up capital, though the absolute amounts are still relatively small. These differences may arise because female entrepreneurs face difficulties in accessing financial capital. Studies of gender discrimination in debt finance have produced mixed conclusions, with some evidence that supports the proposition that females are discriminated against in accessing finance (Fay and Williams, 1993; Carter and Rosa, 1998). A UK study found gender differences in business financing: females were less likely to use overdrafts, bank loans and supplier credit, while males used a larger amount of capital at start-up (ibid.). Furthermore, this study found that females were more likely to be refused bank credit based on a lack of business experience and domestic circumstances, whereas males were more likely to be refused credit based on their lack of education attainment and choice of business sector. Fabowale et al. (1995) found that females were more likely to perceive that they were being treated disrespectfully by lending officers, suggesting that females perceive gender discrimination, though this does not, in and of itself, imply gender discrimination.

Access to external equity financing is linked to social networks, an area where it is suggested females are disadvantaged (Brush et al., 2002). Carter et al. (2003) found that human capital in the form of graduate education increased the likelihood that females used equity financing while social capital increased the likelihood of bootstrapping. In an exploratory study of female entrepreneurs' experiences of the process of search, negotiation and obtaining business angel financing, Amatucci and Sohl (2004) found that females reported gender-related bias in obtaining equity finance. Venture capitalists are interested in investing in firms with rapid growth potential, which is not necessarily aligned to female entrepreneurs who have been found to have lower needs for achievement (Luthans et al., 1995). Minniti et al. (2005) recently reported that across 34 countries a majority of female entrepreneurs personally provide all of their own start-up capital.

However, others conclude that differences in the funding requirements of females and males do not necessarily mean that females are discriminated against in accessing finance (Buttner and Rosen, 1988; Haynes and Haynes, 1999) and that the differences in the capitalization between businesses started by females and those started by males may not be due to gender (Birley, 1989; Read, 1998; Coleman, 2002). The influence of confounding effects such as sector of activity, age, prior business experience and prior start-up experience may explain why female businesses typically start with less capital. For example, it is suggested that as females typically have less experience and are more likely to start in service sectors (and therefore with fewer assets) they might be expected to use less finance, and to use less bank finance during the start-up process. In terms of access to debt finance, females' comparative disadvantage may be linked to factors such as small business size, limited growth potential and profitability (ibid.). Read (1998) found more similarities than differences between males and females in the financing of their businesses, suggesting that gender plays little role in explaining differences in the financing of small business. Read advocates caution in interpreting prior research that has sought to infer gender-based differences but that has failed to control for the influence of factors such as sector, education and age.

Based on the above literature, we expect differences between male and female entrepreneurs in terms of how they finance their new venture. We hypothesize:

H1a: Female nascent entrepreneurs expect to employ less start-up capital, as compared to male nascent entrepreneurs.

H1b: Female nascent entrepreneurs expect to provide more of the required start-up capital from their own financial resources, as compared to male nascent entrepreneurs.

H1c: Female nascent entrepreneurs expect to raise their external finance from their immediate family, and not from other external sources of capital such as banks and government programmes, as compared to male nascent entrepreneurs.

THE SUPPLY OF FINANCE: INFORMAL INVESTMENT

We now turn to another source of financing, informal investment. Informal investors are both 'private individuals (termed business angels) using their own money, directly in unquoted companies in which they have no family connection' (Mason and Harrison, 1999, p. 95) and individuals who invest in family members' ventures. Informal finance is the principal source of external equity finance for new ventures (Bygrave et al., 2003), yet there is relatively little research on informal investors (Mason and Harrison, 1999), particularly studies that include females (Greene et al., 2001; Brush et al., 2002).

The seminal studies of informal investment came from the United States and focused on business angels who filled the 'finance gap' for new technology entrepreneurs (Wetzel, 1981). A key area of interest in the research on informal investors is the relationship between the informal investor and the entrepreneur. Informal investors typically identify opportunities through personal and business networks (ibid.). Knowing the entrepreneur personally is likely to make an investor feel more comfortable with sharing personal funds. Informal investment is hampered by poor familiarity with entrepreneurs (Mason and Harrison, 2002).

External investors face a number of difficulties in identifying and investing in new ventures. These include information asymmetries between the entrepreneur and the investor, and expectation asymmetries between the entrepreneur and the investor (Mason and Harrison, 1999; Bhidé, 2000), and the liability of newness that characterizes new ventures (Aldrich and Fiol, 1994). Sætre (2003) argues that entrepreneurs adopt different perspectives to external equity investment. He suggests that some entrepreneurs treat the capital as a commodity and seek investors who provide not just finance but also expertise and access to contacts.

Female Informal Investors: Supply of Start-up Capital

There is little research on the motivations of female informal investors and the characteristics of their investments. In a study of male and female business angels in the UK, Harrison and Mason (2005) recently concluded that female business angels differ from their male counterparts in only very limited respects, and that gender is not a major issue in determining the supply of informal investment. Rather, Harrison and Mason reported gender differences in networking behaviours, with females less well connected or familiar with other business angels. Given the lack of prior research on informal investment activity by females, formulating hypotheses is problematic. Therefore we assume that there are no differences between female and male informal investors in terms of the amounts invested. However, given that we expect network differences between male and female nascent entrepreneurs, we might anticipate that these differences also apply to informal investors. Female informal investors may prefer to finance entrepreneurs with whom they share strong personal ties as they may have less experience with informal investment, or less access to investment opportunities outside their personal social ties. Based on the above, we hypothesize:

H2a: Female informal investors invest equal amounts, as compared to male informal investors.

H2b: Female informal investors are more likely to invest in the business of a close family member, as compared to male informal investors.

LEVELS OF ENTREPRENEURIAL ACTIVITY AND INFORMAL INVESTMENT BY FEMALES

Females are less likely to engage in nascent entrepreneurial activity, new-firm entrepreneurial activity and informal investment activity. In each of 34 countries' population surveys, male entrepreneurs outnumber female entrepreneurs (Minniti et al., 2005). In developed 'high-income' economies, males are 33 per cent more likely to be engaged in entrepreneurial activity compared to females (ibid.). In Ireland, the GEM study has reported that the mean rate of entrepreneurial activity (both nascent and new-firm entrepreneurs) for 2002–04 for females is 4.73 per cent, while for males it is 11.77 per cent (Fitzsimons and O'Gorman, 2005). Extrapolating to the total adult Irish population, the data suggest that there are approximately 200 000 people in Ireland involved in start-up activities (nascent entrepreneurs and entrepreneurs with new businesses that are less than 42 months old), of whom about 60 000 are females.

We now explore why females, as compared to males, might have a lower demand for entrepreneurial finance and why they are typically less involved in informal investment activity. We argue that differences between individuals in terms of access to resources are important determinants of entrepreneurial propensity. However, access to finance is only one such resource. In seeking to start a new business, entrepreneurs require access to a range of resources, including opportunities, management and business knowledge, and financial resources. Such resources are acquired through education, work experience and exposure to role models.

Reynolds et al. (2004) argue that personal context is an important determinant of propensity to engage in entrepreneurial activity. They demonstrated that individuals that perceive opportunity in their local environment, perceive that they have the knowledge and skills to start a business, and know a recent entrepreneur, are significantly more likely to be entrepreneurs. That is, variation in entrepreneurial activity partly reflects variation in the personal context of the adult population in a country. Furthermore, an aggregated study of 34 countries found that females who know an entrepreneur are more likely to engage in entrepreneurial activity (Minniti et al., 2005).

In Ireland, females have historically been less active in the labour force. Ireland's low rate of female employment, 55.3 per cent as compared to 74.7 per cent among men (Central Statistics Office, 2004), has, until recently, trailed the EU average. Female participation in the Irish labour market is concentrated in health (18 per cent) and wholesale and retail trade (16.6 per cent) and is lowest in construction (1.2 per cent) and agriculture, forestry and fishing (1.8 per cent) (Government of Ireland, 2003). Furthermore, only 29 per cent of those in managerial roles are female (Central Statistics Office, 2004). These statistics suggest that females in Ireland may not have equal opportunities to access human capital in the form of industry, management and start-up experience, which have been found helpful to entrepreneurs seeking to start and grow new businesses (Carter et al., 2003; Terjesen, 2005).

However, Irish females have acquired comparable levels of another aspect of human capital, formal education. In fact, compared to males, a slightly higher percentage of all females have as their highest level of education 'Third-level degree or higher', 'Third-level non-degree', and 'Upper secondary', while slightly fewer will have 'Lower secondary' and 'Primary (including no formal education)' as their highest level of education (Central Statistics Office, 2004). That is, 54 per cent of these females have at least completed 'Upper secondary', compared to 50.5 per cent for males, while 26 per cent of these females have some form of third level, compared to 23.5 per cent for males. There are nearly equal numbers of male and female graduates in the social sciences, business and law, though females remain underrepresented in areas such as science and engineering (ibid.).

Given the lower labour force participation by females we expect that they have less access to the resources needed to invest in a new business, their own or others'. We hypothesize:

H3a: In Ireland, females are less likely to perceive entrepreneurial opportunities, as compared to males.

H3b: In Ireland, females are less likely to have the skills and knowledge needed to start a new business, as compared to males.

H3c: In Ireland, females are less likely to have a 'recent' entrepreneur in their personal network, as compared to males.

METHODOLOGY AND DATA

Sample

Our analysis is based on a representative sample of the adult population aged 18 to 64 in Ireland, using Global Entrepreneurship Monitor (GEM) data. GEM measures levels of entrepreneurial activity and levels of informal investment activity based on a representative telephone survey of the adult population. The GEM survey requests a broad array of information related to individuals' demographics, perceptions of the country environment for entrepreneurship, attitudes and awareness of entrepreneurship, as well as participation in new business activity as an entrepreneur or as an informal investor. The GEM study tracks entrepreneurship in over 40 countries, including Ireland. See Reynolds et al. (2005) for a detailed overview of the GEM methodology and approach and a discussion of the reliability and validity of GEM data.

In 2002, 2003 and 2004, a standardized telephone survey was conducted of a representative sample of 5949 people of whom 4856 were between the ages of 18 and 64. We follow Maula et al. (2005) and Acs et al. (2007) in aggregating the data from all three years. The initial sample is weighted to account for age and gender distributions in the adult population, yielding a representative sample of 245 nascent entrepreneurs, 73 females and 172 males. In addition, 131 informal investors were identified, 40 females and 91 males. While the absolute number of nascent entrepreneurs and informal investors is small, this reflects the relative rareness of the phenomenon of nascent entrepreneurial activity and of informal investment. From 2006, the data used for this survey will be publicly available at www.gemconsortium.org.

Variables

Nascent entrepreneurs are identified as those individuals (aged 18–64) who have, in the past year, undertaken some activities towards starting a new business. These individuals expect to own a share of the business, which has not paid any wages or salaries for more than three months.

The survey identifies individuals (aged 18–64) who have recently made an investment in a new venture. To be considered an informal investor, an individual must respond positively to the following question: 'You have, in the past three years, personally provided funds for a new business started by someone else, excluding any purchases of stocks or mutual funds'.

For the nascent entrepreneurs and the informal investors we report basic demographic data, including *age* (a scaled variable from 18 to 64, computed from the respondent's year of birth), *education* (a categorical variable based on the respondent's highest level of education completed: no education, some secondary education, secondary degree, post-secondary education and graduate degree), and *work status* (a categorical variable based on the individual's current work status: full or part time, part time only, retired or disabled, homemaker, student or other). Individual attitudes towards entrepreneurship are reported based on the following dichotomous variables: *know an entrepreneur* ('You know someone personally who started a business in the past two years'); *good opportunities* ('In the next six months, there will be good opportunities for starting a business in the area where you live'); *skills* ('You have the knowledge, skill and experience required to start a new business'); and *fear of failure* ('Fear of failure would prevent you from starting a business').

A series of questions about financing are asked of the nascent entrepreneurs. For nascent entrepreneurs financing activity reflects anticipated levels of finance. First, *total investment required* is a scaled variable based on the response to the question: 'How much money, in total, will be required to start this new business?' Next, *personal investment provided* is a scaled variable to the question, 'How much of your own money, in total, do you expect to provide to this new business?' For both variables, the amounts are given in euros. Following arguments by Bygrave et al. (2003) that it is appropriate to exclude the very small number of new ventures that receive very large investments, we exclude investments over €1 million. We also restrict the amount to include only those investments over €100 as amounts less than this are not thought to constitute a meaningful response. The investment data are presented as a median as start-up capital distributions are right skewed. The variable, *financing sources*, is the response to the following question: 'Have you received or do you expect to receive money from any of the following to start this business: close family member, other relatives, work colleagues, an employer, friends or neighbours, banks or other financial institutions, government programmes, or other?'

For the informal investors, the scaled variable *informal investment* captures responses to the question: 'How much, in total, have you provided in the last three years?' For the reasons described above, the range of investments was restricted to all amounts between one hundred and one million euros, and reported as medians. The categorical variable *investee relationship* captured response to the question: 'What was your relationship with the person that received your most recent personal investment? Was this a close family member such as spouse, brother, child, parent or grandparent, some other relative, kin or blood relation, work colleague, friend or neighbor, or a stranger with a good business idea?'

The types of business to which the investment related were captured for both the nascent entrepreneurs and the informal investors. *Firm type* was based on the following 10 categories based on the SIC code: agriculture/forestry/hunting/fishing, mining/construction, manufacturing, transport/communications/utilities, wholesale/motor vehicle sales/repair, retail/hotel/management, finance/insurance/real estate, business services, health/education/social services, and consumer services.

Analysis

We used the statistical package SPSSx to conduct simple statistical tests for differences between our respondents. While we use gender to discriminate between our samples, this does not allow us to infer that any differences we report are due to gender. As our data are representative of the adult population, we are interested in absolute differences between the groups. To make gender-based inferences we would need to control for factors such as sector, education, age and prior work experience. While such an approach has merit, our sample size limits our ability to control for such factors. Our approach is as follows. First we compare female and male nascent entrepreneurs in terms of personal demographics (age, education and work status), sectors of entrepreneurial activity, and personal context (know an entrepreneur, good opportunities, skills and fear of failure). In terms of finance, we compare nascent entrepreneurs in terms of the amount of finance required, the planned investment by the entrepreneur and the sources of finance. We then turn to informal investment, comparing female and male investors in terms of demographics (age, education and work status), personal context and current entrepreneurial activity. Gender comparisons of amounts invested, relationship with the entrepreneur and sectors invested in are reported. At the population level, we then compare the males and females in the sample in terms of personal context. Finally, we compare employed males with employed females to see whether any differences we identify persist. We provide cross-tabulation tables and measure differences using chi-square and *t*-tests.

RESULTS

Nascent Entrepreneurs in Ireland

In Ireland, female nascent entrepreneurs differ from male nascent entrepreneurs in terms of education, work status and firm type (Table 7.1). We

Table 7.1 Irish nascent entrepreneurs' demographics

Variables	Female nascent entrepreneurs	Male nascent entrepreneurs	Significance
Age of Entrepreneur (Mean)	35.07 ($n=73$)	34.05 ($n=172$)	None
Highest Education Completed	($n=70$)	($n=171$)	‡
Some secondary	5.7%	17.0%	
Secondary	34.3%	33.3%	
Post-secondary	44.3%	39.8%	
Graduate	15.7%	9.9%	
Work Status	($n=75$)	($n=172$)	***
Full or part time	48.0%	71.5%	
Part time only	24.0%	6.4%	
Retired or disabled	0%	0.6%	
Homemaker	6.7%	1.2%	
Student	8.0%	5.2%	
Other	13.3%	15.1%	
Firm Type	($n=66$)	($n=156$)	***
Agriculture/Forestry/Hunting/ Fishing	3.0%	4.5%	
Mining/Construction	1.5%	10.9%	
Manufacturing	6.1%	5.8%	
Transport/Communications/Utilities	1.5%	8.3%	
Wholesale/Motor Veh. Sales/Repair	0%	7.7%	
Retail/Hotel/Restaurant	30.3%	16.0%	
Finance/Insurance/Real Estate	1.5%	3.8%	
Business Services	16.7%	23.7%	
Health/Education/Social Services	16.7%	1.3%	
Consumer Services	22.7%	17.9%	
Personal Context			
Know an entrepreneur (% yes)	56.0% ($n=50$)	77.2% ($n=136$)	**
Good opportunities (% yes)	63.3% ($n=49$)	53.3% ($n=122$)	None
Skills (Have knowledge and skills to start) (% yes)	92.0% ($n=50$)	89.2% ($n=130$)	None
Fear of failure (% yes)	24.0% ($n=50$)	24.4% ($n=135$)	None

Note: *** $p<0.001$; ** $p<0.01$; * $p<0.05$; ‡ $p \leq 0.10$.

find that female nascent entrepreneurs are more likely than the men to have a higher degree of education, though only at the $p < 0.10$ level of significance. Female and male nascent entrepreneurs also have significantly different current work status ($p < 0.001$). Females are less likely to be in full-time employment, and more likely to work part time or as a home-maker. We find significant differences ($p < 0.001$) between the types of businesses started by males and females. Female nascent entrepreneurs are more likely to start firms in retail/hotel/restaurants, health/education/social services and consumer services. Male nascent entrepreneurs are more likely to be starting businesses in mining/construction, transport/communications/utilities and business services. We find no difference in terms of age; the mean age of Irish female nascent entrepreneurs is just over 35 years as compared to males who are, on average, just over 34 years of age. In terms of personal context, female nascent entrepreneurs are significantly ($p < 0.01$) less likely to report knowing an individual who has started a business in the last two years: only 56 per cent of female entrepreneurs report knowing another entrepreneur compared to 77 per cent for males. We find no differences between female and male entrepreneurs in terms of perception of opportunity; perception of possessing the skills and knowledge to start a business; and whether fear of failure would prevent them starting a business.

Demand: New Venture Financing

The financing requirements of the nascent entrepreneurs are reported in Table 7.2. We follow Bygrave et al. (2003) in presenting the results in categories. We use the following two categories for assessing average funds required for start-up: €100 to €100 000, and €100 000 to €1 000 000. We find no overall differences in the level of funding that entrepreneurs expected to need to start their new business. The median required investment for both females and males is €20 000. Of those expecting to start up with between €100 and €100 000, the median reported amount required by female entrepreneurs is €12 012 as compared to €20 000 for males; and for those expecting to need between €100 000 and €1 000 000, the median required amount by female entrepreneurs is €285 587, as compared to €250 000 for males. As these differences are not statistically significant, we conclude that H1a is not supported.

Next, we examine the amount of funding that nascent female entrepreneurs plan to personally invest in their new business. Overall we find that the median planned investment by the nascent entrepreneurs is €10 000 for females and €15 000 for males (though the difference is not statistically significant). However, the median amount for those requiring between

Table 7.2 Demand: Irish nascent entrepreneurs' new venture financing

Investment variables	Female nascent entrepreneurs	Male nascent entrepreneurs	Significance
Total Investment Required			
Range: €100–€1 000 000 (median)	€20 000	€20 000	None
(Std dev.)	(225 268) ($n=47$)	(159 674) ($n=121$)	
Range: €100–€100 000 (median)	€12 012	€20 000	None
(Std dev.)	(26 392) ($n=39$)	(30 958) ($n=97$)	
Range: €100 000–€1 000 000 (median)	€285 587	€250 000	None
(Std dev.)	(338 711) ($n=11$)	(205 883) ($n=33$)	
Total Personal Investment Provided			
Range: €100–€1 000 000 (median)	€10 000	€15 000	None
(Std dev.)	(79 889) ($n=43$)	(49 616) ($n=121$)	
€100–€100 000 (median)	€7 500	€15 000	*
(Std dev.)	(22 287) ($n=40$)	(21 849) ($n=112$)	
€100 000–€1 000 000 (median)	€245 000	€150 000	None
(Std dev.)	(149 724) ($n=4$)	(60 699) ($n=12$)	
Financing Sources			
Close family (% yes)	42.1% ($n=19$)	23.7% ($n=59$)	None
Other relatives, kin (% yes)	5.0% ($n=20$)	10.2% ($n=59$)	None
Work colleague (% yes)	5.0% ($n=20$)	18.6% ($n=59$)	None
Employer (% yes)	5.0% ($n=20$)	5.2% ($n=58$)	None
Friends/neighbours (% yes)	5.0% ($n=20$)	11.9% ($n=59$)	None
Banks/other financial institutions (% yes)	57.9% ($n=19$)	50.0% ($n=58$)	None
Government programmes (% yes)	15.8% ($n=19$)	38.3% ($n=60$)	None
Other (% yes)	15.0% ($n=20$)	15.5% ($n=58$)	None

Note: *** $p<0.001$; ** $p<0.01$; * $p<0.05$; ‡ $p\leq 0.10$.

€100 and €100 000 was €7500; in contrast, male entrepreneurs planned to personally invest about €15 000 (the difference is statistically significant at the $p < 0.05$ level). For those planning on using between €100 000 and €1 000 000, the median amount that females planned to personally invest was €245 000, while males planned to invest €150 000, though this does not constitute a statistically significant difference (and the sample sizes are very small). Therefore, we find no support for H1b. In fact we find that female entrepreneurs expect to invest smaller amounts of money in their new ventures.

Table 7.2 also presents the start-up entrepreneurs' sources of financing. We find no statistically significant differences between females and males in terms of where they expect to source their required capital. We reject H1c.

Informal Investors

We find no differences between male and female informal investors in terms of age, education, personal context (know an entrepreneur, good opportunities, skills and fear of failure) or current entrepreneurial activity (as either a nascent or new-firm entrepreneur) (Table 7.3). The one exception is work status; like their female nascent entrepreneur counterparts, female investors are significantly ($p < 0.001$) less likely to be in full-time employment, and more likely to work part time or as a homemaker.

Supply: Informal Investors' New Venture Financing

The financing activities of informal investors are reported in Table 7.4. We report no significant differences in the amounts invested by males and females; the median investment for females is €10 185, while for males it is €10 000. While the sample sizes are very small, given the relative rareness of reported female informal investment activity, we reject H2a. We also find no differences between male and female investors in terms of their relationship to the entrepreneur. H2b is not supported.

Female Entrepreneurial Activity and Informal Investment Activity

We find that the personal context of males and females in the population is different (Table 7.5). Irish females are less likely to perceive entrepreneurial opportunity ($p < 0.001$); they are less likely to have the skills and knowledge needed to start a new business ($p < 0.001$); and they are less likely to know a recent entrepreneur ($p < 0.001$). This supports H3a, H3b and H3c.

Finally, we find that employed females and employed males also differ in terms of entrepreneurial personal context (Table 7.6). Employed females are

Table 7.3 Irish informal investors

	Female investors	Male investors	Significance
Age (mean)	37.61 ($n=40$)	38.78 ($n=91$)	None
Highest Education Completed	($n=40$)	($n=90$)	None
Some secondary	15.0%	12.2%	
Secondary	37.5%	32.2%	
Post-secondary	25.0%	40.0%	
Graduate	22.5%	15.6%	
Work Status	($n=39$)	($n=89$)	***
Full or part time	53.8%	85.4%	
Part time only	20.5%	2.2%	
Retired or disabled	0%	5.6%	
Homemaker	17.9%	0%	
Student	5.1%	3.4%	
Not Working	2.6%	3.4%	
Personal Context	($n=40$)	($n=91$ unless stated)	
Know an entrepreneur (% yes)	80.0%	85.7%	None
Good opportunities (% yes)	55.0%	54.7% ($n=86$)	None
Skills (Have knowledge and skills to start) (% yes)	82.5%	76.9%	None
Fear of failure (% yes)	12.5%	23.3% ($n=90$)	None
Classified as an Entrepreneur	20.0% ($n=40$)	17.6% ($n=90$)	None

Note: *** $p<0.001$; ** $p<0.01$; * $p<0.05$; ‡ $p \leq 0.10$.

less likely to perceive entrepreneurial opportunity ($p < 0.05$); they are less likely to have the skills and knowledge needed to start a new business ($p < 0.001$); and they are less likely to know a recent entrepreneur ($p < 0.001$).

DISCUSSION

Extant research has suggested that female entrepreneurs face difficulties in accessing finance, and that difficulties in accessing finance may explain lower levels of female entrepreneurial activity. What do our findings allow us to say about either of these issues?

Table 7.4 Supply: Irish informal investors' new venture financing

	Female investors	Male investors	Significance
Total Investments	($n=17$)	($n=62$)	
Range: €100–€1 000 000 (Median)	€10 185	€10 000	None
(Std dev.)	(55 410)	(88 690)	
Investee Relationship	($n=17$)	($n=52$)	None
Close family	64.7%	50.0%	
Other relative	17.6%	7.7%	
Work colleague	5.9%	5.8%	
Friend/neighbour	5.9%	28.8%	
Other	5.9%	7.7%	
Firm Type	($n=16$)	($n=52$)	None
Agriculture/Forestry/Hunting/Fish	6.3%	11.5%	
Mining/Construction	18.8%	5.8%	
Manufacturing	6.3%	15.4%	
Transport/Communications/Utilities	0%	9.6%	
Wholesale/Motor Veh. Sales/Repair	0%	5.8%	
Retail/Hotel/Restaurant	12.5%	15.4%	
Finance/Insurance/Real Estate	0%	7.7%	
Business Services	18.8%	11.5%	
Health/Education/Social Services	18.8%	3.8%	
Consumer Services	18.8%	13.5%	

Note: *** $p<0.001$; ** $p<0.01$; * $p<0.05$; ‡ $p\leq 0.10$.

First, do female nascent entrepreneurs face barriers in accessing finance? Our results suggest that this is not the case in Ireland. While we expected that female nascent entrepreneurs would report using less finance and be more dependent on their own finance, we find that female and male nascent entrepreneurs have similar planned capitalization. Furthermore, our results suggest that female nascent entrepreneurs expect to raise more of the required finance from external sources. We also find no differences in the sources of finance used by females. Similarly we did not find that female informal investors invest smaller amounts of capital.

That females plan to use similar amounts of capital does not exclude the possibility that they find it harder to access finance. It could be argued that the demographic differences between male and female nascent entrepreneurs suggest that females find it more difficult to access finance. We reported that females that are active as nascent entrepreneurs are on average more educated (though only at the $p < 0.10$ level of significance). It may be that to access similar levels of finance females need to be more

Table 7.5 The personal context of the Irish adult population

Personal context	Adult females	Adult males	Significance
Know an entrepreneur (% yes)	36.7% ($n = 1683$)	63.1% ($n = 1921$)	***
Good opportunities (% yes)	35.8% ($n = 1527$)	43.9% ($n = 1733$)	***
Skills (Have knowledge and skills to start) (% yes)	46.7% ($n = 1663$)	53.3% ($n = 1895$)	***

Note: *** $p<0.001$; ** $p<0.01$; * $p<0.05$; ‡ $p \leq 0.10$.

Table 7.6 The personal context of the Irish adult population classified as working (either full or part time)

Personal context	Adult females	Adult males	Significance
Know an entrepreneur (% yes)	44.0% ($n = 638$)	58.5% ($n = 1406$)	***
Good opportunities (% yes)	40.2% ($n = 575$)	45.2% ($n = 1263$)	*
Skills (Have knowledge and skills to start) (% yes)	31.1% ($n = 629$)	68.9% ($n = 1393$)	***

Note: *** $p<0.001$; ** $p<0.01$; * $p<0.05$; ‡ $p \leq 0.10$.

educated, that is, females find it more difficult than males to raise finance. Education may give females increased confidence to seek external financing or may be associated with increased own resources, or increased creditability and legitimacy with providers of informal venture capital. However, female nascent entrepreneurs may have higher levels of education for reasons other than the need to access finance. Factors such as career preferences or family commitments might explain the higher levels of education reported for female nascent entrepreneurs. Our results cannot reconcile these conflicting arguments.

Second, is difficulty in accessing finance a barrier to females engaging in entrepreneurial activity? Females participate less in entrepreneurial activity and this may suggest that there is a prima facie case that the inability to access finance prevents them from starting new businesses. While we cannot measure directly whether the lack of access to finance has prevented females from becoming entrepreneurs, we can report differences between males and females in terms of their personal entrepreneurial context. Irish females perceive fewer entrepreneurial opportunities, are less likely to have the knowledge and skills needed to start a business, and are less likely to know a recent entrepreneur. These differences in personal context might explain the significant differences in levels of female participation in entrepreneurial activity. The difference in the levels of participation in entrepreneurial activity reported between males and females may be due to factors other than difficulties in accessing finance. So rather than arguing that females face barriers in accessing finance, we suggest that there may be less demand from females for entrepreneurial finance.

If these differences in personal context are important to understanding why females have less demand for entrepreneurial finance, we should ask why they exist. Such differences are most likely to reflect differences in education and in labour force participation. While females have similar levels of educational attainment as males, they have historically had much lower levels of active involvement in the workforce. We therefore sought to explore whether by controlling, as best as we can, for current labour force participation, the differences in personal context reduce. While the differences between working (full and part time) males and females are less than the differences between males and females, there are still differences. However, this may be because current labour force participation does not capture cumulative workforce participation or type of participation. These later factors might have a more important bearing on personal context, and therefore on the demand for entrepreneurial finance.

CONCLUSIONS AND IMPLICATIONS

In this chapter we have responded to calls for research on the demand for finance from female entrepreneurs and the supply of finance, including informal investment, by females. We make several contributions to the existing body of knowledge. First, we provide a description of both female and male informal investors in Ireland. To the best of our knowledge, this study is the first to profile Irish informal investors, including a gendered analysis. Second, in terms of the demand for finance we do not find capitalization differences between male and female nascent entrepreneurs. We find that both female and male nascent entrepreneurs have similar funding requirements in terms of the absolute amount of investment required. However, we find that females expect to invest fewer personal resources in their new business. We find no significant network differences between female and male nascent entrepreneurs in terms of their planned sources of finance. Third, in terms of the supply of finance we find that male and female informal investors invest similar amounts in new ventures. Fourth, we offer an explanation for the very different levels of demand for, and supply of, entrepreneurial finance by females. We have shown that females have different personal entrepreneurial contexts than males. Therefore we suggest that females might have lower demand for entrepreneurial finance.

There are a number of limitations to the data used in this study. First, while nascent entrepreneurial activity is an important context for research, these entrepreneurs are by definition engaged in starting the business and have yet to fully realize their financing ambitions. Therefore it is likely, given entrepreneurs' inexperience, that they will not attract the external financing they anticipate and that entrepreneurs may have under- or overestimated the amount of funds needed to start up. Second, this study did not explore either debt financing or the use of bootstrapping strategies. Debt finance is a common source of finance among entrepreneurs. Bootstrapping activity includes finding creative ways of attracting external finance (Freear et al., 1994) and finding ways to minimize the costs of start-up (Winborg and Landström, 2001). These activities appear to be critical in the financing of new ventures. Third, consistent with earlier studies of informal investment, informal investors may not always wish to identify themselves, and may be underreported in the telephone survey. Fourth, in comparing the nascent entrepreneurs and the informal investors we did not control for factors such as sector, age, or prior work experience – factors that might explain variation in financing.

The implications of this research for female entrepreneurs are as follows. In seeking to start a new business, the absolute amount of finance required by the majority of entrepreneurs is relatively low (the median in our sample is €20 000). Further, for new ventures, the most frequent source of finance is the entrepreneur's own resources. Where external informal venture capital is raised, the most likely source is close family members. As argued by Bhidé (2000), recognizing these realities and concentrating efforts into developing the emerging business rather than diverting attention to seeking external finance, may result in a faster-growing business, reduced uncertainties around the business idea, and ultimately a more attractive investment prospect for external investors and providers of debt and equity finance.

The implications of this research for policy makers are as follows. As policy makers seek policies that increase levels of entrepreneurship (Gilbert et al., 2004) they may seek to encourage more females to become entrepreneurs and informal investors. We suggest that narrowly focused policies that seek to ease access to finance for female entrepreneurs may only partially increase female entrepreneurial activity. We make this assertion for several reasons. First, most female nascent entrepreneurs require relatively little capital and are likely to use their own resources and the resources of their family to meet their capital requirements. Second, the female nascent entrepreneurs in our study did not have lower expectations regarding the capitalization of their business, suggesting that they believed that they would be able to raise the finance they required. Third, we suggest that the low levels of entrepreneurial activity by females is not explained solely by problems in the supply of capital, but also that there may be a lack of demand for entrepreneurial finance from females. This may be because females have less access to entrepreneurial opportunities, are less likely to have the skills and knowledge needed to start a business, and are less likely to have a recent entrepreneur in their personal network.

Finally, what do our findings imply for female entrepreneurial activity in Ireland? In the near future can we expect that the Celtic Tiger will be populated with increased numbers of female entrepreneurs and investors? More Irish females are obtaining university qualifications and there has been a rapid increase in female participation in the labour force. The combination of these factors might suggest that females will be better equipped to identify opportunities and to finance such entrepreneurial businesses through accessing their own resources and the resources of others. Therefore, we speculate that the rate of entrepreneurial activity, both in terms of entrepreneurs and informal investors, by females in Ireland will increase over the coming decades.

ACKNOWLEDGEMENTS

The authors contributed equally to this chapter. A similar version of this chapter was previously published in *Venture Capital*, **8** (1), 2006, pp. 69–88, as O'Gorman and Terjesen, 'Financing the Celtic Tigress: venture financing and informal investment in Ireland'. See www.tanjdf.co.uk/journals.

REFERENCES

Acs, Z., P. Arenius, M. Hay and M. Minniti (2005), *Global Entrepreneurship Monitor: 2004 Executive Report*, Wellesley, MA: Babson College and London, UK: London Business School.

Acs, Z., C. O'Gorman, L. Szerb and S. Terjesen (2007), 'Could the Irish miracle be repeated in Hungary?', *Small Business Economics*, **28** (2/3), 123–42.

Ahl, H. (2004), *The Scientific Reproduction of Gender Inequality: A Discourse Analysis of Research Texts on Women's Entrepreneurship*, Copenhagen: Copenhagen Business School Press.

Aldrich, H. (1999), *Organizations Evolving*, London: Sage.

Aldrich, H. and C. Fiol (1994), 'Fools rush in? The institutional context of industry creation', *Academy of Management Review*, **19** (4), 645–70.

Amatucci, F. and J. Sohl (2004), 'Women entrepreneurs securing business angel financing: tales from the field', *Venture Capital*, **6** (2/3), 181–96.
Baker, T., H. Aldrich and N. Liou (1997), 'Invisible entrepreneurs: the neglect of women business owners by mass media and scholarly journals in the United States', *Entrepreneurship and Regional Development*, **9** (3), 221–38.
Bhidé, A. (2000), *The Origin and Evolution of New Businesses*, Oxford and New York: Oxford University Press.
Bird, B. and C. Brush (2002), 'A gendered perspective on organizational creation', *Entrepreneurship Theory and Practice*, **26** (3), 41–65.
Birley, S. (1989), 'Female entrepreneurs: are they really any different?', *Journal of Small Business Management*, **27** (1), 32–7.
Birley, S., C. Moss and P. Sanders (1987), 'Do women entrepreneurs require different training?', *American Journal of Small Business*, **12** (1), 27–35.
Brush, C. (1992), 'Research on women business owners: past trends, a new perspective and future directions', *Entrepreneurship Theory and Practice*, **16** (4), 5–30.
Brush, C., N. Carter, P. Greene, M. Hart and E. Gatewood (2002), 'The role of social capital and gender in linking financial suppliers and entrepreneurial firms: a framework for future research', *Venture Capital*, **4** (4), 305–23.
Buttner, E. and B. Rosen (1988), 'Bank loan officers' perceptions of characteristics of men, women and successful entrepreneurs', *Journal of Business Venturing*, **4** (4), 249–61.
Bygrave, W. (2005), *Financing Entrepreneurial Ventures: Global Entrepreneurship Monitor Financing report*, Wellesley, MA: Babson College and London, UK: London Business School (with S. Hunt).
Bygrave, W., M. Hay, E. Ng and P. Reynolds (2003), 'Executive forum: a study of informal investing in 29 nations composing the Global Entrepreneurship Monitor', *Venture Capital*, **5** (2), 101–16.
Carter, N., C. Brush, P. Greene, E. Gatewood and M. Hart (2003), 'Women entrepreneurs who break through to equity financing: the influence of human, social and financial capital', *Venture Capital*, **5** (1), 1–28.
Carter, S. and P. Rosa (1998), 'The financing of male and female owned-businesses', *Entrepreneurship and Regional Development*, **10** (3), 225–41.
Casson, M. (1982), *The Entrepreneur: An Economic Theory*, Oxford: Martin Robertson.
Center for Women's Business Research (2005), *Top Facts about Women Owned Businesses*, Silver Spring, MD: Center for Women's Business Research.
Central Statistics Office (2004), *Women and Men in Ireland 2004*, Dublin: Stationery Office, Government of Ireland.
Coleman, S. (2002), 'Constraints faced by women small business owners: evidence from the data', *Journal of Developmental Entrepreneurship*, **7** (2), 151–74.
Cowling, M. and M. Taylor (2001), 'Entrepreneurial women and men: two different species?', *Small Business Economics*, **16** (3), 167–76.
Fabowale, L., B. Orser and A. Riding (1995), 'Gender, structural factors, and credit terms between Canadian small businesses and financial institutions', *Entrepreneurship Theory and Practice*, **19** (4), 41–65.
Fay, M. and L. Williams (1993), 'Gender bias and the availability of business loans', *Journal of Business Venturing*, **8** (4), 363–76.
Fitzsimons, P. and C. O'Gorman (2005), *How Entrepreneurial Was Ireland in 2004: The Global Entrepreneurship Monitor Irish Annual Report*, Dublin: Enterprise Ireland.

Freear, J., J. Sohl and W. Wetzel (1994), 'Angels and non-angels: are there differences?', *Journal of Business Venturing*, **9** (2), 109–24.

Gender Equality Unit (2003), *Women and Men in Ireland as Entrepreneurs and as Business Managers*, Dublin: Department of Justice and Law Reform.

Gilbert, B., D. Audretsch and P. McDougall (2004), 'The emergence of entrepreneurship policy', *Small Business Economics*, **22** (3/4), 313–23.

Government of Ireland (2003), *Ireland North and South: A Statistical Profile*, Northern Ireland, UK: Statistics and Research Agency and Cork, Ireland: Central Statistics Office.

Greene, P., C. Brush, M. Hart and P. Saparito (2001), 'Patterns of venture capital funding: is gender a factor?', *Venture Capital*, **3** (1), 63–83.

Greene, P., M. Hart, E. Gatewood, C. Brush and N. Carter (2004), 'Women entrepreneurs: moving front and center: an overview of research and theory', Working Paper, University of Missouri, Kansas City, MO.

Harrison, R. and C. Mason (2005), 'Does gender matter? Women business angels and the supply of entrepreneurial finance', Working Paper, Centre for Entrepreneurship Research, University of Edinburgh Management School/ Hunter Centre for Entrepreneurship, University of Strathclyde, April.

Harrison, R., C. Mason and P. Girling (2004), 'Financial bootstrapping and venture development in the software industry', *Entrepreneurship and Regional Development*, **16** (4), 307–33.

Haynes, G. and D. Haynes (1999), 'The debt structure of small businesses owned by women in 1987 and 1993', *Journal of Small Business Management*, **37** (2), 1–19.

Henry, C. and S. Kennedy (2003), 'In search of a new Celtic Tiger: female entrepreneurship in Ireland', in J.E. Butler (ed.), *New Perspectives on Women Entrepreneurs*, Greenwich, CT: Information Age Publishing, pp. 203–24.

Kalleberg, A. and K. Leicht (1991), 'Gender and organizational performance: determinants of small business survival and success', *Academy of Management Journal*, **34** (1), 136–61.

Landström, H. (1998), 'Informal investors as entrepreneurs', *Technovation*, **18** (5), 321–33.

Levesque, M. and M. Minniti (2006), 'The effect of aging on entrepreneurial behavior', *Journal of Business Venturing*, **21** (2), 177–94.

Loscocco, K., J. Robinson, R. Hall and J. Allen (1991), 'Gender and small business success: an inquiry into women's relative disadvantage', *Social Forces*, **70** (1), 65–85.

Luthans, F., B. Envick and R. Anderson (1995), 'The need for achievement and organizational commitment of entrepreneurs: a gender comparison', in W. Bygrave, B. Bird, S. Birley, N. Churchill, M. Hay, R. Keeley and W. Wetzel, Jr (eds), *Frontiers of Entrepreneurship Research*, Babson Park, MA: Center for Entrepreneurial Studies, Babson College, 379–80.

Mason, C. and R. Harrison (1999), 'An overview of informal venture capital research', *Venture Capital*, **1** (2), 95–100.

Mason C. and R. Harrison (2002), 'Barriers to investment in the informal venture capital sector', *Entrepreneurship and Regional Development*, **14** (3), 271–87.

Maula, M., E. Autio and P. Arenius (2005), 'What drives micro-angel investments?', *Small Business Economics*, **25** (5), 459–75.

Minniti, M., P. Arenius and N. Langowitz (2005), *Global Entrepreneurship Monitor 2004 Report on Women and Entrepreneurship*, Wellesley, MA: Babson College and London, UK: London Business School.

Organisation for Economic Cooperation and Development (OECD) (2001). 'Female entrepreneurship indicator: Benchmarking enterprise policy: Results from the 2001 scoreboard', Commission Staff Working Document, Brussels.
Read, L. (1998), *The Financing of Small Business: A Comparative Study of Male and Female Business Owners*, London: Routledge.
Reynolds, P., N. Bosma, E. Autio, S. Hunt, N. De Bono, I. Servais, P. Lopez-Garcia and N. Chin (2005), 'Global Entrepreneurship Monitor: data collection design and implementation 1998–2003', *Small Business Economics*, **24** (3), 205–31.
Reynolds, P., W. Bygrave and E. Autio (2004), *Global Entrepreneurship Monitor: 2003 Executive Report*, Wellesley, MA: Babson College and London, UK: London Business School.
Sætre, A. (2003), 'Entrepreneurial perspectives on informal venture capital', *Venture Capital*, **5** (1), 71–94.
Shane, S. and S. Venkataraman (2000), 'The promise of entrepreneurship as a field of research', *Academy of Management Journal*, **25** (1), 217–26.
Terjesen, S. (2005), 'Senior women managers' transition to entrepreneurship: leveraging embedded career capital', *Career Development International*, **10** (3), 246–59.
Thornton, P. (1999), 'The sociology of entrepreneurship', *Annual Review of Sociology*, **25** (19), 19–26.
Watkins, J. and D. Watkins (1986), 'The female entrepreneur: her background and determinants of business choice – some British data', in S. Curran, J. Stanworth and D. Watkins (eds), *The Survival of the Small Firm, Vol. 1: The Economics of Survival and Entrepreneurship*, Aldershot: Gower, pp. 220–32.
Wetzel, W., Jr (1981), 'Informal risk capital in New England', in K. Vesper (ed.), *Frontiers of Entrepreneurship Research*, Wellesley, MA: Babson College, pp. 217–45.
Winborg, J. and H. Landström (2001), 'Financial bootstrapping in small businesses: examining small business managers' resource acquisition behaviors', *Journal of Business Venturing*, **16** (3), 235–54.

8. Organization context and knowledge management in SMEs: a study of Dutch technology-based firms

Lorraine Uhlaner and Jerry van Santen

INTRODUCTION

Policy makers and analysts alike have come to the growing consensus that the future strength of 'developed' Western economies depends increasingly upon an effective knowledge-based economy. In the initial decades of the information and communication technology (ICT) revolution (that is, in the 1970s and 1980s) its major impact was to stimulate entrepreneurship; scale and largeness were no longer required in many sectors to deliver complex products and services (Audretsch and Thurik, 2001, 2004). However, in the second wave of ICT development, with its proliferation into less-developed economies, entrepreneurs themselves, especially those located in geographic regions with high labour and operating costs, are under pressure to shift production to lower-cost regions and/or to change focus to more knowledge-based activities. Both these related trends, that is, internationalization of competition, and proliferation of explicit knowledge via ICT innovations, make conscious and top-quality knowledge management an increasingly critical factor in the competitive performance of both large and small firms.

Perhaps more aptly referred to as knowledge strategy, knowledge management (KM) is a relatively new term that encompasses not only the related notions of knowledge transfer and knowledge sharing (externally from other firms to the small firm and/or internally among firm members), but also the entire knowledge acquisition and utilization process, beginning with locating and capturing knowledge (including tacit knowledge which is difficult to codify), and followed by the enabling of that knowledge within the firm (Choo and Bontis, 2002; Takeuchi and Nonaka, 2004). KM is especially critical for small and medium-sized enterprises (SMEs) who are suppliers of complex goods and/or services. In addition to providing inputs to the products and services of multinational and other smaller firms, these firms are increasingly expected to contribute innovation and knowledge to the development and improvement of the products and product designs.

The purpose of this chapter is to develop and perform a preliminary test of a predictive model of KM practices of SMEs based on certain aspects of organizational context. The main research question is as follows: 'How is organizational context related to KM practices in small to medium-sized technology-based firms?' The answer to this question provides an understanding of the level of sophistication or maturity of KM within technology-based SMEs and shows certain predictors of various formal KM practices adopted by them. This chapter is designed to obtain a better understanding of the relationship between KM and organizational context.

Organizational context variables include company size, company age, family business, growth orientation and networking – especially with larger organizations. Some of these variables have been identified as having an influence on KM practices (mostly in large firms) in several studies (Mohan-Neill, 1995; Sparrow, 2000; Nooteboom, 2001; Yli-Renko et al., 2001). Others are derived from theoretical reasoning by the authors.

In the first part of the chapter, an eclectic model is presented which draws from various theoretical perspectives, including the resource-based approach, the dynamic-capabilities perspective and transaction cost economics. The introduction also includes relevant empirical research on KM antecedents and consequences. In the second part, we present qualitative and quantitative results of a pilot study of KM practices in a sample of 16 Dutch technology-based SMEs – all of which are suppliers to a large multinational chemicals manufacturer – intended as a first test of the model. The chapter concludes with recommended directions for future research.

BACKGROUND

The Importance of Knowledge Management in SMEs

To date, perhaps some of the most extensive research on knowledge transfer and sharing relates to the nature of networks among (larger) firms and between such firms and public institutions (research institutes, universities and so on). However, research over the past 30 years repeatedly shows patterns that a disproportionate amount of innovation (including new patents and other inventions and discoveries) comes from SMEs. Small firms make impressive contributions to innovation (Thompson and Leyden, 1983; Acs, 1996). According to an OECD report (2002), for instance, small businesses create as much as one-half of all innovations in the United States. Because small firms have such an important share in innovations, it is helpful to know how they perceive and practise knowledge management. So, in addition to knowledge transfer between large firms and from large to small firms, it is of interest how small firms themselves capture, share and enable knowledge to foster innovation within their own firms, and how they transfer their own knowledge and innovations back to other firms.

Research on size effects in effective knowledge management is still in its infancy. Some research suggests that small size might be an advantage because small firms often have a flat and simple organizational structure and more open culture, which might allow for more efficient sharing of information (Bhidé, 2000; Wong and Aspinwall, 2004). However, other research suggests that small firms may lag in the adoption of new technologies (Nooteboom, 2001). Some explain the innovativeness of SME suppliers in particular, due to the demand-pull of large-firm client demands (Boersema and Stegwee, 1996). According to Sparrow (2001), SMEs need to address their KM practices, but based on a three-year qualitative research study into knowledge practices, he also finds that the issues they face are far from simply a scaled-down replica of large company experiences. Sparrow adds that the adoption of particular KM practices in small businesses may be led by large customers and suppliers.

SMEs are especially vulnerable to the erosion of knowledge, particularly as a result of losing key employees. In these instances companies not only lose the person's knowledge; they also lose that person's competence to capture knowledge (Wickert and Herschel, 2001). Recent studies recognize the problems that small firms face in sharing know-how and retaining knowledge when experienced staff move on or retire (Uit Beijerse, 1999); SMEs must develop particular skills for turning tacit knowledge within a company into explicit, accessible information and know-how for new project and product development. These skills can play an important role in the initial stages of the innovation processes of small technology enterprises (Koskinen and Vanharanta, 2002). Therefore it is important for SMEs to pay particular attention to KM. In the case of SMEs, it is not only the employees but the owner-managers themselves that pose a risk when good KM is neglected. In the family firm, for instance, the owner-manager holds a lot of tacit knowledge that must be transferred in a timely manner to a successor to avoid its loss (Varamäki et al., 2002).

In sum, although KM has always been a useful tool, it is becoming an increasing imperative for SME suppliers. Four drivers of the increasing importance of KM for SMEs can be distinguished. First, innovation has become one of the most important factors in the competition between companies. Today's SME customers demand increasing customized products to match specific preferences. SMEs play an important role as a supplier not only of the specific product but also of the related know-how to big companies. Second, SMEs suffer from the increasing mobility on the labour market. This development forces SMEs to look to internalizing tacit knowledge of key employees through KM. Third, developments in ICT and an increasing emphasis on 'knowledge workers' require SMEs to consider implementation of KM practices. Finally, some evidence to date, though largely case based, suggests that KM practices of SMEs should not be simply a scaled-down version of large company solutions.

The Concept of Knowledge Management as used in this Study

This research study builds on the definitions of knowledge management of Uit Beijerse (1999), von Krogh et al. (2000), van Santen (2002) and Takeuchi and Nonaka (2004). This research stream identifies three phases of KM to unlock tacit knowledge including: (i) capturing and locating; (ii) transferring and sharing; and (iii) enabling knowledge.

The first phase of the adapted model of von Krogh et al. (2000), 'knowledge capturing and locating practices', is mainly concerned with unlocking tacit knowledge into explicit knowledge, as 'tacit knowledge yields an obstacle for the absorption of novelty' (Nooteboom, 2001, p. 10). Nooteboom points out that the limitation of tacit knowledge is that by its nature it does not allow for critical reflection and debate, since it represents knowledge difficult to articulate into words. Tacit knowledge can be externalized, however, with a knowledge audit (von Krogh et al., 2000), that is, via discussions among colleagues which result in a sharing of information. Data warehousing is another capturing and locating practice identified by von Krogh et al. Data warehousing refers to a system which holds or stores knowledge, in repositories of books and manuals, knowledge management systems (KMS), Enterprise Resource Planning (ERP) and/or other information management systems (both computerized and non-computerized).

Knowledge transferring and sharing practices, the second phase of KM practices, involve a combination of ICT and non-ICT solutions. Non-ICT solutions are important for a variety of reasons – but not only due to a lack of technological sophistication. Some knowledge just cannot be transferred easily, as it cannot be recorded in a database (Davenport and Prusak, 1998). One cannot make such knowledge explicit and so one has to share it in order to get it transferred from one person to the next. Some researchers suggest that it takes more than merely deploying technology for knowledge to be successful in transferring and sharing. For instance, Nooteboom (2001) states that knowledge may only be transferred by comparatively lengthy, direct, on-line, real-time interaction, with demonstration, trial, error and correction, which is a problem in the codification of tacit knowledge. One remedy is to transfer knowledge embodied in a worker, who then carries it into the firm while practising it, and transfers it on the basis of the ongoing interaction needed. Research conducted by Chen (2004) suggests that knowledge transfer performance is positively affected by the explicitness of knowledge and the firm's absorptive capacity.

Knowledge enabling practices comprise the third phase. Managers must set up the means for making knowledge accessible and easy to accumulate in the organization (von Krogh et al., 2000), by, for instance, promoting lateral communication and dialogue rather than vertical communication (Hedlund, 1994; Davenport et al., 1998). The use of an ICT system is one way to disseminate knowledge but there are also low-technology practices, including informal conversations and formal meetings (von Krogh et al., 2000), especially those which allow each participant to share new ideas and/or reflect on other people's viewpoints. One can connect one's ideas to those of another participant, and see how these ideas take on a life of their own (ibid.).

Organizational Contextual Variables and KM: Theoretical Background

The main goal of this study is to create a better understanding of the role of organizational context in predicting the variation of KM practices among a small group of technology-based SMEs. This subsection provides a rationale for the relationship between organizational context and KM from theories drawn from the management literature. The resource-based view (Barney, 1991; Barney et al., 2001) is used to show the importance of knowledge as a strategic resource for the firm and its environment (customers and partners) (von Krogh and Roos, 1995; Hitt et al., 2001). The dynamic capabilities approach (Prahalad and Hamel, 1990; Teece et al., 1997) highlights the problem that knowledge erodes and needs to be renewed by learning or creating new knowledge (Huysman et al., 1998). This approach also helps to explain why one would expect a positive relationship between KM and firm performance.

Transaction cost economics is especially helpful for understanding how certain players from both the internal and external environment serve to mediate the disadvantages of size and scale effects in SMEs (Nooteboom, 1993; Mohan-Neill, 1995), especially through cooperation with major outside firms (De Kok and Uhlaner, 2001). Various interorganizational contacts that can be important for knowledge acquisition and organizational learning include training, consulting and research institutions (Kailer and Scheff, 1999), local development agencies (Collinson and Quinn, 2002) and major customers (Yli-Renko et al., 2001).

Finally, the behavioural perspective focuses on the role of the chief executive officer (CEO) in selecting strategy, more generally, or KM practices more specifically. For instance, Wong and Aspinwall (2004) conclude that the management style of owner-managers can have far-reaching implications on the transfer and sharing of knowledge in SMEs as knowledge sharing is mostly bounded to those areas determined by the owner-managers. On the other hand, in a variant of the resource-based view, Alvarez and Busenitz (2001) point out that it is the owner-manager who often recognizes the value and the opportunity of knowledge and whose function it is to organize knowledge.

Overall Degree of Formalization of KM Practices

The primary dependent variable of interest in this study is formalization of KM practices. De Kok and Uhlaner (2001) conclude that there is no universally accepted definition of formalization or 'sophistication'. However, in the context of human resource management (HRM) practices, they note that formalization has been referred to as: (i) the degree to which a procedure is regularly applied within the organization; (ii) the extent to which a rule or procedure is written down; and/or (iii) the degree to which the employee versus the employer takes the initiative to ensure that an activity takes place. Similarly, in this study it is assumed that formalization is not a homogeneous concept and thus should be treated as a cluster of variables and not as single variables. Degree of formalization addresses all three aspects in the current study.

THE PROPOSED MODEL AND HYPOTHESES

The objective of this study is to examine the relationships between organizational context and formalized KM practices. The proposed model explains the level of formalization of KM, combining elements from the resource-based view, dynamic capability approach, transaction cost economics (TCE) and behavioural perspectives (see Figure 8.1).

In particular, organizational context variables such as age, size, family business, having a growth orientation and networking – especially with a (large) firm (henceforth referred to as 'large firm associate') – are thought to influence the overall degree of formalization of KM practices. The reader should note that the model is not intended as a comprehensive list of all possible contextual predictors, but rather as a starting-point upon which other research can build. Furthermore, although we are most interested in the prediction of KM practices, and assume that organization context is

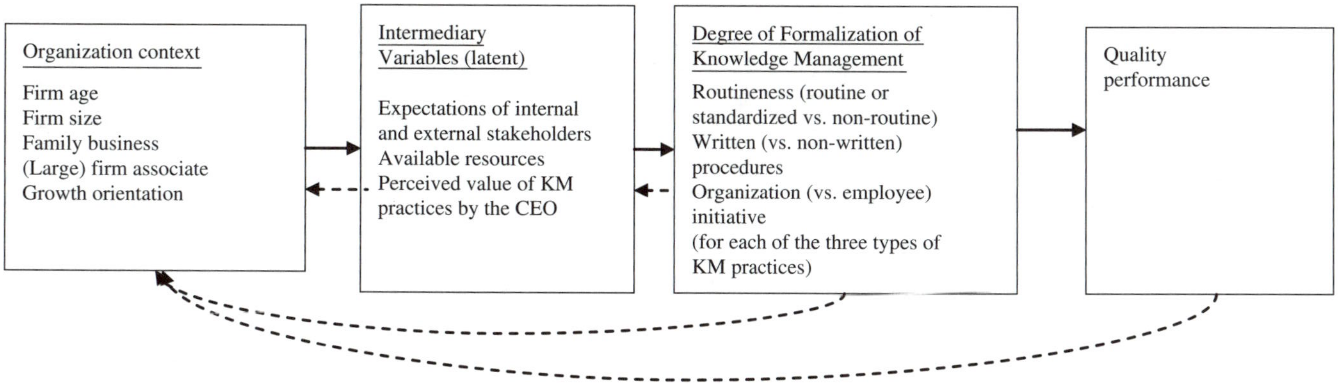

Figure 8.1 A model of KM practices in the technology-based SME

likely to influence those practices, given the nature of organizations as open systems, we can presume bidirectional relationships among a number of the variables, as represented by the dashed feedback loops from KM practices to organization context and the intermediary variables feedback loop from quality performance to context (quality in particular may lead to larger firm size for instance), and feedback from intermediary variables (such as resources) to organization context. However, these links are not specifically proposed as hypotheses nor tested in this study.

KM practices are operationalized according to the model of von Krogh et al. (2000), including representative items from all three phases of KM: capturing and locating systems and practices, transferring and sharing tools and practices, and knowledge-enabling practices. The overall degree of formalization of KM practices is measured in terms of a combination of types of formalization, namely 'non-routine vs. standardized work', 'non-written vs. written procedures', and 'employee vs. organization initiative', as well as frequency of KM practices.

The model also contains three intermediary 'latent' variables, which were first introduced in research of organizational contextual variables and the formalization of HRM practices (De Kok and Uhlaner, 2001). These intermediary variables may also play an important role in predicting the use of (formalized) KM practices. The resource-based view provides a rationale for the role of internal and external stakeholders on KM practices. The influence of resources on KM practices is explained by the resource-based view as well as the TCE perspective (the latter especially with respect to the effect of networking with larger firms), whereas the behavioural perspective explains the influence of the perceived value that the CEO may have regarding KM.

Intermediary variables are not directly measured in this research. These show the effects of resources, know-how and recognition of the importance of more formalized KM practices, on the relationship between the independent and dependent variables. Finally the model suggests a relationship between 'formalization of KM practices' and quality performance. The remainder of the section discusses the hypotheses tested using the proposed model.

Age and Formalization of KM

According to the behavioural view, in a start-up the founder's focus is typically on resource acquisition and market strategy (Hendrickson and Psarouthakis, 1998). When a firm grows older, the CEO shifts focus towards internal issues including among other things, technical mastery, which implies formalization of KM practices. Sparrow (2000) supports this view by saying that KM needs to recognize the current level of maturity of a firm and the drivers in its context. This perspective is also in line with the resource-based view, which asserts that KM is expected to relate to the firm's age, because of the importance of knowledge build-up over the years and the important role played by present and former employees in this process. Furthermore, consistent with the TCE view, Mohan-Neill (1995) finds that older firms use formal methods more frequently than do younger firms. She argues that start-ups often have limited resources, so they concentrate on what appears to be of immediate relevance to the problem at hand. Taking these views and findings together, we propose the first hypothesis, Hypothesis 1, as follows:

H1: The older the SME, the more formalized the KM practices are likely to be.

Size and KM

Nooteboom (1993) argues that firm size correlates strongly with scale and scope, but less strongly with limited experience and learning. Penrose (1995), however, taking the resource-based view, argues that when a firm grows in size, it will reorganize its resources to take advantage of more obvious opportunities for specialization. This implies that larger companies are likely to formalize KM practices following growth in firm size. In a growing firm, the internal stakeholders (one of the intermediary variables) expect the firm to introduce KM practices. When the firm grows, more knowledge is available to the firm. The firm's size as measured by the number of full-time employees is also positively correlated with the collection of information (Mohon-Neill, 1995).

The relationship between size and formalization more generally, is widely supported in the literature. Most formal organization structures require considerable development costs requiring financial resources typically more available to larger firms (Klaas et al., 2000). These structures often lead to a further cost advantage. The classical argument is as follows: as firms increase in size and complexity, they typically develop more layers of management and they become more formalized in order to process information more effectively within the organization (Galbraith, 1973; Tidd and Hull, 2002). Even among SMEs, this trend is so powerful that it is easily replicated in empirical work. Thus, for instance, in a recent study of SMEs, De Kok et al. (2006) confirm the positive relationship between firm size and sophistication of HRM practices.

From both the transaction cost and dynamic capabilities perspectives, smaller firms may be able to go into partnership with external (often larger) partners to obtain new knowledge when their capability to generate knowledge internally is more limited. Such a situation calls for more formalized KM practices (monitoring and control) to reduce the risk of spillover (Nooteboom, 2001). More specifically, TCE suggests that SMEs lack the resources for development of specialized programmes such as formalization of KM practices. With the advantages of scale, larger companies have more resources to (re)cover development costs (Nooteboom, 1993). Availability of resources thus also affects formalization of KM practices (see the intermediary variable in Figure 8.1). Empirical support for the relationship between firm size and KM practices, *per se*, is lacking. However, given this overall trend in the literature, we would still expect a positive relationship between firm size and formalization of KM, stated as follows:

H2: The larger the SME, the more formalized the KM practices are likely to be.

Family Business and KM

Previously published research empirically supports the proposition that family businesses are more informally structured than their non-family counterparts (De Kok et al., 2006). For instance, they are likely to have less formal HRM practices and more informal accounting practices (ibid.). Findings from past research provide various theoretical explanations, including, for example, the resource-based model (ibid.). Donckels (1998) suggests that family-owned companies may be particularly strong in passing knowledge and experience from generation to generation, but occasionally fall short in some areas of knowledge. The resource-based model provides an explanation for less formal practices, due to scarcer resources often found in the family-owned firm. Nooteboom (2001, p. 2) states: 'an entrepreneur who emerged from a traditional craft environment, often continuing a family tradition, with limited formal training, faces more obstacles, especially in absorptive capacity, than a university graduate (manager) who escapes from a large bureaucratic firm to spin off a firm of his own'. In spite of these explanations, we note that due to limited past empirical research, we cannot be sure of the direction of the relationship between family business and knowledge management. Nevertheless, based on other research on the negative relationship between family business and formalization of business practices, more generally, we state Hypothesis 3 as follows:

H3: In family business, less formalized KM practices are present compared to non-family business.

Networking (with Larger Firm Associates) and KM

Recent research shows that most of a start-up's (SMEs) strategic alliances are with other small firms, and so are ties that do not provide a great deal of resources (Lee et al., 2001). Alliance partners are found to be a particularly important source of new, external knowledge (Inkpen and Dinur, 1998). Von Hippel (1988) finds that organizations' suppliers and customers are their primary sources of ideas for innovations. According to von Hippel, a network with excellent knowledge transfer among users, manufacturers, and suppliers will out-innovate networks with less-effective knowledge-sharing activities. Yli-Renko et al. (2001) find that interaction between a technology-based SME and its key customer increases the knowledge the SME acquires through that relationship by intensifying role interactions. The latter touches upon the value of the external relationship with respect to lack of resources, consistent with the dynamic capabilities perspective and TCE view. SMEs working with a larger private firm or institute benefit from the knowledge available with that larger firm or institute. In particular, SMEs working closely with a larger company, such as customers, suppliers, investors, government institutions, trade organizations and the like, benefit from a reduction of the transaction costs of acquiring knowledge. This relationship, however, requires management of the knowledge transfer and sharing process (governance) to prevent knowledge leakage and spillover. This leads us to the expectation that SMEs with a large associate are more likely to have more formal KM practices implemented. Hypothesis 4 therefore is as follows:

H4: SMEs associated with a larger firm (customer, supplier, innovation centre or trade organization) are likely to have more formalized KM practices than those companies that lack such an association.

Growth Orientation and KM

Seen from a dynamic capabilities perspective, firms that are more growth orientated than others are more likely to perceive the value of KM practices because KM practices are a primary predictor of growth. They are thus aware of the sustained competitive advantage that knowledge and knowledge development can bring to the firm. KM is especially important in technology-based firms (Lane and Lubatkin, 1998). This is because its competition is more knowledge based than in other industries and changes in the firms' context may reduce the strategic value of knowledge. Thus firms with a growth orientation are more likely to develop more formalized

KM practices than are SMEs without a growth-orientated strategy. Hypothesis 5 is therefore proposed as:

H5: SMEs with a growth orientation are likely to have more formalized KM practices than SMEs without a growth orientation.

KM and Quality Performance

It is generally assumed that KM affects organizational performance positively. Bassi (1997, p. 26) defines performance as the ultimate object of KM: 'KM is the process of creating, capturing and using knowledge to enhance organizational *performance*' (italics added). Outcomes of effective KM practices have been variously stated as creating some kind of competitive advantage (Connor and Prahalad, 1996) enhancing performance (Teece, 1998; Wiig, 1999); enabling a firm to be more innovative (Dove, 1999; Carneiro, 2000; Takeuchi and Nonaka, 2004) allowing a firm to better anticipate problems (Carneiro, 2000); and enabling a firm to better analyse and evaluate information (ibid.). Hitt et al. (2001) find that the transfer of knowledge within a firm builds human capital (employees' capabilities) and contributes to higher firm performance. When one talks about performance and KM, one has to be careful not to confuse KM performance, the effectiveness of KM, and organizational performance as a result of KM.

Organizational performance may be defined as the degree to which a company achieves its business objectives (Elenkov, 2002). It may be measured in terms of organizational learning, profitability, or other financial benefits in knowledge management (Simonin, 1997; Davenport, 1999). Without measurable success, passion from employees and managers might vanish (O'Dell and Grayson, 1999). For example, Darroch (2004) examines the effect of different KM styles on performance, finding that with one exception, all correlations between KM and comparative performance measures (that is, relative to the industry average) are positive and significant. However, she finds only a limited number of significant correlations between KM and internal measures of performance (relative to past performance of the same firm).

According to Buckley and Carter (1999), it is not possible to quantify the performance of KM. It is, however, possible to comment on the effectiveness, speed and costliness of alternative approaches. Quality performance is one of the dimensions identified by Elliott (1999). Taking into account this rationale and the above presented findings leads us to Hypothesis 6:

H6: The degree of formalized KM practices in SMEs is positively associated with the quality of its performance.

METHODOLOGY

Sample and Data Collection Techniques

To test the model and hypotheses presented in the previous section, a series of semi-structured interviews were conducted in the spring of 2002 with 17 technology-based suppliers to a large international chemicals manufacturer. A rather broad definition of an SME was used, to range between one and 500 employees. One company, however, was excluded from analyses, as it was a member of an international group. All but one of the firms fit the more narrow definition used in Europe of less than or equal to 250 employees. Given the small sample size, a company that had recently grown to exceed the 250 employee size limit was included in analyses. The remaining 16 companies in the sample vary in size from eight to 300 employees. They represent the following technology-orientated sectors: engineering and consulting; panel construction and electrical installation; mechanical construction and machine manufacturing; and audiovisual techniques.

Given the exploratory nature of the research and the small sample size, companies were not selected randomly, but rather were selected to ensure variation on the previously mentioned criteria. For instance, within the SME size range it was decided to include a number of relatively large companies because they were assumed to have more formalized KM practices. Only technology-based firms were selected for study because it is expected that, in these types of firms, knowledge plays a prominent role and changes rapidly. The study was further limited to SMEs. In addition, to ensure variation in selected independent variables, an effort was made to seek out firms varying in size (within the range of SME), status as a family business and age of the firm. Table 8.1 provides a description of the participating companies by sector, size and age.

The semi-structured interview was based on a model developed by the authors, since no prior research measured formalization of KM practices. The model or questionnaire of the semi-structured interview is divided into three parts: the first deals with organization context and consists of open-ended questions; the second deals with KM and is semi-structured; and the third and last part contains two questions aimed at testing the size of the firm according to the EU definition of SMEs. (European Commission, 2001).

Variables

Box 8.1 gives a summary of how each of the independent and dependent variables are measured.

Table 8.1 Sector, company size and age statistics for the sample

Sector	Firms	Size (no. of employees)		Age	
		Mean	Range	Mean	Range
Engineering and consulting	3	152.6	8–300	25.6	8–40
Panel construction and electrical installation	5	32.0	12–62	25.5	17–34
Mechanical construction and machine manufacturing	6	59.2	10–200	38.5	16–74
Audiovisual techniques	2	24.5	9–40	35	35–35
Total	16	63.9	8–300	31.7	8–74

Firm size is measured as the number of full- and part-time employees. *Firm age* is measured as the number of years since start-up. The concept of networking is captured by the variable, *large firm associate*, whether or not the firm associates with a larger firm in any of the following categories: trade organization, large customer, innovation centre, university or supplier. The interviewer made sure that these were direct relationships with the respondent, not just one at arm's length, related for example to compliance requirements. To meet the criterion of being a *family business*, first, one family or owner must own more than half of the firm; and second, either the present owner(s) must intend to pass on the firm to the next generation or the next generation must already be working within the firm. *Growth orientation* is measured on a two-point scale based on whether the firm intends to remain stable or to grow.

KM practices were examined initially in six categories, including between seven and nine specific KM methods related to: (i) recording; (ii) locating by knowledge audits; (iii) determining the knowledge gap; (iv) sharing and transferring; (v) managing conversations; and (vi) having facilities promoting knowledge development.[1] For each category, respondents were asked which of a list of specific methods are used and if so, how frequently (1 = seldom, 2 = regularly, 3 = often). At the end of each of the six sections, respondents were then asked to describe the overall degree of formalization for those practices mentioned as being used by that firm. This two-step process was designed in order to obtain detailed information about KM practices while at the same time keeping an eye on the total length of the interview. For each of the six categories, formalization was rated on a five-point scale on the basis of three aspects: (i) 'non-routine vs. standardized work'; (ii) 'non-written vs. written procedures'; and (iii) 'employee vs. organization

BOX 8.1 THE INDEPENDENT AND DEPENDENT VARIABLES USED IN THE PILOT STUDY

Independent variables

Firm size	Number of full- and part-time employees
Firm age	Years since start-up
Large firm associate	No association with an outside firm Association with a larger firm, categorized by: trade organization; large customer; innovation centre; university; and/or supplier
Family business	Non-family business; family business (see text for explanation)
Growth orientation	1 = intention to remain stable 2 = intention to grow

Dependent variables

Formalization of Knowledge Management

For the following questions, these scales were used:

Frequency of practices:	Type of formalization:
1 = seldom	1 = non-routine / non-written / employee initiative
2 = regularly	2 = more non-routine / non-written / employee initiative
3 = often	3 = some of both sides, neutral (undecided)
	4 = more standardized / written procedures / organization initiative
	5 = only standardized / written procedures / organization initiative
Phase 1: Locating and capturing practices:	Q1: Knowledge recording Q2: Knowledge locating (knowledge audits)
Phase 2: Transferring and sharing practices:	Q3: Determining the knowledge gap Q4: Knowledge sharing and transferring
Phase 3: Knowledge enabling practices:	Q5: Managing conversations Q6: Facilities promoting knowledge development
Quality performance	1 = bad; 2 = not satisfactory; 3 = satisfactory; 4 = good; 5 = excellent

initiative'. Past research questions whether these three types of formalization are highly correlated (De Kok and Uhlaner, 2001). Therefore the three types of formalization are treated as separate variables.

The degree of formalization variables for each of the six categories of KM methods were computed as follows. First an average was computed of the frequency of the seven to nine methods within each of the six categories. Then the overall degree of formalization per category was calculated by multiplying this average frequency with the ratings, in turn, for each type of formalization, including routineness, extent of written procedures, or organization initiative. This approach in essence weights the type of formalization by the frequency of KM practices.[2]

Quality performance was based on an assessment by the procurer, a multinational enterprise (MNE) served by all but two of the respondents participating in the study. These data were derived from separate archival sources based on an assessment carried out routinely by the MNE to determine whether a particular supplier can become and/or remain a preferred vendor. In the assessment, short interviews with a representative from the purchasing department and two engineers from the technical department of the MNE were carried out to measure each SME's performance with respect to meeting the MNE's specifications – in particular, supply of goods and/or services according to the company's specifications and inspection methods, and delivery of the appropriate technical service. At the end of these interviews, each of the interviewees was asked to give a global quality performance rating for each supplier ranging from 1 = bad, to 5 = excellent. These confidential data were made available for the present study by special arrangement with the authors.

Data Analysis

Both qualitative and quantitative analysis techniques are applied to the dataset. In the qualitative analysis, company responses are examined on a case-by-case basis to identify patterns and trends. Hypotheses are tested using Pearson product moment correlation coefficients.

RESULTS

Qualitative Analysis

This subsection describes four cases to illustrate the different approaches taken to knowledge management within the firm sample.[3]

Case 1, a 55-year-old mechanical construction company with 45 employees, is not growth orientated, but does fit the criteria for a family business. It uses few KM practices. Those that are implemented have a low degree of formalization. This firm is a member of a trade organization, but the organization does not appear to influence the firm's KM practices. However, the company does depend strongly upon the knowledge of customers and suppliers, which – according to the company – occurs on a daily basis. KM capturing practices are practised more frequently than transferring, sharing and enabling practices. Most practices asked about in the interview are seldom used. In spite of its limited use of KM – the lowest among the 16 cases – this firm still received a good rating (that is, a 4 on a 5-point scale) for quality performance by the MNE.

By contrast, Case 2 is a younger (eight years old) small (eight employees) technical consulting firm and is not a family firm. Case 2 has more formalized KM practices than Case 1. Since its employees frequently work outside the office, its CEO thinks it is important to manage conversations and standardize transferring and sharing practices, although the practices are low in frequency and these are not communicated through written procedures. Rather, informal means are used, such as having lunch together. Trade fairs and exhibitions are seldom visited due to the perceived high cost of sending employees to such activities; nor do employees choose to attend such activities in their own time. Although the CEO has close contacts with government labour agencies,[4] no relationship is mentioned between these contacts and the KM practices of the firm. A key service offered by this firm is the certification of installations and working procedures for its customers. As part of this service, one of its major competencies is thus to convert *tacit* knowledge regarding machine design of working methods from its customers into *explicit* knowledge that is recorded in certificates and manuals. This might explain why it shows a higher degree of capturing practices. However, negligible effort is put into consulting strategic studies and involving advisers, which seems inconsistent with the firm's main business. Nevertheless, Case 2 also has a good rating for quality performance, as assigned by the MNE.

Case 3 is a 34-year-old, Heating Ventilation and Air-Conditioning (HVAC) certified subcontractor with 62 employees, located in the panel construction and electrical installation sector. It works as a subcontractor for a large firm, other than the MNE in this study. The main contractor introduced Case 3 to a number of KM practices, especially for capturing and locating knowledge. For instance, it operates an ERP system and other software to aid the process of knowledge capturing. This may indicate that formalization bears a relation to size. In determining the knowledge gap, research and development and technological reconnaissance practices are not carried out. The practices that are present are highly formalized, receiving maximum scores for all three items. The sharing and transferring practices, although high in frequency, are much less formalized. The enabling practices are not particularly formalized, although the frequency of 'facilitating development of knowledge' is high. This might be explained by the fact that Case 3 carries out a lot of installation work as subcontractor to its major customer, a large firm used to formalizing such information. To achieve its HVAC certificate, furthermore, it must provide full training for all of its employees. This company receives an excellent rating (5 on the five-point scale) from the MNE for its ability to meet customer specifications.

In contrast to Cases 1 and 2, Case 4, which is a much bigger firm, shows more formalized KM practices both in formalization and in frequency. This firm reports that it has a lot of knowledge captured in software of production machinery that was originally developed by one of the CEOs of the firm in combination with their machine suppliers. Use of such software has led to a loss of craftsmanship over the years; employees are no longer able to make the airshafts without the help of these machines and the built-in software. This firm is the market leader in its field; it plays a prominent role within its trade organization by serving as a member of the trade organization's technical committee which determines the standards in the markets. There are, however, no specific practices mentioned that emphasize the relationship of the associate, a large trade association, and the formalization of the transferring and sharing practices. Case 4 received an excellent score (5 of 5 rating) on quality performance, in part, it would appear, due to its greater use of formalized KM practices.

These four cases illustrate variation in the types of KM practices found among the supplier studies for this project. The four cases share certain elements with respect to KM practices. They all receive a good or excellent rating. This is not too surprising since those with weaker ratings usually do not last too long in a very competitive environment. Another similarity is that most do not have a growth orientation, at least not with respect to aggressive growth. However, these firms do vary with respect to the degree of formalization of different KM practices.

Quantitative Analysis

Table 8.2 provides an overview of the sample according to the key independent variables in the study. Half of these firms are family businesses based on the definition used in this study. About a third report the intention to grow. Eleven of the 16 firms report a link with a '(large) firm associate', eight are associated with a trade organization, and five are associated with a (large) customer and about 25 per cent with a (large) supplier. One

Table 8.2 Other descriptive statistics of the sample

Variable	Valid observations	Characteristic present	Valid per cent (%)
Family business	16	8	50
(Large) firm associate	16	11	69
Trade organization		8	50
Large customer		5	31
Innovation centre		0	0
University		0	0
Supplier		4	25
Other		1	6
Growth orientation	16	5	31
Innovation strategy	16	6	31

Table 8.3 Relationships[a] between the overall degree of formalization of different groups of KM practices

Overall degree of formalization of:	1	2	3	4	5
1 Knowledge recording practices (Q1)					
2 Knowledge locating practices (Q2)	0.74**				
3 Practices to determine the knowledge gap (Q3)	0.57*	0.48			
4 Knowledge sharing and transferring practices (Q4)	0.49	0.44	0.74**		
5 Practices to manage conversations (Q5)	0.18	0.26	0.10	0.16	
6 Practices to promote knowledge development (Q6)	0.39	0.24	0.25	0.23	0.74**

Note: [a] Listwise $N=16$; * $p<0.05$; ** $p<0.01$.

company is related to another type of large associate, namely a working condition service.

Table 8.3 presents correlations among the six groups of KM practices, with respect to the overall degree of formalization. These results show significant relations between certain groups of practices. This suggests that the values assigned to the KM categories are homogeneous according to this definition and justifies the formation of these scales for the respective KM practices. Therefore for further analyses, a new scale was created combining the first two categories, knowledge recording practices and knowledge locating practices, to form the combined category referred to henceforth as 'capturing and locating practices'. The second scale, 'sharing and transferring practices', was created by averaging scores for the third category (practices to determine the knowledge gap) and the fourth category (knowledge sharing and transferring practices). The third scale, 'enabling practices', was formed by averaging responses for the remaining two categories. For each of these three sets of KM practices, the ratings for the three types of formalization are averaged together. Thus, nine KM formalization variables are created in total (three aspects of formalization, routineness, written procedures, and organization initiative) for each of the three scales.

In Table 8.4 the results of the quantitative test for the six proposed hypotheses based on the overall degree of formalization are presented, as well as the tests for the interrelationships among the independent, the nine dependent variables for KM formalization, and finally, the quality performance variable. Looking first at the interrelationships among the independent variables, no statistically significant relationships were found.

Due to relatively low correlations and conceptual differences between the variables, hypotheses were tested for each of the nine KM formalization dependent variables separately (Table 8.4). Degree of support for each of the hypotheses is discussed in the next section.

DISCUSSION

Support for Hypotheses

Age and KM

Hypothesis 1 posits that age is associated with more formalized KM practices. No support is found for this hypothesis. Given the small sample size, lack of support may be due to lack of power in the study. However, the inconsistency of sign and rather small average size of coefficient provides little support for this hypothesis.

Size and KM

By contrast, in spite of the small sample, the relationship between company size and written formalization seems reasonably well supported, especially for capturing and locating practices ($r = 0.65$; $p < 0.01$), and enabling practices ($r = 0.51$; $p < 0.05$). This finding is consistent with, for instance, the resource-based view (as well as transaction cost perspective) that resources may play a key role in formalization of KM practices.

It should be noted that formalization of sharing and transferring practices is not related to size. This seems consistent with a dynamic capabilities

Table 8.4 Correlations[a] between the independent variables and overall degree of formalization of KM practices

	1	2	3	4	5	6	7	8	9	10	11	12	13	14
1 Size (no. of employees)														
2 Age (in years)	0.23													
3 Family business	−0.16	0.25												
4 Growth orientation	0.12	−0.42	−0.14											
5 (Large) firm associate	0.17	0.21	0.41	−0.42										
Capturing & Locating Practices, formalization by														
6 non-routine vs. standardized work	0.21	−0.29	−0.11	−0.13	0.40									
7 non-written vs. written procedures	0.65***	0.01	−0.16	0.16	0.31	0.46*								
8 employee vs. organization initiative	−0.14	−0.18	−0.02	−0.35	0.34	0.80***	0.137							
Sharing & Transferring Practices, formalization by														
9 non-routine vs. standardized work	−0.37	−0.02	0.23	−0.43*	0.45*	0.50**	0.04	0.59						
10 non-written vs. written procedures	0.24	0.05	−0.28	−0.15	0.22	0.42	0.42	0.42	−0.05					
11 Employee vs. organization initiative	0.36	0.36	0.38	−0.23	0.54**	0.44*	0.38	0.42	0.31	0.29				
Enabling Practices, formalization by														
12 non-routine vs. standardized work	−0.09	−0.31	0.32	−0.24	0.45*	0.55**	0.13	0.35	0.52**	−0.06	0.12			
13 non-written vs. written procedures	0.51**	−0.17	0.28	0.41	0.27	0.22	0.64***	−0.19	−0.29	0.14	0.36	0.22		
14 employee vs. organization initiative	−0.09	−0.32	0.67***	0.16	0.34	0.22	0.01	0.00	0.17	−0.16	0.19	0.71***	0.57**	
15 Quality performance	0.30	0.21	0.00	−0.25	0.25	0.69***	0.52*	0.67**	0.17	0.46	0.67***	0.00	0.26	0.64**

Note: [a] Listwise $N=16$ for all relations except performance, which has $N=13$; * $p<0.10$; ** $p<0.05$; *** $p<0.01$.

perspective, which says that smaller firms also need sharing and transferring practices, due to their need for external partners. Nooteboom (2001) states that it is a caveat that the notion of firm size as a distinguishing characteristic is becoming obsolete as a result of the development of a 'network economy'. Therefore the conclusion is drawn that size bears a certain relationship to KM practices, but only when it concerns capturing and locating, and enabling practices.

Family business and KM

Hypothesis 3 states that family business and KM formalization are negatively related. This is not supported in the present study, with the one significant finding, regarding formalization of enabling practices and family business, opposite to the predicted direction ($r = 0.67$; $p < 0.01$), based on the 'employee vs. organization initiative' type of formalization. This finding seems to be in line with the view that family businesses may be able to pass knowledge and experience from generation to generation through the organization without necessarily having to write down its procedures. This finding further highlights the need to review the concepts of formalization as a homogeneous one.

Networking and KM

Regarding Hypothesis 4, having a (large) associate, irrespective of the type of the associate, is positively related to the overall degree of formalization of sharing and transferring practices based on formalization by 'employee vs. organization initiative' ($r = 0.54$; $p < 0.05$). There are also positive suggestions that the overall degrees of formalization of sharing and locating ($r = 0.45$; $p < 0.10$), and enabling practices ($r = 0.45$; $p < 0.10$) based on formalization by 'non-routine vs. standardized work' are related to having a (large) firm associate. A cautionary note should be given in interpreting the data since in eight of the 11 firms reporting a relationship with a large firm associate, this relationship pertains to a large trade organization. That such a linkage may lead to more formal KM practices may be expected since firms usually join a trade organization with the specific intention of gaining specific knowledge from the organization. On the other hand, some firms have multiple large firm linkages. With such a small sample, it was not possible to tease apart the effects of different types of large firms on the firms under study but this would be wise in future research.

Support for the effect of a large firm associate on more formalized KM practices is consistent with findings by De Kok and Uhlaner (2001), with respect to HRM practices and was explained by them using transaction cost economics. According to the rationale presented by De Kok and Uhlaner, SMEs which have large firm associates generally have more sophisticated practices (in the case of their research, HRM practices) because they benefit from the support and knowledge provided by these larger firms. It would stand to reason that such firms could also provide guidance regarding KM practices. Whether all large associates (that is, suppliers, versus customers, versus trade associations) benefit the smaller firm equally could not be tested, however, given the limited sample size in the current study.

Growth orientation and KM

Other than a suggestion on a negative relationship with the overall degree of formalization of sharing and transferring practices with regard to formalization through 'non-routine vs. standardized work' ($r = -0.430$; $p < 0.10$), no support for Hypothesis 5 is found. Combined with the fact that several of the examined firms mentioned not having a growth orientation, this hypothesis warrants further testing.

KM and quality performance

Relationships between overall degree of formalization of KM practices and quality performance are found most consistently with respect to capturing and locating practices, with a positive relationship found between quality performance and routineness ($r = 0.69$; $p < 0.01$), written procedures ($r = 0.52$; $p < 0.1$) and organization initiative ($r = 0.67$; $p < 0.05$). A positive relationship is also found between the organization initiative aspect for formalization of sharing and transferring practices ($r = 0.67$; $p < 0.05$) as well as enabling practices ($r = 0.64$; $p < 0.05$). From these results we conclude that results are mixed, but that the formalization of KM practices, especially with respect to setting up practices by the organization versus employee initiative may be beneficial to a firm's quality performance, consistent with Hypothesis 6.

Further Discussion and Suggestions for Future Research

The results of this study point to a number of interesting directions for further research. First, consistent with other research, even within a small sample, company size appears to be an important predictor of the formalization of at least two categories of KM practices. This confirms the importance of scale in predicting the overall shape of organizations.

Second, even though KM practices were tested in a small sample, the SMEs studied in this research demonstrate that small firms vary widely in the types of KM practices used and in the way these KM practices are formalized. Thus, in spite of the importance of firm size, this variation suggests that other factors may also shape KM practices and their formalization in the organization. In particular, the findings point to the possible fruitfulness of other organization contextual variables, including other firm characteristics and aspects of the firm's environment and strategy as explanatory factors.

Third, there is still a lack of interrelationship shown among the three categories of KM practices. For instance, firms that have more (formalized) enabling practices do not necessarily have more (formalized) sharing and transferring practices. These results suggest that, in spite of the theory of von Krogh et al. (2000) the notion of KM, as a homogeneous and related concept based on the frequency of KM practices only, must be questioned.

Fourth, when considering the formalization of each category of KM practices, results vary depending upon the way in which formalization is defined. Thus, results vary, depending upon whether formalization refers to routineness, use of written procedures, or organization (versus individual or employee) initiative. This is a more pervasive problem with the concept of formalization that has yet to be resolved in the literature (see De Kok et al., 2006).

Fifth, the current dataset does not allow testing for the impact of the three latent intermediary variables (resources, internal and external stakeholder expectations, and the perceived value of KM practices by the CEO). These variables might be operationalized and measured in future research in order to improve our understanding of the types of KM practices.

Sixth, since KM is a broadly defined concept and time was limited, in this research a choice of KM practices had to be made from each of the three KM categories to be included in the dataset. With hindsight, this may have led to a less optimal or less well-balanced set of KM practices. As a result of these choices, the tests for homogeneity of both KM and formalization may have suffered, and certain relations and/or influences of intermediary variables may have been underexposed. It is recommended that future research should involve a larger sample and include as many practices as possible for each category (preferably all 79 practices described in Uit Beijerse's research, 1999). Then, testing for formalization based on frequency of KM practices, in line with the model of Von Krogh and colleagues would be feasible. An alternative would be to research KM and formalization extensively, while each KM practice is questioned with regard to the way it is formalized.

Seventh, given the wide variation in KM practices in SMEs, future research is required to clarify the relationship between the various KM practices and small-firm performance. Although it is tested in this thesis on a limited basis, future research should validate the effect of formalization or KM practices on firm performance. Nevertheless, even with a rather limited dataset, the patterns of results regarding quality performance are compelling and bear further exploration in future research.

In sum, future research using larger, randomly drawn samples from multiple sectors is required to test the hypotheses and tentative conclusions outlined here. Additionally, longitudinal research may provide a better understanding of the directions of cause and effect among the proposed linkages, and it may provide more understanding of the linkages between KM categories and formalization types. Future research needs to examine both organizational contextual variables measured in this chapter as well as other contextual variables not included in this research. Such variables might include sector, innovation orientation and legal liabilities faced by the firm and region. Nevertheless, the trends reported here suggest that the use of organizational contextual variables in addition to company size may be a promising line of research in an effort to predict KM practices in SMEs.

CONCLUSION

This chapter aims at the empirical testing of a set of hypotheses relating organization context and formalization of knowledge management practices, as well as the possible further relationship between formalization of KM practices and quality performance. Specific organization context variables chosen for testing include company age, company size, family ownership, growth orientation and networking with a large firm associate. The results most clearly support the positive relationship between company size and formalization of KM practices as well as the positive relationship between networking with a large firm associate and formalization of KM practices. Although there are only a few empirical studies with respect to formalization of KM practices, these findings are consistent with other research on formalization in SMEs (De Kok and Uhlaner, 2001; De Kok et al., 2006). Various theories may be used to explain these findings, simplest perhaps being that of the resource-based view and transaction cost economics. Furthermore, the research provides intriguing support, in spite of a very small sample size, for the positive relationship between KM practices and the quality of performance. Although the sample size is quite limited, the source of data for the dependent variable in this case is unusual, given the archival nature of the rating and the fact that it is based on an extensive assessment carried out by the same procurer, overcoming the problem of common method bias often found in other studies of firm performance (Podsakoff et al., 2003).

The admittedly small, non-random sample used for this study should caution the reader regarding the weight to which practical implications should be given. Nevertheless, preliminary findings suggest that KM practices may well be an important way to leverage a small firm's competitive advantage, especially where quality is important to success of the firm.

Firm size and the supplier's relationships with a larger firm are the most influential organizational contextual characteristics that predict more formalized KM practices, and thus better performance or quality. In particular, even among smaller firms, larger SMEs are more likely to have implemented more formalized KM practices, ensuring that valuable knowledge is preserved. This may be due to the fact that a large firm generally has more resources available to implement these KM practices. Larger firms may also be more likely to have employees or internal stakeholders whose expectations keep the management on their toes when it comes to KM practices.

Although size is important, its impact can be offset by the degree of networking by the firm, that is, a membership of a trade organization or some form of association with a (large) supplier or customer. A membership of a trade organization indicates that the SME has access to all kinds of best practices in a specific industry. It is likely that an SME uses that kind of information to run its company efficiently and to raise its level of performance. Having links with a supplier may provide the SME with earlier access to new kinds of technology and/or an extensive backup when this new technology or its application leads to unforeseen problems.

The conclusions of this study presume that more formal KM practices are beneficial, and that we have an understanding of what those practices entail. However, shortcomings in definition and measurement suggest the need for further validation of KM practices in SMEs, and a more careful definition of what is meant by formalization of KM practices. Future research should address these issues more systematically.

NOTES

1. The specific items are included in Van Santen (2002) and/or available from the authors.
2. More detailed information about the measurement of the knowledge management variable is available from Van Santen (2002).
3. All companies were originally analysed in this way but due to page limitations for this chapter, only four cases are included for illustrative purposes.
4. These agencies are semi-government agencies that can be used by firms to examine whether their working conditions are at the appropriate level according to government regulations; the Dutch term is *ARBO-dienst*, or *arbeidsomstandigheden dienst*.

REFERENCES

Acs, Z.J. (1996), 'Small firms and economic growth', in Z.J. Acs, B. Carlsson and A.R. Thurik (eds), *Small Business in the Modern Economy*, Padstow, UK: T.J. Press, pp. 1–62.

Alvarez, S.A. and L.W. Busenitz (2001), 'The entrepreneurship of resource-based theory', *Journal of Management*, **27**, 755–75.

Audretsch, D.B. and A.R. Thurik (2001), 'What is new about the new economy: sources of growth in the managed and entrepreneurial economies', *Industrial and Corporate Change*, **10**, 267–315.

Audretsch, D.B. and A.R. Thurik (2004), 'A model of the entrepreneurial economy', *International Journal of Entrepreneurship Education*, **2** (2), 143–66.

Barney, J. (1991), 'Firm resources and sustained competitive advantage', *Journal of Management*, **17** (1), 99–120.

Barney, J., M. Wright and D.J. Ketchen Jr (2001), 'The resource-based view of the firm: ten years after 1991', *Journal of Management*, **27**, 625–41.

Bassi, L.J. (1997), 'Harnessing the power of intellectual capital', *Training and Development*, **51** (12), 25–30.

Bhidé, A. (2000), *The Origin and Evolutions of New Business*, Oxford and New York: Oxford University Press.

Boersema, J.S.K.T. and R.A. Stegwee (1996), 'Exploring the issues in knowledge management', *Information Resources Management Association International Conference, in Information Technology Management and Organizational Innovations: Proceedings of the 7th May*, Washington, DC, Harrisburg, PA: Idea Group Publishing, pp. 217–22.

Buckley, P.J. and M.J. Carter (1999), 'Managing cross-border complementary knowledge – conceptual developments in the business process approach to knowledge management in multinational firms', *International Studies of Management and Organization*, **29** (1), 80–104.

Carneiro, A. (2000), 'How does knowledge management influence innovation and competitiveness?', *Journal of Knowledge Management*, **4** (2), 87–98.

Chen, C.J. (2004), 'The effect of knowledge attribute, alliance characteristics, and absorptive capacity on knowledge transfer performance', *R&D Management*, **34** (3), 311–22.

Choo, C.W. and N. Bontis (2002), *The Strategic Management of Intellectual Capital and Organizational Knowledge*, Oxford and New York: Oxford University Press.

Collinson, E. and L. Quinn (2002), 'The impact of collaboration between industry and academia on SME growth', *Journal of Marketing Management*, **18**, 415–34.

Connor, K.R. and C.K. Prahalad (1996), 'A resource-based theory of the firm: knowledge versus opportunism', *Organization Science*, **7** (5), 477–501.

Darroch, J. (2004), 'Developing a measure of knowledge management behaviours and practices', *Journal of Knowledge Management*, **7** (5), 41–54.

Davenport, T.H. (1999), 'Knowledge management and the broader firm: strategy, advantage, and performance', in J. Liebowitz (ed.), *Knowledge Management Handbook*, Boca Raton, FL: CRC Press, pp. 2-1–2-11.

Davenport, T.H., D.W. de Long and M.C. Beers (1998), 'Successful knowledge management projects', *Sloan Management Review*, **39** (2), 43–57.

Davenport, T.H. and L. Prusak (1998), *Working Knowledge: How Organizations Manage What They Know*, Boston, MA: Harvard Business School Press.

De Kok, J. and L.M. Uhlaner (2001), 'Organization context and human resource management in the small firm', *Small Business Economics*, **17**, 273–91.

De Kok, J.M.P., L.M. Uhlaner and A.R. Thurik (2006), 'Professional HRM practices in family owned–managed enterprises', *Journal of Small Business Management*, **44** (3), 441–60.

Donckels, R. (1998), 'Ondernemen in het familiebedrijf', in D.P. Scherjon and A.R. Thurik (eds), *Handboek Ondernemers en Adviseurs in het MKB*, Deventer: Kluwer Bedrijfsinformatie, pp. 86–9.

Dove, R. (1999), 'Knowledge management, response ability, and the agile enterprise', *Journal of Knowledge Management*, **3** (1), 18–35.

Elenkov, D.S. (2002), 'Effects of leadership on organizational performance in Russian companies', *Journal of Business Research*, **55** (6), 467–80.

Elliott, T. (1999), 'Business performance and viability', in F. Dawes (ed.), *Small Business Management: An Overview*, Dublin: Blackhall, pp. 92–115.

European Commission (2001), 'Commission Recommendation of amending Recommendation 96/280/EC concerning the definition of small and medium-sized enterprises', European Commission, Brussels.

Galbraith, J.R. (1973), *Designing Complex Organizations*, Reading, MA: Addison-Wesley.

Hedlund, G. (1994), 'A model of knowledge management and the *N*-form corporation', *Strategic Management Journal*, **15**, 73–90.

Hendrickson, L.U. and J. Psarouthakis (1998), *Dynamic Management of Growing Firms: A Strategic Approach*, 2nd edn, Ann Arbor, MI: University of Michigan Press.

Hitt, M.A., R.D. Ireland, S.M. Camp and D.L. Sexton (2001), 'Guest editor's introduction to the special issue: strategic entrepreneurship: entrepreneurial strategies for wealth creation', *Strategic Management Journal*, **22**, 479–91.

Huysman, M., M. Creemers and F. Derksen (1998), 'Learning from the environment: exploring the relation between organizational learning, knowledge management and information/communication technology', in E.D. Hoadley and I. Benbasat (eds), *Proceedings of the Fourth Americas Conference on Information Systems*, Association for Information Systems, Baltimore, MD, 14–16 August, pp. 598–600.

Inkpen, A.C. and A. Dinur (1998), 'Knowledge management processes and international joint ventures', *Organization Science*, **9** (4), 454–68.

Kailer, N. and J. Scheff (1999), 'Knowledge management as a service: co-operation between small and medium-sized enterprises (SMEs) and training, consulting and research institutions', *Journal of European Industrial Training*, **23** (7), 319–28.

Klaas, B.S., J. McClendon and T.W. Gainey (2000), 'Managing HR in the small and medium enterprise: the impact of professional employer organizations', *Entrepreneurship: Theory and Practice*, **25** (1), 107–24.

Koskinen, K.U. and H. Vanharanta (2002), 'The role of tacit knowledge in innovation processes of small technology companies', *International Journal of Production Economics*, **80** (1), 57–64.

Lane, P.J. and M. Lubatkin (1998), 'Relative absorptive capacity and interorganizational learning', *Strategic Management Journal*, **19**, 461–77.

Lee, C., K. Lee and J.M. Pennings (2001), 'Internal capabilities, external networks, and performance: a study on technology-based ventures', *Strategic Management Journal*, **22**, 615–40.

Mohan-Neill, S.I. (1995), 'The influence of firm's age and size on its environmental scanning activities', *Journal of Small Business Management*, **33**, 10–21.
Nooteboom, B. (1993), 'Firm size effects on transaction costs', *Small Business Economics*, **5**, 283–95.
Nooteboom, B. (2001), *Problems and Solutions in Knowledge transfer*, ERIM Report Series Research in Management, Rotterdam, NL: Erasmus Research Institute of Management (ERIM).
O'Dell, C. and J. Grayson (1999), 'Knowledge transfer: discover your value proposition', *Strategy and Leadership*, **27** (20), 10–15.
Organisation for Economic Cooperation and Development (OECD) (2002), *OECD Small and Medium Enterprise Outlook*, Paris: OECD.
Penrose, E. (1995), *The Theory of the Growth of the Firm*, 3rd edn, Oxford: Oxford University Press.
Podsakoff, P.M., S.B. MacKenzie, J.Y. Lee and N.P. Podsakoff (2003), 'Common method biases in behavioral research: a critical review of the literature and recommended remedies', *Journal of Applied Psychology*, **88** (5), 879–903.
Prahalad, C.K. and G. Hamel (1990), 'The core competence of the corporation', *Harvard Business Review*, **68** (3), 79–91.
Simonin, B. (1997), 'The importance of collaborative know-how: an empirical test of the learning organization', *Academy of Management Journal*, **40** (5), 509–33.
Sparrow, J. (2000), 'Knowledge features of small firms', Paper presented at the Operations Research Society KMAC conference, University of Aston, Birmingham, 17–18 July.
Sparrow, J. (2001), 'Knowledge management in small firms', *Knowledge and Process Management*, **8** (1), 3–16.
Takeuchi, H. and I. Nonaka (2004), *Hitotsubashi on Knowledge Management*, Singapore: John Wiley & Sons.
Teece, D.J. (1998), 'Capturing value from knowledge assets: the new economy, markets for know-how and intangible assets', *California Management Review*, **40** (3), 55–79.
Teece, D.J., G. Pisano and A. Shuen (1997), 'Dynamic capabilities and strategic management', *Strategic Management Journal*, **18** (7), 509–33.
Thompson, J.H. and D.R. Leyden (1983), 'The United States of America', in D.J. Storey (ed.), *The Small Firm: An International Survey*, London: Croom Helm, pp. 7–45.
Tidd, J. and F. Hull (2002), 'Organizing for service innovation: best-practice or configurations?', SPRU Electronic Working Paper Series, no. 77, Science and Technology Policy Research Unit, University of Sussex, Brighton.
Uit Beijerse, R.P. (1999), 'Questions in knowledge management: defining and conceptualizing a phenomenon', *Journal of Knowledge Management*, **3** (2), 94–110.
Van Santen, J. (2002), 'An exploratory study of Dutch technology-based firms', unpublished Master's thesis, Rotterdam School of Management, Erasmus University, Rotterdam.
Varamäki, E., T. Pihkala and V. Routamaa (2002), 'Knowledge transfer in small family businesses', in M. Koiranen and N. Karlsson (eds), *Research Forum Proceedings, Family Business Network, 13th Annual World Conference, 11–14 September*, Helsinki: University of Jyväskylä.
Von Hippel, E. (1988), *The Sources of Innovation*, Oxford and New York: Oxford University Press.
Von Krogh, G., K. Ichijo and I. Nonaka (2000), *Enabling Knowledge Creation*, Oxford and New York: Oxford University Press.

Von Krogh, G. and J. Roos (1995), 'A perspective on knowledge competence and strategy', *Personnel Review*, **24** (3), 56–76.
Wickert, A. and R. Herschel (2001), 'Knowledge-management issues for smaller businesses', *Journal of Knowledge Management*, **5** (4), 329–37.
Wiig, K.M. (1999), 'What future knowledge management users may expect', *Journal of Knowledge Management*, **3** (2), 155–65.
Wong, K.Y. and E. Aspinwall (2004), 'Characterizing knowledge management in the small businesses environment', *Journal of Knowledge Management*, **8** (3), 44–61.
Yli-Renko, H., A. Erkko and H.J. Sapienza (2001), 'Social capital, knowledge acquisition, and knowledge exploitation in young technology-based firms', *Strategic Management Journal*, **22**, 587–613.

9. Refugee entrepreneurship: the case of Belgium

Bram Wauters and Johan Lambrecht

INTRODUCTION[1]

An increased interest in entrepreneurship among refugees at the diverse policy levels in Europe aims at killing two birds with one stone. By promoting this kind of entrepreneurship, both the integration of refugees into society can be aided and entrepreneurship in general can be boosted.

The number of refugees entering Western societies has increased enormously during the last decade, although it should be noted that in recent years it has again slightly decreased. The case of Belgium is well chosen since it is a country that receives a relatively high number of asylum seekers. During 2000–04, Belgium was the eighth country worldwide in the number of received asylum seekers, with a total of 118 400 (UNHCR, 2005). The integration of refugees into Western societies is often seen as problematic, both by the refugees themselves and by the native population of the host society. Refugees encounter several problems in their new society, among others obtaining a good job. This is due to a combination of a lack of knowledge and skills, and discrimination on the labour market (Pécoud, 2003). Setting up an own business can provide a valuable way out of this economic uncertainty and in that sense it can be seen as stimulating further integration of the refugees into their new society (Kloosterman and van der Leun, 1999).

On diverse policy levels in Europe there is a rising awareness of the need to enhance entrepreneurship in general in order to consolidate and strengthen the domestic economy. The rate of new entrepreneurship is perceived as too low in several Western European countries. There is general agreement that the potential for entrepreneurship is insufficiently put into practice. Diverse studies have shown that entrepreneurship in Belgium has a low profile in comparison with other countries. The Global Entrepreneurship Monitor (GEM) (Vlerick Leuven Gent Management School, 2005), for instance, shows that from the EU countries under investigation only Hungary performs worse than Belgium. With a percentage of

3.9 per cent of the population at working age involved in setting up an enterprise, Belgium lags far behind the European average of 5.2 per cent.

Entrepreneurship among *immigrants* has attracted a lot of scientific attention during the last few decades, while scientific interest for *refugee* entrepreneurship has been limited. There is an extensive literature on so-called 'ethnic entrepreneurship' (Waldinger et al., 1990a; Kloosterman and van der Leun, 1999; Li, 2000; Masurel et al., 2002; Kontos, 2003; Leung, 2003; Pécoud, 2003). In these research articles, however, little attention has been paid to refugees *per se*. Generally, they have been seen as an integral part of the immigrant population with little attempt to treat them as a distinct group. Although there has been some scientific interest in the employment positions of refugees in general, self-employment has mostly taken a marginal place in these analyses (Hauff and Vaglum, 1993; Valtonen, 1999; Beiser and Hou, 2000; Bollinger and Hagstrom, 2004; DeVoretz et al., 2004). A notable exception is Gold (1988, 1992), who undertook extensive research on entrepreneurship in the US among Vietnamese refugees and Soviet Jews.

One could question whether a separate analysis for refugees is necessary. There are indeed some observations, phenomena, difficulties and so on that are similar for immigrants and refugees. Nevertheless, there are arguments for undertaking a separate analysis (Bernard, 1977; Gold, 1992; Cortes, 2001). Refugees flee their country because they are being persecuted and, as a consequence, they leave for humanitarian reasons. Economic immigrants, on the other hand, leave their country in search of a (better) job and for (more) economic security. One can sum up six differences between refugees and immigrants that have consequences for starting up and running a business of their own:

- The social network of refugees in the new host country is likely to be less extensive than that of immigrants. Often, refugees flee their country on an individual basis and come from a wide range of countries (Gold, 1992).
- Refugees flee their country of origin because of persecution. As a consequence, it is usually no longer possible for them to return to their country in order to acquire funds, capital or a labour force for their business.
- Refugees have experienced traumatic events, both in their country of origin as well as during the flight out of the country. These traumatic experiences can cause psychological problems, which hamper self-reliance and self-employment (Bernard, 1977; Hauff and Vaglum, 1993).
- Because refugees often have to leave their home country without knowing exactly where they are going, they have had less

opportunity to prepare in advance for their stay in the host country (Gold, 1988).

- Another consequence of their unexpected flight is that they were unable to bring much with them. They have often had to leave various valuable items behind, such as capital and education certificates.
- A considerable number of refugees are not suitable for undertaking paid labour. This also applies to refugees with country-specific skills and qualifications, who in normal circumstances would never leave their home country (ibid.).

In general, one can say that refugees encounter more problems than immigrants. Cortes (2001: 25) concludes her research as follows: 'I can only stress the importance of not aggregating immigrants into one general category because this fails to take into account the enormous variation that exists among immigrants'.

THEORETICAL FRAMEWORK

This chapter aims to contribute to an underinvestigated domain of research by sketching an image of refugee entrepreneurship in Belgium, paying attention to both the potential and the practice. The focus will be on two research questions: first, whether there exists a potential for entrepreneurship among refugees and what kind of refugees are more likely to have an appetite for entrepreneurship; and second, how many and what kind of refugees managed to set up a business of their own in the host country and whether these businesses allow them to earn a decent income. We shall make use of theories on ethnic entrepreneurship and on entrepreneurship in general.

Regarding the motivations for starting a business, one can make a distinction between four groups of explanations, which have been used for the analysis of ethnic entrepreneurship (Bovenkerk, 1983; Ward and Jenkins, 1984):

- The cultural model or the model of entrepreneurship migration: this theory states that one immigrates with the explicit goal of setting up an own business in another country.
- The economic chances model or the theory of ethnic infrastructure: ethnic entrepreneurs respond to the demands and needs of the ethnic community by offering specialized products for sale to this group.
- The reaction model or the theory of reaction to unemployment and discrimination: immigrants experience difficulties in accessing the

labour market, and as a reaction they start a business of their own in order to survive (Borjas, 1986; Gold, 1988). Shapero (1982) predicts entrepreneurial behaviour in general on the basis of a (mostly negative) event that changes the original situation. In Shapero's model, the main condition is that entrepreneurship is perceived as a credible career alternative. To be credible, entrepreneurship has to be considered as attractive and feasible.

- The entrepreneur model or the theory of the entrepreneurship instinct: like Belgians, some immigrants appreciate the advantages of self-employment (to be one's own boss, self-realization and so on) and want to become self-employed.

We add here another explanation, namely the desire to integrate into the host society, the so-called 'integration model'. Ajzen and Fishbein (1980) mention the subjective norm as a predictor for intentions: it denotes the combination of the perceived social pressure to behave in a certain manner and of the motivation to meet that pressure. People will be more inclined to behave in a certain way when they evaluate the expected results of the behaviour positively and when they believe that others find that important. In this study, social integration can be a motive. Refugees are encouraged to integrate into their new society and entrepreneurship can be seen, according to this model, as an instrument for realizing the goal of integration. It will be investigated which of these five motivation theories apply for refugee entrepreneurship.

The profile of refugees interested in setting up an own business will also be investigated. A short overview of some earlier findings about appetite for entrepreneurship in general will be given. According to the demographic approach, entrepreneurship is influenced by the presence of a role model, by gender and by experience (Robinson et al., 1991; Tkachev and Kolvereid, 1999).

According to the social learning theory, parents, other family members and friends can act as *role models*. Those who value highly entrepreneurship by their parents have a higher probability of choosing entrepreneurship (Scherer et al., 1991; Delmar and Davidsson, 2000; Lambrecht et al., 2004). Moreover, research has revealed that refugees often find inspiration in their family to respond to the social and economic challenges posed by migration and resettlement (Kibria, 1995).

Concerning *gender*, female students have a lower probability than their male colleagues of considering entrepreneurship (Lambrecht et al., 2004). GEM also showed that men are twice as likely as women to be involved in entrepreneurship (Vlerick Leuven Gent Management School, 2005).

Tkachev and Kolvereid (1999) showed that *experience* in self-employment is a statistically significant determinant for entrepreneurship intentions. Likewise, Westhead and Wright (1999) found that in Great Britain a third of the surveyed businesses were founded by entrepreneurs with prior business experience. This phenomenon can be denoted as 'serial entrepreneurship'. Tienda and Raijman (2004) identified prior business experience as an important variable for entrepreneurial intentions in a study about ethnic entrepreneurship in Chicago.

It will be tested whether these three dimensions of the demographic approach (role model, gender and experience) also apply for refugees. Although intentions can determine behaviour, they cannot predict behaviour perfectly. The prediction accuracy is dependent on the stability of the intentions and on contextual factors (Ajzen and Fishbein, 1980; Bird, 1988; Katz, 1989). The second part of the analysis will focus on the practice of refugee entrepreneurship. It seems likely that the actual number of refugee entrepreneurs will be rather limited. Refugees have often left all their valuables (capital, relevant networks, diplomas and so on) behind. Time and skills are needed to obtain financial means to invest, to assess the market potential and to acquire the necessary resources to establish a business in their new country. Waldinger et al. (1990b) have developed a framework to analyse the barriers faced by ethnic entrepreneurs. This model contains two groups of variables that influence the success rate of ethnic businesses: opportunity structure and group characteristics. These concepts refer more specifically to market opportunities and the extent to which one is able or allowed to make use of them. Refugees are in general not familiar with the market potential in the host country. As a consequence, they are often not capable of profiting from possible market opportunities. Group characteristics can explain why some people anticipate market opportunities and others do not. Two factors are relevant in this respect: human capital and social networks. Human capital consists of characteristics, skills, competencies, education and so on that are inextricably tied up with the individual and that have a positive impact on him/her (Becker, 1975). Social networks, on the other hand, are important sources of information, can be a basis for attracting customers and suppliers, and can provide access to capital.

Kloosterman et al. (1999) have amended Waldinger et al.'s (1990b) model by adding the concept of 'mixed embeddedness'. Their main criticism of Waldinger et al.'s framework is the latter's almost exclusive attention to social and cultural characteristics of groups. Analysis of refugee entrepreneurship should take into account the broader society with its own morphology, its own socio-economic, cultural and political dynamics and its sectors with existing business customs. This aspect can be split into two parts: the institutional environment, that is, everything that has to do with legal requirements, and the social environment. This concept is thus broader than just policy measures and also contains, among others, the compostion of urban districts, the presence of organizations and entrepreneurial habits.

Studies show that, as a consequence, the percentage of immigrant entrepreneurs is often much lower than that of the native population. An exception is immigrant groups who have been in the country for a very long period – they have had time to overcome the drawbacks mentioned earlier (Borjas, 1986; Hammarstedt, 2001).

Given the abundance of difficulties that refugee entrepreneurs have to overcome (in comparison with the native population and other immigrants), it can be expected that they will be more limited in number and they will earn less. Li (2000) found that self-employed immigrants in Canada earned less than their salaried counterparts. A study in Chicago shows that the average income of Hispanic entrepreneurs is considerably lower than that of Asian entrepreneurs because they experience more barriers (Tienda and Raijman, 2004). It will be investigated whether this also applies for refugees in Belgium who generally experience more difficulties than do immigrants.

Regarding the differences within the group of refugee entrepreneurs, one might expect that the standard human capital characteristics, such as age, gender and education, will play a role. As we mentioned earlier, an individual needs time, experience and skills to set up an own business. Therefore, one can expect the self-employment ratio to increase with age (Hammarstedt, 2001; Lunn and Steen, 2005). It is also a fact that in general, entrepreneurship remains a male-orientated career choice. There are several possible explanations for this phenomenon, such as traditional role patterns and a more limited network. Studies have also shown that immigrants often start a business in a sector where the threshold to start is low. These are sectors where businesses require little investment and where there are not many formal requirements. These can largely be described as 'inferior' sectors where competition is hard (Kloosterman and van der Leun, 1999).

Taking the specific situation of refugees into account, we hypothesize that most refugee entrepreneurs will tend to be male, belong to an older generation and be active in rather 'inferior' sectors.

METHODOLOGY

We used two different methods: one to measure the potential for refugee entrepreneurship and one to analyse the actual self-employed refugees.

In order to measure the potential for refugee entrepreneurship, we conducted a survey among refugees and asylum seekers in the Reception Services for Newcomers in Flanders, one of the three regions in Belgium. From 2004, all refugees and asylum seekers in Flanders have been obliged to follow courses at the Reception Services for Newcomers to facilitate their integration into the new society. A short and standardized questionnaire was presented to the newcomers in the course of May and June 2005. Ultimately, 462 people filled out a questionnaire, among them 232 asylum seekers and refugees, and 221 immigrants, mainly people within the scope of family reunification, and a few with an unknown status. As far as possible, the questionnaires were translated into the mother tongue of the asylum seekers and refugees. Questionnaires were available in Dutch, French, English, Russian, Arabic, Turkish, Farsi (Persian), Serbo-Croatian, Spanish and German. The results of the survey should indicate the potential for entrepreneurship among refugees and asylum seekers. First, we look at some raw tables showing the potential and motives of refugees to set up a business of their own. Where appropriate, we make a comparison with other immigrants, who are mostly people coming to Belgium within the scope of family reunification. Next, based on theoretical insights, we analyse the relationship between the appetite for entrepreneurship and some background variables and past experiences of the refugees.

Second, to get an idea of the actual number of self-employed refugees, we examine the data of the Social Security Services for Self-employed (RSVZ). Since every person in Belgium who is self-employed is included in the RSVZ datasets, we shall use the term 'self-employed' instead of the more specific term 'entrepreneur' for the analyses using these data. We used RSVZ datasets from 1997 to 2003, which included all refugees who have a self-employed social status. This allows us to draw a profile of self-employed refugees and also to analyse their (officially declared) income. Unfortunately, the nationality of the refugees is not included in these datasets. The revenue of the self-employed equals the gross enterprise income less the gross enterprise expenditures and any possible enterprise losses. Therefore, it is possible that this becomes negative. Those self-employed who have a negative income are treated as if they have no income because the RSVZ datasets only indicate that there is a negative revenue, but do not indicate the extent of this loss. For the revenue analysis, only people with self-employment as their main activity are included. The data are always from the year of reference, which is used to calculate the amount of social contributions a self-employed person has to pay. The year of reference is always three years before the actual year. For instance, social contributions paid in 2003 are calculated on the revenues of the year of reference, 2000.

We should, however, interpret the figures with caution. The data concern only the formal self-employed activities of refugees, not their activities in the informal economy. Moreover, many recognized refugees who have been in the country for several years have, since the so-called 'fast Belgian law' of 2000, availed themselves of the opportunity to get Belgian nationality quickly and easily. Once they are granted Belgian nationality, they are no longer registered as a refugee in the RSVZ dataset. It is thus possible that the self-employment rate of refugees is slightly higher than the figures indicate.

POTENTIAL FOR ENTREPRENEURSHIP AMONG REFUGEES

We start our analysis by measuring the potential for refugee entrepreneurship. The newcomers were asked, first, whether they had ever considered becoming an entrepreneur in the host society. The percentage of refugees who take into consideration the possibility of self-employment is quite high. Only 25 per cent of them declare that they would rather not or definitely not consider this option (see Table 9.1). Some 19 per cent declare that they will definitely consider setting up an own business, while more than a third claim that they will probably or definitely start up as an entrepreneur. It can be concluded that many of the refugees show at least some interest in working as an entrepreneur. This percentage significantly outnumbers the appetite-for-entrepreneurship percentage of other immigrants, who largely comprise people entering Belgium within the scope of family reunification.

Table 9.1 Have you ever considered becoming self-employed?

	Refugees ($N=223$)		Immigrants ($N=189$)	
	%	Cumulative %	%	Cumulative %
Definitely	18.83	18.83	16.93	16.93
Probably	17.49	36.22	6.88	23.81
Perhaps	38.12	74.44	46.56	70.37
Rather not	14.35	88.79	16.40	86.77
Definitely not	11.21	100.00	13.23	100.00

Notes: The categories 'don't know' and 'no answer' are omitted here. They contain 0.43% and 3.45% of the refugees and 0% and 5.03% of the immigrants.
$Chi^2 = 11.6931$, $df = 4$, $p < 0.05$.

Next, we examine the reasons why refugees want to set up a business of their own, and we investigate which of the theories holds for refugee entrepreneurship.

The reason for entrepreneurship with the highest score is to expedite integration into Belgian society (see Table 9.2). This reason can be classified in the integration model and refers to one of the assumptions of this research, namely that entrepreneurship can help integration. As we apply a *t*-test, it becomes clear that this is the only reason that differs significantly between immigrants and refugees. Negative reasons (entrepreneurship as a way out of unemployment, the reaction model) score relatively low, although there is evidence that in practice these reasons often prevail, but with a minimal chance of success (Gold, 1988). Reasons from the entrepreneur model about the perceived attractiveness of entrepreneurship (be one's own boss, execute a profitable activity and so on) rank quite high as motives for considering setting up a business. Reasons from the economic chances model rank lower

Table 9.2 Why have you considered becoming self-employed?

	Refugees ($N=113$)		Immigrants ($N=97$)	
	Average score	Rank	Average score	Rank
To expedite my integration into Belgian society*	3.23	1	2.91	3
Because this can be a profitable activity	3.02	2	3.12	1
Because I like to be my own boss	2.99	3	2.86	4
To execute a similar activity as in my country of origin	2.87	4	2.58	7
Because I think there is a demand for my products/services	2.84	5	2.95	2
Because it is the only way out of unemployment	2.79	6	2.67	6
Entrepreneurship runs in my blood	2.64	7	2.77	5
To become rich	2.52	8	2.44	9
For the benefit of other refugees	2.42	9	2.32	10
Because there are not enough possibilities on the labour market	2.29	10	2.51	8
I came here to set up a business of my own	1.58	11	1.70	11

Note: Average score on a four-point-scale (4 = highest score) (only respondents who have definitely, probably or perhaps considered becoming self-employed). Only significant differences are reported: * $t=-2.27$, variances are equal, df = 222, $p<0.05$.

(respond to a demand of products), because refugees are often not well integrated into a tight ethnic network. As already said, the cultural model scores low for refugees, but this also applies for immigrants.

Let us now turn to the reasons why refugees are *not* inclined to become an entrepreneur. Factors related directly to the status of refugees rank highest in Table 9.3 as reasons to abandon the possibility of entrepreneurship. Uncertainty about the future scores significantly lower among immigrants, because they have more certainty about their stay in Belgium. This justifies

Table 9.3 Why would you not *consider becoming self-employed?*

	Refugees ($N=40$)		Immigrants ($N=42$)	
	Average score	Rank	Average score	Rank
Because this is too difficult for a refugee/immigrant	3.08	1	2.77	2
Because there is too much uncertainty about my future here*	3.03	2	2.53	4
Because I lack the financial means to start up a business	2.95	3	3.14	1
Because of red tape and other administrative formalities	2.84	4	2.53	4
Because the risk is too high	2.50	5	2.70	3
Entrepreneurship doesn't run in my blood***	2.48	6	1.84	13
To execute a similar activity as in my country of origin	2.45	7	2.43	7
Because there are enough other possibilities on the labour market	2.39	8	2.32	9
Because I do not think it can be a profitable activity	2.29	9	2.11	12
Because the workload of a self-employed person is too heavy	2.28	10	2.34	8
I've never thought about that	2.25	11	2.47	6
Because the demand for my products/services is too small	2.16	12	2.14	10
Because I already have a good job**	1.56	13	2.14	10

Note: Average score on a four-point-scale (4 = highest score) (only respondents who have, would rather not, or would definitely not consider becoming self-employed). Only significant differences are reported: * $t=-1.86$, variances are equal, df $=75$, $p<0.1$; ** $t=2.10$, variances are unequal, df $=61.7$, $p<0.05$; *** $t=-2.25$, variances are equal, df $=65$, $p<0.05$.

our approach to treat refugees and immigrants separately in the analysis of entrepreneurship. Another factor impeding the start-up of a business for both refugees and immigrants is a lack of capital. Immigrants also seem to have more job alternatives than refugees, because they more often cite already having a good job as a reason why they are not considering starting as an entrepreneur. Here again, for each variable a *t*-test was conducted to compare the means of refugees and immigrants.

We now look at factors influencing the appetite for refugee entrepreneurship. To test the above-mentioned hypotheses based on the demographic approach, we develop a cumulative logit model. The appetite for entrepreneurship is the dependent ordinal variable in this model and has five categories: definitely not, rather not, perhaps, probably and definitely. The independent variables in the model are the gender of the respondents (0 = male, 1 = female), the self-employed activity in the past (0 = has not been active as an entrepreneur, 1 = has been active) and the self-employed activity of parents, brothers and sisters (0 = not active as an entrepreneur, 1 = active). The three elements of the demographic approach, that is, role model, gender and experience, can be found in this analysis of appetite for refugee entrepreneurship.

In this way, we obtain four estimated equations, that is, one less than the number of categories of the dependent variable. We show only the one that is relevant in this context:

logit 2 = log (*P* definitely or probably becoming self-employed
/ 1 − *P* definitely or probably becoming self-employed)
= −0.4145 + 0.8030*** self-employment in the past
+ 0.7844*** self-employment of family −0.5899** gender
likelihood ratio = 23.9400, 3 degrees of freedom,
$p < 0.01$, $N = 180$; ** significant at 5%, *** significant at 1%.

The estimated chances and the confidence intervals for the 'odds ratios' are shown in Table 9.4. The chance that refugees have more appetite for entrepreneurship is 2.23 times higher when people have been self-employed in the past in comparison with people who have not been self-employed. If a family member has an own business, the chance that a refugee has the appetite for setting up an own enterprise is 2.19 higher than a refugee whose family members are not self-employed. The likelihood that a woman will start up an enterprise is 55 per cent of the likelihood that a male refugee will do it.

On the basis of the following formula, the chances can be calculated:

$$P \text{ (appetite for entrepreneurship)} = \exp(\text{logit}) / 1 + \exp(\text{logit}).$$

Table 9.4 Odds ratios and confidence intervals for the cumulative logit model explaining the appetite for entrepreneurship

	Odds	Confidence intervals of 95 %	
Self-employment in the past	2.232	1.264	3.942
Self-employment of family	2.191	1.277	3.760
Gender	0.554	0.320	0.961

Table 9.5 Likelihood of the appetite for entrepreneurship (logit 2: definitely or probably thinking of becoming an entrepreneur) (%)

		Family self-employed	Family not self-employed
Has not been self-employed	Male	44.52	26.81
	Female	30.79	16.88
Has been self-employed	Male	64.18	44.98
	Female	49.83	31.19

This formula allows us to present results that are more easily interpretable. For each equation a table can be constructed where for every combination of the independent variables a chance can be calculated. We shall do it here only for logit 2 (definitely or probably becoming self-employed).

Male refugees who have been self-employed in their country of origin and whose family members are self-employed have the greatest likelihood of being interested in entrepreneurship: they have a 64 per cent chance of falling into the category of people who probably or definitely want to start a business of their own (see Table 9.5). Conversely, female refugees who have not been active as an entrepreneur and whose family was not self-employed, have slightly more than a 16 per cent chance of definitely or probably starting an own business.

In conclusion, factors that influence starting up as an entrepreneur (self-employed activity in the past, entrepreneurship in the family and gender) do not vary much between Belgian people and refugees. This also proves that there is a realistic potential among refugees for entrepreneurship. If more than a third of the refugees had an independent business in their home country and this past activity enhances considerably the appetite for entrepreneurship in the new host society, then it will be evident that many refugees want to become an entrepreneur.

NUMBER, CHARACTERISTICS AND REVENUES OF SELF-EMPLOYED REFUGEES

In this section, we focus on refugees in Belgium who have a self-employment status. Table 9.6 shows that the total number of self-employed refugees is very limited and this number has even decreased in recent years. In 2003, for instance, throughout Belgium there were no more than 152 self-employed refugees. Of the total population of self-employed people, no more than 0.04 per cent are refugees, which is a very small percentage.

Taking into account that the total number of refugees amounted to 10 288 in 2003, the percentage of self-employed refugees is only 1.48 per cent. This is very low, especially taking into account the high percentage of refugees who claim that they are interested in becoming an entrepreneur. In comparison, the percentage of self-employed in the total Belgian population amounts to 8.24 per cent.

The figures about refugees should, however, be interpreted with caution (see Methodology, above). Nevertheless, the conclusion that too few refugees manage to become self-employed still holds.

Let us now turn to some background variables of the self-employed refugee. As we are working on the total population of self-employed and self-employed refugees, respectively, it is not necessary to run statistical analyses. First, we consider the gender of the self-employed.

The percentage of female self-employed refugees is clearly lower than the same percentage over the whole population of self-employed, which is about 30 per cent (see Table 9.7). The percentage of female refugees fluctuates around 15 per cent. This is higher than the percentages among

Table 9.6 Number of self-employed and refugee entrepreneurs in Belgium, 1997–2003

	1997	1998	1999	2000	2001	2002	2003
Total number of self-employed	787 171	792 806	793 854	794 923	793 481	795 257	856 655
Number of self-employed refugees	345	300	222	200	178	159	152
Percentage of self-employed refugees to the total number of self-employed	0.04	0.04	0.03	0.03	0.02	0.02	0.02

Source: Own calculations based on RSVZ data.

self-employed Turkish and Moroccan immigrants, which amounted in 1997 to 12 and 10 per cent, respectively (Lambrecht et al., 2002).

With regard to age, self-employed refugees are overrepresented in the category of people who are in their thirties and forties (see Table 9.8). They are, on the other hand, underrepresented in the categories of people in their twenties and above 50 years old. In other words, there is a strong concentration of self-employed refugees in the categories of people at their most active age. A similar phenomenon can be found among self-employed Belgians, although the concentration there is less extreme than among refugees. This also confirms the hypothesis we formulated in the theoretical framework.

Self-employed refugees are not equally spread among the different sectors in which they are active. If we take a look at the sector where refugee entrepreneurs are active, then it becomes clear that they are overrepresented in trade and in industry and handicrafts (see Table 9.9). In agriculture, services and liberal professions, they are clearly underrepresented. This confirms our hypothesis that refugee entrepreneurs are more likely to end up in 'inferior' sectors.

Following the profile of self-employed refugees, we turn now to an analysis of their revenues in order to get an indication of the success rate of refugee entrepreneurship. The average income of self-employed refugees is each year considerably lower than that of all self-employed people in Belgium (see Table 9.10). Earlier research also revealed that the average income of ethnic self-employed is lower than that of the

Table 9.7 Percentage of female self-employed to the total number of self-employed, self-employed refugees, and self-employed Moroccan and Turkish immigrants, 1997–2003

Population on which percentage of women is calculated	1997	1998	1999	2000	2001	2002	2003
All self-employed	28.27	28.46	28.71	28.90	29.05	29.23	33.93
Self-employed refugees	16.23	17.67	16.67	15.50	16.29	14.47	14.47
Moroccan immigrants	10.14	–	–	–	–	–	–
Turkish immigrants	12.05	–	–	–	–	–	–

Sources: Own calculations based on RSVZ data and Lambrecht et al. (2002).

Table 9.8 *Percentage per age category of the total number of self-employed (Tot) and self-employed refugees (Ref), 1997–2003*

Age	1997		1998		1999		2000		2001		2002		2003	
	Ref	Tot	Ref	Tot	Ref	Tot	Ref	Tot	Ref	Tot	Ref	Tot	Ref	Tot
< 30	6.96	13.86	5.00	13.32	3.60	12.00	3.00	11.54	2.25	10.91	2.52	10.27	5.92	9.60
30–39	43.19	29.09	41.00	28.92	37.84	28.28	33.00	28.01	28.65	27.61	20.75	26.97	17.11	25.97
40–49	33.91	26.71	36.33	27.05	33.33	27.67	37.50	28.05	39.89	28.57	45.91	29.11	42.11	29.81
50–59	10.72	17.97	12.33	18.35	18.92	19.11	20.00	19.70	20.79	20.28	21.38	20.85	23.68	22.02
60–64	1.74	5.66	1.67	5.68	3.15	5.86	3.00	5.71	3.93	5.65	5.03	5.72	5.26	5.93
65–69	0.58	3.09	0.67	3.07	0.45	3.20	1.00	3.07	1.12	3.02	1.26	3.07	2.63	3.00
70–79	2.61	2.93	2.67	2.99	1.35	3.20	1.50	3.21	2.25	3.20	1.89	3.22	1.97	2.95
> 79	0.29	0.65	0.33	0.61	1.35	0.68	1.00	0.71	1.12	0.76	1.26	0.79	1.32	0.72
Unknown	0.00	0.04	0.00	0.01	0.00	0.00	0.00	0.00	0.00	0.00	0.00	0.00	0.00	0.00

Source: Own calculations based on RSVZ data.

Table 9.9 Percentage per sector of the total number of self-employed and the total number of self-employed refugees, 1997–2003

		1997	1998	1999	2000	2001	2002	2003
Agriculture	Total population	10.99	10.77	10.57	10.36	10.19	10.00	10.47
	Refugees	1.16	1.00	0.45	0.00	0.00	0.00	0.00
Fisheries	Total population	0.13	0.12	0.13	0.13	0.13	0.12	0.19
	Refugees	0.29	0.33	0.45	0.50	0.56	0.00	1.32
Industry and handicrafts	Total population	21.19	20.93	20.56	20.26	20.01	20.09	20.03
	Refugees	28.99	29.67	31.53	32.00	30.34	27.04	28.29
Trade	Total population	40.56	40.67	40.80	40.78	40.73	40.54	40.24
	Refugees	51.59	49.00	50.45	53.00	53.93	56.60	53.95
Liberal professions	Total population	18.03	18.43	18.94	19.45	19.91	20.26	20.16
	Refugees	12.46	14.00	10.36	10.50	10.67	11.32	11.18
Services	Total population	8.59	8.68	8.67	8.69	8.69	8.70	8.62
	Refugees	3.48	4.33	4.50	4.50	4.49	5.03	5.26
Other	Total population	0.52	0.39	0.34	0.33	0.33	0.29	0.29
	Refugees	2.03	1.67	2.25	0.00	0.00	0.00	0.00

Source: Own calculations based on RSVZ data.

whole population of self-employed, although without providing concrete evidence (Lambrecht et al., 2002). The median income of self-employed refugees differs considerably from the average income of this group of self-employed. This leads us to the conclusion that the income distribution is uneven among self-employed refugees. This is a phenomenon that often occurs with regard to the income of self-employed people, and we shall address this issue in more detail below.

A possible explanation for the difference in revenues between refugees and other self-employed people can be found in the sector where they work. The reason behind this explanation is that self-employed refugees are more active in sectors where revenues are low. According to this reasoning, there are relatively more refugees active in less-profitable trade businesses than in, for example, liberal professions. We shall test this explanation by comparing per sector the average income of self-employed refugees with that of all the self-employed. If these average incomes are equal, then the difference in overall average income is solely due to a sector effect.

Table 9.11 shows that for every sector there is a difference in income between self-employed refugees and the total population of self-employed. This has as an implication that the overall income difference between self-employed refugees and others cannot be explained exclusively by a different distribution of the self-employed over the sectors. The

Table 9.10 *Annual average revenue (€) for total self-employed and self-employed refugees, 1997–2003, standard deviations and quartiles (without entrepreneurs with no or negative revenue)*

Year of reference	1994	1995	1996	1997	1998	1999	2000
Actual year	1997	1998	1999	2000	2001	2002	2003
Average revenue for all self-employed	–	19 233.59	19 645.55	20 403.64	21 271.45	22 163.31	22 685.34
Average revenue for refugee entrepreneurs	10 501.19	10 906.74	10 779.34	13 802.44	12 123.33	14 857.54	14 772.98
Standard deviation refugees	12 798.27	12 100.61	11 447.91	31 086.35	12 704.34	17 567.82	15 715.27
First quartile refugees (25%)	1 940.21	4 288.56	4 632.96	5 156.19	5 259.82	6 035.84	6 390.46
Median refugees (50%)	8 082.77	8 539.94	8 437.48	9 580.35	9 062.89	10 105.74	10 668.28
Third quartile refugees (75%)	12 952.44	13 857.25	13 455.73	15 249.42	15 787.57	17 355.84	17 712.31

Source: Own calculations based on RSVZ data.

Table 9.11 Annual average revenue (€) per sector for total self-employed and self-employed refugees, 1997 (without entrepreneurs with no or negative revenue)

	Total population of self-employed	Refugees
Agriculture	8 880.04	5 985.04
Fisheries	25 317.02	–
Industry and handicrafts	16 502.50	10 462.10
Trade	13 529.61	11 951.04
Liberal professions	27 323.47	22 550.03
Services	10 235.37	7 758.39
Other	14 030.65	6 731.76

Source: Own calculations based on RSVZ data.

income of self-employed refugees is on average always lower than that of other self-employed, even when we control for the sector in which they are active. The factors outlined in the theoretical framework (market opportunities, access to entrepreneurship, human capital, social networks and institutional and social environment) provide an explanation for this phenomenon.

Let us now turn again to the distribution of incomes of self-employed refugees, and investigate whether these incomes are spread or concentrated. In order to evaluate the income concentration, we develop a Lorenz curve representing the income distribution of self-employed refugees.

Figure 9.1 shows that 48 per cent of the total income of the self-employed refugees is in the hands of 70 per cent of them. This implies conversely that slightly more than half of the total income belongs to 30 per cent of the refugees with a business of their own.

The income inequality can also be expressed in quantitative terms. The Gini coefficient (twice the surface of the Lorenz curve) is the most appropriate instrument to measure this inequality. The Gini coefficient of incomes for refugee self-employed for all years under investigation is equal to 0.33. In comparison, for the total Belgian population (either self-employed or others) in 2000 this coefficient was equal to 0.31 (Vranken et al., 2002). We can state that the incomes of self-employed refugees are spread in a similar way to those of the total population. The income distribution of all Belgian self-employed, with a coefficient of 0.50, is much more unequal than these two distributions (Lambrecht and Beens, 2005). This implies that the incomes of self-employed refugees are more equally spread than those of all Belgian self-employed.

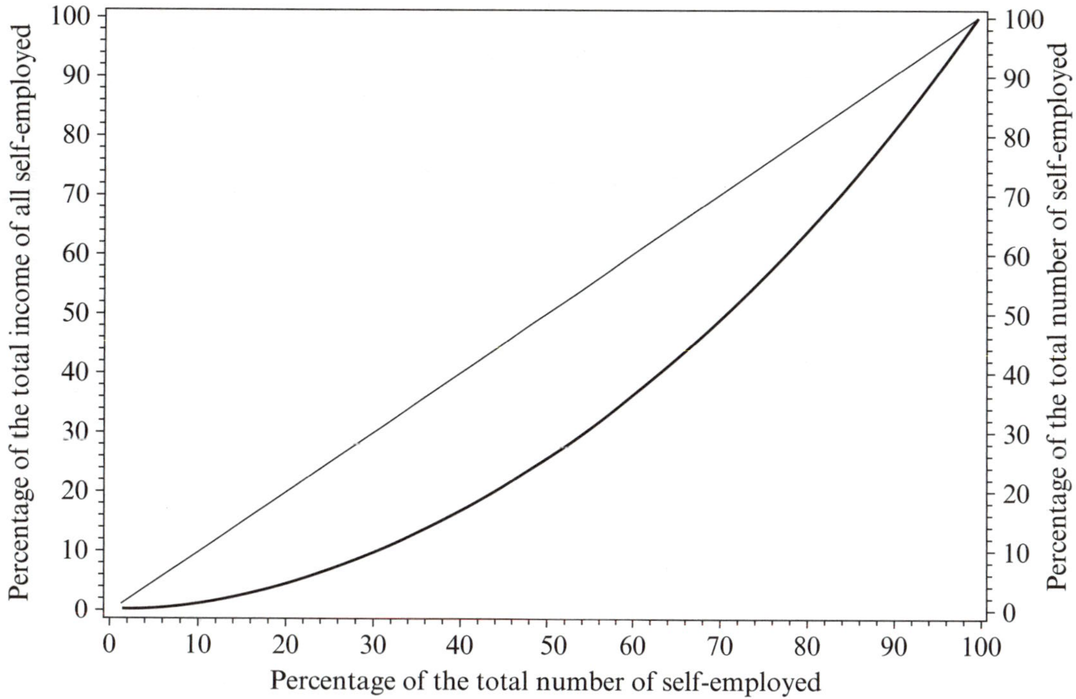

Source: Own calculations based on RSVZ data.

Figure 9.1 Lorenz curve: revenues of self-employed refugees (year of reference: 2000)

CONCLUSIONS AND SUGGESTIONS FOR FURTHER RESEARCH

In this contribution, the focus was on refugee entrepreneurship in Belgium. Refugee entrepreneurship is an underdeveloped scientific domain of research. Until now, attention has largely been on ethnic entrepreneurship in general or on the employment position of refugees in general. Refugees encounter additional difficulties in setting up and running an own business in comparison with immigrants and therefore a separate analysis is justified. The aim of this chapter was to illustrate the current state of affairs of refugee entrepreneurship. Belgium is well chosen since it is among the top countries in the world as a host society for refugees and domestic entrepreneurship would benefit from a boost.

We have focused on both the potential and the practice of refugee entrepreneurship.

It was found that more than a third of all new refugees consider self-employment a viable option. We tested five motivational theories for becoming an entrepreneur. Refugees' main motive was that they hope in this way to expedite their integration into the host society (the integration model). Reasons that also apply to native entrepreneurs, such as being their own boss (the entrepreneur model), are also high scoring. Negative motives (a way out of unemployment) are low scoring in this form of self-reporting.

With regard to the profile of refugees considering starting a business, we used the demographic approach. Refugees who have been self-employed in the past, whose direct family members have been or still are self-employed, and who are male, are more likely to have an appetite for entrepreneurship. The demographic approach is confirmed.

It is clear that there is a potential for entrepreneurship among refugees in Belgium. In the second part of this chapter, we investigated to what extent the potential for refugee entrepreneurship is put into practice and what are the characteristics of refugee self-employed. Based on the thresholds as described by Kloosterman et al. (1999) and Waldinger et al. (1990b), we expect that both the number of self-employed refugees as well as their revenues will be lower than the native population. They even suffer from additional difficulties in comparison with other ethnic entrepreneurs.

The number of self-employed refugees in Belgium is extremely low: in 2003 only 152 refugees, or only 1.48 per cent of the total number of refugees, were self-employed. Women and refugees in their twenties and older than 50 are underrepresented in the population of self-employed refugees. Self-employed refugees are concentrated in the sectors of trade, and industry and handicrafts. They are clearly underrepresented in a sector such as the liberal professions. These findings confirm our hypotheses that older male refugees were most likely to set up an own business in rather 'inferior' sectors.

The average yearly income of self-employed refugees is considerably lower than that of self-employed Belgians. This is not due to a sector effect, since in all sectors refugees earn less than other self-employed people. The revenues of all self-employed refugees do not vary widely.

This was a first analysis of refugee entrepreneurship investigated in one particular country. This analysis is only a first step and would benefit from additional analyses in other countries. In addition, other aspects of refugee entrepreneurship should be investigated in the future. Among others, the thresholds that self-employed refugees have to overcome and the consequences of the differences between immigrants and refugees are interesting aspects for further research.

NOTE

1. This is a slightly revised version of an article that appeared earlier as: B. Wauters and J. Lambrecht (2006), 'Refugee entrepreneurship in Belgium: potential and practice', *International Entrepreneurship and Management Journal*, **2** (4), 509–25, published here by kind permission of Springer. The research is part of the Rainbow economy project, which is funded by the Equal programme of the European Social Fund (ESF) and the Flemish Community Commission of the Brussels Capital Region. The Federal Impulse Fund for Immigrant Policy provided financial aid.

REFERENCES

Ajzen, I. and M. Fishbein (1980), *Understanding Attitudes and Predicting Social Behavior*, Englewood Cliffs, NJ: Prentice-Hall.

Becker, G.S. (1975), *Human Capital*, New York: NBER.

Beiser, M. and F. Hou (2000), 'Gender differences in language acquisition and employment consequences among Southeast Asian refugees in Canada', *Canadian Public Policy*, **26** (3), 311–30.

Bernard, W.S. (1977), 'Immigrants and refugees: their similarities, differences and needs', *International Migration*, **14** (4), 267–81.

Bird, B. (1988), 'Implementing entrepreneurial ideas: the case for intention', *Academy of Management Review*, **13** (3), 442–53.

Bollinger, C.R. and P. Hagstrom (2004), 'Poverty rates of refugees and immigrants', UK Centre for Poverty Research (UKCPR) Discussion Paper Series, London.

Borjas, G.J. (1986), 'The self-employment experience of immigrants', *Journal of Human Resources*, **21** (4), 487–506.

Bovenkerk, F. (1983), 'De sociologie van de allochtone onderneming', *Sociologische Gids*, **30** (3–4), 264–75.

Cortes, K. (2001), 'Are refugees different from economic immigrants? Some empirical evidence on the heterogeneity of immigrant groups in the United States',

Center for Labor Economics (University of California at Berkeley) Working Paper.

Delmar, F. and P. Davidsson (2000), 'Where do they come from? Prevalence and characteristics of nascent entrepreneurs', *Entrepreneurship and Regional Development*, **12** (1), 1–23.

DeVoretz, D., Pivnenko, S. and M. Beiser (2004), 'The economic experiences of refugees in Canada', Institute for the Study of Labor (IZA) Discussion Paper.

Gold, S.J. (1988), 'Refugees and small business: the case of Soviet Jews and Vietnamese', *Ethnic and Racial Studies*, **11** (4), 411–38.

Gold, S.J. (1992), 'The employment potentials of refugee entrepreneurship: Soviet Jews and Vietnamese in California', *Policy Studies Review*, **11** (2), 176–86.

Hammarstedt, M. (2001), 'Immigrant self-employment in Sweden – its variation and some possible determinants', *Entrepreneurship and Regional Development*, **13** (2), 147–61.

Hauff, E. and P. Vaglum (1993), 'Integration of Vietnamese refugees into the Norwegian labor market: the impact of war trauma', *International Migration Review*, **27** (2), 388–405.

Katz, J.A. (1989), 'Intentions, hurdles, and start-ups: an analysis of entrepreneurial follow-through', in Robert A. Brockhaus Jr, Neil C. Churchill, Jerome A. Katz, Bruce A. Kirchhoff, Kail H. Vesper and William E. Wetzel Jr (eds), *Proceedings of the Ninth Annual Babson College Entrepreneurship Research Conference Frontiers of Entrepreneurship Research*, Wellesley, MA: Babson College, pp. 43–57.

Kibria, N. (1995), *Family Tightrope: The Changing Lives of Vietnamese*, Princeton, NJ: Princeton University Press.

Kloosterman, R. and J. van der Leun (1999), 'Just for starters: commercial gentrification by immigrant entrepreneurs in Amsterdam and Rotterdam neighbourhoods', *Housing Studies*, **14** (5), 659–77.

Kloosterman, R., J. van der Leun and J. Rath (1999), 'Mixed embeddedness: (in)formal economic activities and immigrant businesses in the Netherlands', *International Journal of Urban and Regional Research*, **23** (2), 252–67.

Kontos, M. (2003), 'Self-employment policies and migrants' entrepreneurship in Germany', *Entrepreneurship and Regional Development*, **15** (2), 119–35.

Lambrecht, J. and E. Beens (2005), 'Poverty among self-employed businesspeople in a rich country: a misunderstood and distinct reality', *Journal of Developmental Entrepreneurship*, **10** (3), 205–22.

Lambrecht, Johan, Christine Van Liedekerke, Noemi de Guzman and Marc Vanbruwaene (2004), *Ontwikkeling van ondernemerschap tijdens studietijd aan EHSAL*, Brussels: EHSAL.

Lambrecht, H., H. Verhoeven and A. Martens (2002), *Ondernemende allochtonen . . . of allochtone ondernemers? Ondernemers!*, Leuven: Departement Sociologie (KU Leuven).

Leung, M.W.H. (2003), 'Beyond Chinese, beyond food: unpacking the regulated Chinese restaurant business in Germany', *Entrepreneurship and Regional Development*, **15** (2), 103–18.

Li, P.S. (2000), 'Economic returns of immigrants' self-employment', *Canadian Journal of Sociology*, **25** (1), 1–34.

Lunn, J. and T. Steen (2005), 'The heterogeneity of self-employment: the example of Asians in the United States', *Small Business Economics*, **24** (2), 143–58.

Masurel, E., P. Nijkamp, M. Tastan and G. Vindigni (2002), 'Motivations and performance conditions for ethnic entrepreneurship', *Growth and Change*, **33** (2), 238–60.

Pécoud, A. (2003), 'Self-employment and immigrants' incorporation: the case of Turks in Germany', *Immigrants and Minorities*, **22** (2–3), 247–61.

Robinson, P.B., D.V. Stimpson, J.C. Huefner and H.K. Hunt (1991), 'An attitude approach to the prediction of entrepreneurship', *Entrepreneurship Theory and Practice*, **15** (4), 13–32.

Scherer, R.F., J.D. Brodzinski and F.A. Wiebe (1991), 'Examining the relationship between personality and entrepreneurial preference', *Entrepreneurship and Regional Development*, **3** (3), 195–206.

Shapero, A. (1982), 'Social dimensions of entrepreneurship', in C. Kant, D. Sexton and K. Vesper (eds), *The Encyclopedia of Entrepreneurship*, Englewood Cliffs, NJ: Prentice-Hall, pp. 72–90.

Tienda, M. and R. Raijman (2004), 'Promoting Hispanic immigrant entrepreneurship in Chicago', *Journal of Developmental Entrepreneurship*, **9** (1), 1–21.

Tkachev, A. and L. Kolvereid (1999), 'Self-employment intentions among Russian students', *Entrepreneurship and Regional Development*, **11** (3), 269–80.

United Nations High Commissioner for Refugees (UNHCR) (2005), *Asylum Levels and Trends in Industrialized Countries, 2004. Overview of asylum applications lodged in Europe and non-European industrialized countries in 2004*, Geneva: Population data unit/PGDS (UNHCR).

Valtonen, K. (1999), 'The societal participation of Vietnamese refugees: case studies in Finland and Canada (Statistical Data Included)', *Journal of Ethnic and Migration Studies*, **25** (3), 469–91.

Vlerick Leuven Gent Management School (2005), *Global Entrepreneurship Monitor Belgium and Flanders*, Gent: Vlerick Leuven Gent Management School.

Vranken, Jan, Katrien De Boyser, Dirk Geldof and Gerard Van Menxel (eds) (2002), *Armoede en sociale uitsluiting. Jaarboek 2002*, Leuven: Acco.

Waldinger, R., H. Aldrich and R. Ward (eds) (1990a), *Ethnic Entrepreneurs: Immigrant Businesses in Industrial Societies*, Newbury Park, CA: Sage.

Waldinger, R., H. Aldrich and R. Ward (1990b), 'Opportunities, group characteristics, and strategies', in Waldinger et al. (eds), pp. 13–48.

Ward, R. and R. Jenkins (eds) (1984), *Ethnic Communities in Business: Strategies for Economic Survival*, Cambridge: Cambridge University Press.

Westhead, P. and M. Wright (1999), 'Contributions of novice, portfolio, and serial founders located in rural and urban areas', *Regional Studies*, **33** (2), 157–73.

10. The role of gender for entrepreneurship in a transition context

Friederike Welter, David Smallbone, Nina Isakova and Elena Aculai

INTRODUCTION

Female entrepreneurship and gender differences in small business development continue to be at the forefront of research in many countries. Most research so far has been conducted in the context of mature market economies and it is focused on identifying female entrepreneurs' characteristics and gender differences in areas such as sector and business features, motivation, education and previous experience, psychological characteristics, finance, barriers to development and growth, and networking (for example, Scott, 1986; Cromie, 1987; Aldrich, 1989; Fay and Williams, 1993; Catley and Hamilton, 1998). Based on a literature review of some 400 academic articles on female entrepreneurs, Carter et al. (2001) have revealed that literature on the topic is developing in the direction of investigating more specifically gender differences in business management, finance, business networks and performance, but they conclude that cumulative knowledge and explanatory theories are still lacking.

What role does gender play in relation to entrepreneurship in a transition context? In transition environments, the contribution of women in business extends from the economic sphere to include the wider process of social transformation. The wide political, economic and social reforms in former socialist countries deprived many women of the paid jobs and social security provided by government, thereby forcing them to find alternative ways of generating income. Starting a business was one of the options facing entrepreneurial women, shaped by a combination of push and pull factors. Previous research on female entrepreneurs in transition countries has concentrated on their characteristics (for example, Glas and Petrin, 1998; Lokar, 2000). Research on female entrepreneurs in Russia and Ukraine (Ivaschenko, 1994; Babayeva and Chirikova, 1996) as well as in Hungary

(Koncz, 2000) revealed gender differences with respect to the motivation, business sectors, business characteristics and strategies. However, most of these earlier studies neglect both the heterogeneity of female entrepreneurship and the influence of the role attributed to women in society on the nature and extent of their involvement in entrepreneurship. In transition economies it is important to recognize the differing cultural background between, and even within, countries as well as varying historical paths and the previous and current role of women in society. Regional differences could aggravate constraints on female entrepreneurship not only where the business environment and the access to external resources and support are concerned, but also with respect to the role of women when traditional clan and patriarchal family structures restrict female roles.

In this context, this particular chapter sets out to analyse similarities and differences between male and female entrepreneurs, their businesses and strategies such as networking in different transition environments. This is an exploratory study, in which we contrast results from research done in a mature market context with empirical results from different transition countries in Eastern Europe and Central Asia. More specifically, the following issues, which are popular in literature on female entrepreneurship in mature market economies, will be explored: what are the similarities and differences between male and female entrepreneurs and their businesses across a number of countries? In what ways does gender enable or constrain entrepreneurs, with respect to the types of business started? Do problems facing businesses differ across gender groups? Does gender assist/constrain women in dealing with the external business environment? Are female entrepreneurs more or less successful in this regard? Following a review of these themes, based on existing literature on gender differences, these issues will be examined empirically for a transition context, drawing on survey and case-study data from our own studies for three transition countries, supplemented by evidence from other countries where available.

The main empirical data come from an international research project (Intas 00-0843). The survey was conducted in 2002. In Ukraine, a total of 297 female and a control group of 81 male entrepreneurs were surveyed; in Uzbekistan, 200 and 60, respectively; and in Moldova, 218 and 63. Case studies with up to 30 women and five men each were also carried out in each country in spring 2003.

One of the issues this raises concerns the nature of the evidence base. In this regard, Scase (2003) refers to a lack of reliable data leading, among other things, to extremely unreliable estimates of the real significance of entrepreneurship and small business ownership in a transition context. However, while secondary data constraints, and the difficulties of systematically conducting empirical research in some of the former Soviet republics, should not be underestimated, the challenge for researchers is to develop methodological approaches that are appropriate to the context in which they are being used, as well as to the research questions they are addressing. Large-scale surveys can be undertaken in transition circumstances, and can produce potentially useful results, provided that they are interpreted in the context in which the data were gathered, with the limits to generalization clearly defined. At the same time, such methods can benefit from being used in combination with more process-orientated qualitative approaches, which on some issues can produce quite different results from those based on survey responses (Welter and Smallbone, 2003).

The chapter is structured as follows. First, we present results from a literature review on the role of gender for entrepreneurship in mature market economies. Second, we describe the distinctive context for women in a transition country, and third, we explore the issues emerging from the literature review in the light of empirical results for transition countries. The final section indicates implications and conclusions for future research and policy makers.

THE ROLE OF GENDER FOR ENTREPRENEURSHIP IN MATURE MARKET ECONOMIES: REVIEWING THE LITERATURE

Entrepreneurs and their Businesses: Similarities and Differences

Studies of the characteristics of female entrepreneurs and their businesses are one of the most popular topics in the field of female entrepreneurship (Carter et al., 2001). Gender-specific differences have been found by occupation and industry, in business characteristics and in the entrepreneur's characteristics and background. Research indicates the relative youth of female businesses (ibid.); the longer working hours of female entrepreneurs (for example, McManus, 2001); and women's propensity to start businesses in industries with low entry barriers, such as retailing and services (for example, Baygan, 2000; Lohmann and Luber, 2000). Women have also been found to display a greater lack of prior work experience, training and business experience (for example, Jungbauer-Gans and Preisendörfer, 1992). Several studies also confirm gender-specific differences in human, social and financial capital, as well as with respect to access to resources (for example, Brush, 1992; Carter and Rosa, 1998; Verheul and Thurik, 2001).

In summarizing the results from several empirical surveys, Baygan (2000) describes the average female entrepreneur as belonging to the 35–44 age group; being married and having children; having less formal or business-related education or prior work experience; and starting their businesses to generate extra income for the household, as well as for non-economic motives. In terms of business characteristics, female entrepreneurs mainly set up their ventures with lower start-up capital than men; and firms owned by women are generally found to be smaller in size compared to those owned by men. At the same time, female entrepreneurs are increasingly getting involved in less traditional sectors.

Brush (1992), having reviewed 57 papers on female business owners, concludes that women are similar to men in some aspects, such as basic demographic factors, business characteristics and problems, but are different in work experience, education, skills, business goals and performance. Generally, most studies researching personal characteristics of female entrepreneurs find more similarities with than differences from male counterparts.

Entering Entrepreneurship

The individual path into entrepreneurship has an important effect on business development and business performance, because the venture creation process is closely linked to acquiring resources, thus partly determining the development potential of new businesses. Again, gender differences with respect to the motives for starting a business, together with research on differing business aims, is a popular research area, although the evidence shows non-conclusive results. Women start a business because they are looking for job satisfaction, independence and achievement, although men enter business for similar reasons (Carter et al., 2001). Reasons for start-up, such as 'independence', 'controlling time', 'flexibility for personal and family life' and 'freedom to adapt one's own approach to work' have been found to be similar for women and men (Shane et al., 1991). However, there are studies which suggest differences in their motives, and/or the emphasis they attach to particular motives (Catley and Hamilton, 1998). According to other sources (Baygan, 2000), women come into business to generate extra income for their households, or to be independent and creative. Although the 'push group', which includes women who are forced into business, is comparatively larger, the 'pull group' of those who are looking for independence and self-realization in business, is argued to be growing (ibid.).

With regard to objectives, several studies have drawn attention to the fact that women aim at combining both business and family responsibilities, reflecting a more intrinsic goal setting, while men tend to concentrate more on economic objectives (for example, Brush, 1992; Rosa et al., 1994, 1996; Meyer and Harabi, 2000). In this regard, while Rosa et al. (1996) indicate gender-related differences in quantitative economic and financial performance measures, their results are non-conclusive with respect to the more intrinsic goal-setting of female entrepreneurs, thus underlining the complexity of this topic.

Additionally, human capital in the form of education and professional experiences plays a role in shaping women's routes into entrepreneurship. Research demonstrates that especially industry- and activity-related experiences, and the level of education, influence the ways into entrepreneurship and the forms that female entrepreneurship takes, such as the sectors that women enter. With respect to education level, Brush (1992) argues that while women and men display similar levels of education, gender-specific education topics account for the preference that female entrepreneurs display for trade and service industries, because most women still prefer human and social sciences to natural sciences and traditional service professions such as health occupations or hairdressing to innovative service occupations.

At the same time, such issues raise a question concerning how far these differences in founding behaviour can be attributed to gender. Some differences in venture creation appear to be a result of the smaller resource base that women are typically able to access at start-up, which leads to cautious behaviour and a longer venture creation process. However, caution can also be associated with a greater feeling of responsibility with respect to their family/household, which can lead to more risk-averse behaviour, thus influencing paths into entrepreneurship and consequently performance and business success.

Performance and Business Success

Several studies appear to confirm gender differences in business outcomes for female and male entrepreneurs, both across representative samples of firms and within specific business niches (for example, Kalleberg and Leicht, 1991; Srinivasan et al., 1994; Rosa et al., 1996; Du Rietz and Henrekson, 2000; McManus, 2001). Moreover, research often points out different success criteria for male and female entrepreneurs (for example, Stevenson, 1986; Buttner and Moore, 1997; Cliff, 1998; Jennings and Provorny Cash, 2006). However, evidence concerning gender-specific influences on business performance and the growth potential of female-owned businesses is not consistent. Storey (1994) reviewed several studies that examined gender and its influence on firm growth, showing that in most cases, gender was not a significant factor. Gender appears to play a more indirect role, through its influence on the sectoral preferences of female entrepreneurs, for example, and industry environments in turn influence the growth potential of their business. Evidence from different countries indicates that female business owners prefer to start their business in sectors where female employment is concentrated (for example, Lohmann and Luber, 2000; Luber and Leicht, 2000; McManus, 2001; Brush et al., 2006), such as wholesale and retail trades, hotels and restaurants, and services. However, these low-entry threshold sectors are also characterized by high turbulence rates, thus providing few opportunities for rapid business growth (Storey, 1994). In this context, several studies have drawn attention to the fact that gender-specific differences in survival and growth rates disappear when data are controlled for industry and size (for example, Jungbauer-Gans, 1993; Du Rietz and Henrekson, 2000; Rosa et al., 1996).

Gender also plays a role with respect to business performance in so far as it influences the self-perception of women with respect to their ability to realize business growth or to the desirability that society attaches to business success. Additionally, the nature and extent of family support could influence the performance of female-owned businesses, referring to the emotional and financial support that the family may offer, as well as family labour, where previous research has demonstrated that non-formal husband and wife teams can play a vital role in the performance of micro enterprises (Baines and Wheelock, 1998). However, Mirchandani (1999) points to the lower legitimacy of home-based businesses, which might influence their standing with creditors and customers.

Overall, the research evidence suggests that gender differences in organizational performance may be less due to the gender of the business owner and more a result of environmental influences, such as the embeddedness of the business, the location (ibid.), industry differences and the size of the business with individual characteristics of the entrepreneur representing an additional layer (Kalleberg and Leicht, 1991). In addition, as Brush and Hisrich (2000) state, performance differences between male- and female-owned businesses also depend on the measurements used, emphasizing that future research should study outcomes other than financial measures, which draws attention to the interdependence among performance, success and goals.

Networks and Networking

Gender differences in network structures and networking behaviour may influence both the decision to start and to develop a business, as well as business survival and success (Carter et al., 2001). Social contacts play a role in mobilizing complementary resources, getting support and help, and establishing viable business relations (Greve, 1995). In a review on business networks, Blundel and Smith (2001: 37) conclude that during venture creation most entrepreneurs rely on informal sources in their personal networks in order to mobilize resources, especially before the venture is set up. Another study shows that social networks have both a direct and an indirect effect (through access to resources) on the degree of start-up success; this applies in particular to the number of initial weak ties and emerging strong ties (Jenssen, 2001). Moreover, networks play a role in creating legitimacy for new ventures. Although results with regard to the role of strong and weak ties for entrepreneurship are not conclusive, most empirical studies confirm a link between networking and positive business development. Whether it is strong ties and/or weak ties appears to depend to a large extent on the operationalization of network variables (Hoang and Antoncic, 2003).

Network research is a popular topic; however, only a few studies research gender differences in this regard. At first glance, those empirical studies show several gender-related effects. For example, Allen (2000) reports that female networks typically include fewer entrepreneurs, which might restrict their outreach and usefulness for a female entrepreneur. Other studies report more homogeneous and fewer outreaching networks for women, as well as less frequent networking activities (for example, Caputo and Dolinsky, 1998; Carter et al., 2001; Schutjens and Stam, 2003).

While differences in network structures appear to be an accepted empirical result, the results with respect to network content and frequency are not conclusive. For example, Aldrich et al. (1986) did not confirm gender differences in network size and the frequency of networking between entrepreneurs. In addition, Renzulli et al. (2000) indicate that women rely on homogeneous networks with a larger share of kinship relations. According to their results, it is less gender than kinship that creates disadvantages in starting a venture. All this leads McManus (2001: 82) to conclude that with respect to women 'it has yet to be empirically established that these entrepreneurial networks are effective at facilitating the transition to self-employment'.

THE CONTEXT FOR WOMEN'S ENTREPRENEURSHIP IN A TRANSITION ENVIRONMENT

The Transition Process and Entrepreneurship Development

Differences in starting-points, in the nature and pace of market reforms and in the wider process of social and economic change during the transformation period have resulted in considerable differences in transition environments. This affects both the nature and the extent of women's entrepreneurship, reflected in the number of female-owned businesses, and the nature of the contribution of female entrepreneurs to the transformation process. This is very much related to the external conditions in which they are operating, including the extent of market reforms, such as the privatization of former state-owned firms; establishing a legal framework; creating the overall institutional conditions; and the policy stance adopted by government. A comparison between Central European and former Soviet countries reveals considerable differences. For example, in policy terms, female entrepreneurship in EU candidate countries can be expected to contribute to both the competitiveness and social inclusion agendas, while in former Soviet countries the major contribution will be in terms of contributing to income and creating (self-)employment possibilities.

In assessing transition progress, indicators of the European Bank of Reconstruction and Development (EBRD) show wide variation between countries on various dimensions. For example, small-scale privatization varies from Croatia, the Czech Republic, Hungary, the three Baltic states, Poland, the Slovak Republic and Slovenia at one extreme (high) to Belarus and Turkmenistan at the other (low). In terms of price liberalization, the spectrum ranges from Hungary, Poland, Slovenia, Romania and Moldova at one extreme (high) to Belarus, Turkmenistan and Uzbekistan at the other (low).

However, any transition model based solely on economic and political reforms neglects the wider social, historical and cultural context of these countries, which in turn influences their transition path. Transition cannot be explained by economic and political reforms alone. Other researchers have sought to explain a quicker or slower pace of transformation through the differential influence of 'communist legacies' on different transition paths. Thus, in situations where market reforms have been slow or only partially installed, the institutional context becomes a critical factor for entrepreneurship, since government still has to create the framework conditions for private sector development to become embedded and sustained.

In this respect, we differentiate between transition countries whose reform progress is slow and those transition countries where reforms have progressed more quickly, mainly the new member states of the European Union and upcoming candidate countries, taking into account that differences in the extent of market reforms, combined with other economic, social and historical differences limit the scope for generalization across the variety of countries that comprise Central and Eastern Europe and the former Soviet Union. All this contributes to a different background of (female) entrepreneurs in transition conditions, which interacts with characteristics of the institutional environment to influence the nature and extent of women's entrepreneurship.

The Soviet Legacy for Female Entrepreneurs

Gender could represent an additional dimension, in that the evolving institutional framework might affect women's formal integration into the emerging market economy due to redefined and changed gender roles, which restricts their access to the external resources and organizations that are needed in order to realize a venture. Moreover, female entrepreneurship in transition countries such as Ukraine and Moldova or Central European countries differs from that in Central Asian countries, because here traditional cultural values survived throughout the Soviet period, gaining in importance during the transition period.

With respect to women's roles, Fajth (2000: 90) describes many achievements of the Soviet period as superficial and the underlying process as authoritarian rather than rights based. Although the Soviet state sought to redefine the role of women in society, in order to utilize their economic potential, the preferred Soviet role model was still the worker-mother whose duties were to work, produce children and run the household, while the state assisted them in meeting their competing role demands by providing the legal and institutional framework that included benefits for working mothers, job protection and childcare systems (Ashwin, 2000; Zhurzhenko, 2001). Even though the Soviet state partly socialized the male role to provide for the family, traditional gender relations persisted (Kiblitskaya, 2000). During the 1920s, the post-revolution boom in policies and practices with respect to equal rights for men and women was limited geographically to large industrial cities and socially to the working class and professionals ('intelligentsia').

Although theoretically based on concepts of equality, in practice, the Soviet system discriminated against women, who experienced a glass ceiling in politics and economy. Starting from the 1930s, a shift towards a 'double burden' of responsibilities for women occurred, as the state placed on women the responsibility for performing simultaneously the roles of a successful worker and a successful mother. At the same time, men were looked upon as agents of political, economic and social changes and progress. Within families, the patriarchal order prevailed, with women in charge of family budgets, household activities, raising children and serving their husband. The Second World War and the post-war period only added to the double burden, since women needed to work harder in order to replace men, who were serving in the army, or were lost in the war.

Overall, despite an ideological commitment to promoting emancipation through the participation of women in the labour market, Soviet women still faced conflicting roles in economy and society. Thus, the Soviet state left a 'paradoxical legacy' with 'strong and independent women who nevertheless ended up doing all the housework' (Ashwin, 2000: 18), while tacitly acknowledging and supporting male dominance in the public sphere.

Female Roles in the Transition Period

During the transition period, women's double burden was aggravated further when family support systems collapsed. While the Soviet working-mother contract is responsible for the ongoing interest of women in work, the responsibilities of motherhood became redefined. Following the destruction of the state social welfare and childcare system, post-Soviet governments transferred motherhood and family responsibilities back into the private sphere, which post-Soviet society was quick to accept. Theoretically, the contemporary revival of patriarchal values should have given post-Soviet women the choice of staying at home. However, widespread and rising female unemployment, combined with growing labour market discrimination, forced more and more women into business ownership, in order to be able to support their families. This happened especially in the early years of transformation and in countries where reforms did not progress quickly. Moreover, although post-Soviet women look for emotional, practical and financial support from their spouses, they also value the independence that any paid work gives them.

However, in post-Soviet countries, female entrepreneurs often lack the established networks that their male colleagues brought with them from Soviet times (Welter et al., 2003), which disadvantages them in entrepreneurship. Formerly, men held most of the leading positions in politics and in state enterprises, which resulted in women being omitted from the Soviet nomenclatura, from 'parallel circuits' in state firms and other high-level networks, which have been suggested as important influences on the development of entrepreneurship during the transition period (Smallbone and Welter, 2001). As a result, at the beginning of the transition process, women had fewer opportunities to enter entrepreneurship, either through the privatization of large state firms, or through setting up small spin-off firms from larger state enterprises. Only where they could transfer their management position from the Soviet period into ownership, were women successful in entering entrepreneurship through the small-scale privatization of shops, restaurants and pharmacies.

On the other hand, networking contacts, especially where they involve strong ties, might be more important for women in post-Soviet societies than for men, in helping them to overcome traditional role patterns. In general, where the institutional framework for entrepreneurship does not function properly, personal networks and contacts often assist entrepreneurs in getting access to resources (Ledeneva, 1998). Networking can facilitate market entry and influence the business field chosen, as well as assisting daily business operations in such environments.

In a post-Soviet context, business is typically considered a predominantly 'male territory', requiring so-called 'male' qualities, such as strength and assertiveness. This is not surprising in Central Asian countries, for example, where cultural values emphasizing family relations survived throughout the Soviet period, though gaining momentum, once transition started (Tabyshalieva, 2000). However, there is a similar trend in the European post-Soviet countries, such as the Ukraine or Moldova, reflected in 'widely held public assumptions that business is a masculine occupation' (Zhurzhenko, 1999: 246). Akiner (1997: 287) describes this as re-establishing the 'concept of male guardianship', in both public and private life, which is a trend with enormous potential consequences for female entrepreneurship and for the role that social capital tends to play. For example, research on young entrepreneurs in transition economies has revealed that female entrepreneurs in NIS (newly independent states) countries were more likely to pursue a business with their husband/friend or father as partners or guardians, while in Central European countries it was apparently easier for women to act as entrepreneurs on their own (Roberts and Tholen, 1999).

Moreover, Bruno (1997) refers to the distinctive styles of female entrepreneurship in post-Soviet countries because of the effect of women's experiences during the Soviet period in organizing their household consumption. This left women during the post-Soviet period with some experience of managing shortages, through a complicated system of bartering goods and favours and cultivating informal knowledge and information networks. In this respect, female entrepreneurs would have quick access to social capital as well as being able to benefit from their experiences.

Regional variations add another dimension to the distinctiveness of female roles in transition economies (Welter et al., 2003). Core–periphery differences include variations in the pace of institutional change, where access to the external resources needed for business development is typically easier in core regions, because of the quicker path of institutional transition. In addition, there are regional differences in the level of effective demand, which affects the opportunities for entrepreneurship, including the participation of females. Core–periphery differences also reflect cultural traditions, which can vary within countries, as well as between them. In Uzbekistan, for example, 70 per cent of the population live in rural areas which are characterized by strong clan and patriarchal family structures, with major implications for the role for women. This often results in women taking up activities that can be home based, but which are also part time and low income, with relatively low growth opportunities.

THE ROLE OF GENDER FOR ENTREPRENEURSHIP IN A TRANSITION CONTEXT: EMPIRICAL RESULTS

Overall, the results from the literature review are not conclusive in attributing observed differences in the types of businesses established, and also in business behaviour, to gender alone. This particularly applies to differences in size and in the income of female-owned businesses, which are also associated with the general business or industry environment, rather than demonstrating gender-inherent differences. Does this pattern differ in a transition context? This will be explored by drawing on our empirical data for Moldova, Ukraine and Uzbekistan and additional country studies.

Enterprises and Entrepreneurs

The sector distribution of female-owned businesses in transition economies reflects a picture well known in Western countries. In all three countries in our study, most female businesses have been set up in services and trade. At the same time, manufacturing accounts for nearly one-quarter of all surveyed female enterprises, although these are typically involved in low-value-added activities in sectors, such as clothing and food processing.

Where differences across countries occur, they reflect the stage of transition reached as well as country-specific environments. For example, the Ukrainian sample shows the highest share of female entrepreneurs in services (50 per cent, compared with 37 per cent in all countries), while Moldovan women show an above-average propensity to operate in trade (38 per cent, total 30 per cent). In Uzbekistan a comparatively larger share of women set up a business in agriculture (14 per cent, total 5.6 per cent). Manufacturing comprises a wide range of activities such as manufacture of toys, food processing and clothing. In Uzbekistan particularly, traditional crafts (for example, gold embroidery, carpet weaving, silk weaving) feature significantly in women's business activities, reflecting the traditional, housebound role of women especially in rural areas (Welter et al., 2006). Trade includes both retail and wholesale activities, while services range from simple personal and consumer services to more complex, higher-value-added activities, such as medical services, language schools, transport and the law. With respect to size, most surveyed female-owned enterprises (60 per cent) employed between one and nine employees, one-third had 10–49 employees. Only around 9 per cent of the female entrepreneurs worked on their own.

Regardless of gender, entrepreneurs in the three surveyed countries were mainly between 30 and 49 years old; there were few female entrepreneurs below 30 years of age, despite high levels of youth unemployment. In Uzbekistan, this appears to reflect traditional role models, which attribute a housebound role to young girls. In comparison to men (20 per cent), only 6 per cent of Uzbek female entrepreneurs were below 30 years old. Three-quarters of the interviewed women had up to three children. Ukrainian women more frequently had only one child (47 per cent), while Moldovan women mainly had two children. More than one-third of the Uzbek women had four or five children, reflecting traditional values in Uzbekistan. Thus in Moldova and Uzbekistan, in particular, women typically combined entrepreneurship with child-rearing, with implications for the types of activity they were able to engage in, as well as for their motives for engaging in them.

Before starting their business, women were mainly employed in the state sector, although a significant minority (17 per cent) had also worked in private businesses, particularly in the case of Ukrainian and Moldovan women (23 and 19 per cent, respectively). A similar picture emerges for men, although a considerably higher share of Uzbek men had previously worked in private businesses (28 per cent) than their female counterparts, which again emphasizes the dominant values of a traditional society. The majority of women and men had university-level education, followed by nearly 30 per cent of women with secondary vocational education. This especially applied to women entrepreneurs in Uzbekistan (37 per cent), while more Ukrainian women (73 per cent; 50 per cent in Uzbekistan, and 62 per cent in Moldova) had a university degree, reflecting the paucity of opportunities for educated people to find satisfying ways of earning a living in primitive transition conditions.

The well-educated profile of entrepreneurs in transition countries is a commonly described characteristic. At the same time, it has potential implications for business behaviour, because of the human capital involved. Several studies confirm this for female entrepreneurs across a wide variety of transition countries, including new member states: the Czech Republic (Lituchy and Reavley, 2004), Lithuania (Aidis, 2006), Slovenia (Drnovsek and Glas, 2006), Poland (Mrcozskowski, 1997; Lituchy and Reavley, 2004); candidate countries such as Bulgaria (Manolova, 2006); and other former Soviet countries such as Russia (Wells et al., 2003).

The overall conclusion is that the socio-demographic profile of female entrepreneurs emerging from previous empirical studies and supported by our survey data, is similar to the picture from studies on female entrepreneurs in a mature market context. The notable exception is the generally high education level of female (and male) entrepreneurs in transition countries.

Entering and Developing a Business

Until recently, the mass media in transition economies have tended to depict female entrepreneurs as women forced by circumstances to trade in the marketplace in order to provide support for their families or because of their poor employment possibilities. Again, the results of several research studies covering a whole variety of transition countries such as Lithuania (Aidis, 2006), Moldova (Aculai et al., 2006), the Ukraine (Isakova, 2001; Isakova et al., 2006), Poland (Lituchy and Reavley, 2004; Mrcozkowski, 1997), Slovakia (Bliss and Garratt, 2001), Kyrgyzstan (Öczan, 2006) and Uzbekistan (Welter et al., 2006) provide evidence to support this type (among others), particularly in the early stages of transition.

In our survey, the reasons given by female entrepreneurs for entering entrepreneurship included personal 'independence', but also monetary reasons, with the latter being particularly dominant in Moldova, reflecting the extremely poor economic situation in the country. This is illustrated by the case of a woman entrepreneur in Moldova, aged 64, who began trading in second-hand clothes, which were imported from overseas as humanitarian aid. This entrepreneur was forced to start a business because she could not survive on her pension and that of her husband, which together amounted to just $20 per month, while their monthly expenses were $50. She entered this particular business line, which was suggested by one of her relatives, because of easy access, with few resources needed. Her relative assisted her in leasing a trade place at the market in Chisinau.

In Ukraine and Moldova, men gave as their main motive for starting a business 'to increase income' and, in Uzbekistan, a strong desire to have their own business. Again, a case from Moldova throws light on the reasoning behind this. This male entrepreneur, who is now running a successful interurban passenger transportation service, was forced to start his own business in order to earn enough to keep his family. After the state enterprise, where he had previously worked as an engineer, closed down, he went abroad to earn money. He used his earnings to buy a minibus, which he transported back to Moldova in order to start his own business.

Most of the cases demonstrate that neither female nor male entrepreneurs are exclusively driven by push or pull reasons. Instead, case evidence shows more complex relationships between entrepreneurship as an economic necessity, or as a response to potential market opportunities and a desire to realize a 'dream'. One such case refers to a female entrepreneur in

Uzbekistan, who set up a business in 1993, specializing in sewing and selling national costumes and children's trousers. Venture creation was motivated by the entrepreneur's perception of a demand for higher-quality goods at the beginning of the 1990s and by her need to supplement her teaching salary. While initially the business was profitable, this changed after 1997, due to an increase in competition from illegal firms. The entrepreneur now plans to give up her sewing production and instead to settle on food processing, that is, drying tomatoes and processing tomato paste, which she considers more rewarding in terms of income under the current economic circumstances. In this case, the need to generate income appears to be the key driver for her current entrepreneurial activities.

Unlike female entrepreneurs, male respondents also mentioned the availability of resources as one of their main three motives for starting up. This might be a result of women having greater problems in accessing resources to start their business, as has been pointed out in previous research. In terms of the main constraints faced when starting a business, with the exception of Ukrainian male entrepreneurs, both females and males named lack of capital as their priority constraint, followed by lack of premises and then regulations and laws facing female entrepreneurs, while the rank order shows a more diverse picture for male entrepreneurs across countries (Table 10.1).

A key theme emerging from our data, as well as from other studies cited above, is that in hostile institutional environments, the influence of gender for entering and developing a business is perhaps more subtle than in

Table 10.1 Top constraints at start-up (%)

Constraints	Ukraine		Moldova		Uzbekistan	
	Female	Male	Female	Male	Female	Male
Lack of capital, finance	51.2	37.0	49.3	54.0	67.0	45.0
Lack of premises	47.5	49.4	21.9	25.4	25.5	16.7
Lack of equipment/ technology	6.4	11.1	17.2	23.8	11.5	16.7
Lack of skilled employees	29.8	43.2	14.0	17.5	12.0	13.3
Market constraints	6.1	9.9	18.6	19.0	2.5	6.7
Regulation & law	31.2	21.0	20.5	14.3	21.0	20.0
Taxes	31.5	35.8	9.8	4.8	15.5	10.0
No of cases	295	81	215	63	200	60

Note: Multiple responses based on cases. Respondents could give up to three answers.

Source: Own survey 2002.

more benign environments, by reinforcing non-gender-specific issues. This becomes apparent since both male and female entrepreneurs mentioned the same obstacles to doing business, mainly reflecting institutional environments, where business conditions are either not yet installed or not working smoothly. In a situation where the legislation changes constantly, competition is growing and the customer's income remains low, all businesses struggle to retain their existing customer base and to find new ones. This applies to both female and male entrepreneurs, regardless of their sex.

In terms of the effect of gender on business relations, evidence from the case studies shows that female entrepreneurs often perceive their gender as being an advantage in doing business, because of a better feeling for the customer's needs and/or greater success in dealing with authorities and external stakeholders. This is best illustrated by the story of a female entrepreneur from Uzbekistan. Asked whether she thought that authorities, banks and other relevant institutions treat female- and male-owned businesses in the same way, this Uzbek entrepreneur perceived that gender had actually helped her, especially in the beginning when she had little experience in doing business (contrary to her husband, who claimed that gender does not matter). She thought that it is easier for women to communicate with agencies and banks, as men are more friendly and polite with a woman than with another man, citing the example of the first visit by the regional tax agency in 1995. The inspector visiting her found a small mistake in her declaration, asked for $2000 penalty (which, in the eyes of the entrepreneur, was hugely exaggerated, given the amount of tax not paid) and a bribe. She went to the office of the agency herself and asked to see another tax inspector, without telling them about the demand made. When they asked her why, she told them: 'I am a weak woman, just starting a business; I need your help'. Now she has very good contacts with the regional tax agency where she is well known.

In this context, the question of whether women are more inclined to prefer dealing with women in their business affairs, was also investigated, since this might influence them in terms of accessing advice and (emotional) support in a gender-friendly environment. We asked entrepreneurs to estimate the share of women in different business relationships. Our data show that women have a higher share of women than men in terms of their suppliers, customers, business partners and business consultants, which ranges from 38 per cent for Ukrainian suppliers to 77 per cent for Uzbek business consultants. While this is not surprising for customers and suppliers in 'traditionally' female-dominated business fields, the high share of female business consultants indicates a need for gender-specific support in the trust-based advisory and consultancy role.

Performance and Success

Gender differences were also examined with respect to business performance and growth in a transition context. Studies show that in Slovenia, for example, female-managed businesses were smaller with regard to the number of their employees than male-owned firms (Drnovsek and Glas, 2006). They also had lower revenues, significantly lower assets, fewer exports and less profit, although they experienced fewer losses. The Slovenian authors argue that this weaker financial performance, compared with their male-owned counterparts, was partly due to stronger competition in activities where most female-managed businesses were concentrated, as well as generally worse financial results. In addition, women were less profit focused, caring more for employment and a positive organizational culture.

Business performance is influenced by the objectives set by entrepreneurs, as well as by other factors. For our survey, Table 10.2 shows that for female entrepreneurs in the Ukraine and Moldova, financial gain was the most commonly mentioned main business objective, reflecting their motives for entering entrepreneurship in the first place. Interestingly, the share of women wanting to expand their business is high. This is reflected in other studies. For example, studies for Russia (Wells et al., 2003) and Latvia

Table 10.2 Objectives for the past 12 months, 2001–2002 (%)

Objective	Ukraine		Moldova		Uzbekistan	
	Female	Male	Female	Male	Female	Male
To grow	64.8	84.8	62.6	81.7	88.9	88.5
To survive	45.2	19.0	38.3	30.0	19.7	17.3
To prepare for selling	1.1	–	1.9	1.7	0.5	1.9
To reduce shadow operations	2.6	1.3	6.8	10.0	1.0	7.7
To provide a living for family	63.0	57.0	68.9	65.0	47.0	50.0
To improve personal/ family income	66.7	70.9	74.8	68.3	60.1	42.3
Other	10.7	8.9	–	–	5.6	1.9
No of cases*	270	79	206	60	198	52

Note: * Cases of businesses operating 12 months and more. Multiple responses based on cases. Respondents could give up to three answers.

Source: Own survey 2002.

(Welter and Kolb, 2006) show a similar picture, with 60 per cent of the Russian and Latvian female entrepreneurs stating growth-related goals.

Examples from our cases allow us to explore growth and growth orientation in more detail, indicating that in a hostile environment the aim of business growth is often linked to business survival and income reasons rather than business development aims. In other words, with trading at a low level, some growth is necessary in order to survive. For example, a Moldovan woman who set up a construction business was growth orientated from the outset, because she needed her business income to provide a living for her family. Another female entrepreneur, engaged in a personal transport business, borrowed a large sum of money to start the business, stating that growth was a necessary objective in order to repay the debt as quickly as possible.

The question of whether women are more or less successful than men was explored through looking at an objective indicator (that is, business income), as well as self-perceived success. In this regard, entrepreneurs were asked to state whether their business income covered expenses, which allowed us to assess their business performance and success indirectly. Here, our data indicate major differences in business performance not only across gender, but also between countries, reflecting the respective economic situations and business environments. The data illustrate that a large share of male entrepreneurs in the Ukraine and Uzbekistan as well as most Moldovan entrepreneurs of both sexes appear to have been most successful, since the majority stated that their previous year's income exceeded expenditure, although this was even more pronounced in the case of male entrepreneurs. However, it needs to be taken into account that Moldovan entrepreneurs, regardless of their gender, often make low estimates of their personal expenses from business, thus increasing their overall business income. As a result, there may be some positive bias, as in those cases where entrepreneurs are not successful in achieving their objectives, and where businesses do not provide enough income to cover their cost of living, businesses may have been liquidated. This is part of the wider methodological issue of analysing business success by investigating only surviving businesses.

Both male and female entrepreneurs were also asked for their assessment of whether they perceived women to be more or less successful than men with regard to various business spheres, including finance, sales growth, business information, market development, exporting, innovation, networking, production and personnel management. Their answers show that women's and men's perceptions differ in this regard. Generally, men were more likely to state that gender had a negative effect on the success of female-owned businesses. This applied across all spheres, and particularly to production, exporting and innovation. Women mainly perceived a neutral effect. In fields such as sales, networking or personnel management, they considered themselves to be more successful. Comparing female entrepreneurs across countries, more Uzbek women judged themselves as more successful than men with respect to finance and, surprisingly, also innovation. In contrast, around one-third of the Ukrainian and Moldovan women attributed a negative effect to their gender in this field. This is often connected with the traditional upbringing of girls within their families. One female entrepreneur in Moldova described her shyness and lack of self-reliance as great obstacles when she started her business, but these characteristics had been cultivated by her parents on purpose because they had been considered advantageous for a woman.

On the other hand, case-study evidence also demonstrates personal success of female entrepreneurs since setting up a business, in terms of a growth in confidence. A good example is a female-owned enterprise in Uzbekistan, which started wholesale trading in 1994, dealing with imported pharmacy goods, with smaller additional sidelines in selling perfumes, cosmetics and jewellery. The female owner initially described herself as being very reluctant to become an entrepreneur, but now the business has grown to become a full-time activity, both for the woman and for her husband, who had previously worked in the Ministry of Internal Affairs. Initially, the husband encouraged his wife to act as director of their company, because he could not own a business due to his position as a government official. However, since starting the business, her interest, enthusiasm and confidence in running the business had grown considerably, which contributed to a change in her motivation. From the entrepreneur's perspective, her initial reluctance to become an entrepreneur had been replaced by an opportunity-seeking pattern of behaviour.

Networking and Assistance

In her study on Bulgarian female entrepreneurs in the construction business, Manolova (2006) stressed that women felt they were not taking advantage of formal and informal networks in terms of business growth. In our survey, female entrepreneurs drew heavily on informal sources of information and advice, such as family, friends and business partners, typically combining different sources, both in starting and developing a business. This can be illustrated with reference to an interior design business in Moldova. In this case, the father of the entrepreneur proposed the business idea, as the entrepreneur had no previous experience in this field. He also helped her to engage a design specialist and provided a substantial part of the funds necessary to register the firm and renovate the business. Her friend offered space in her own shop, forgoing payments for half a year, while her brother, an artist, made an 'in-kind' contribution, currently also working in her firm. Another example is a small hairdresser's salon in Chisinau, Moldova. In this case, a brother helped his sister during the initial stage of setting up the business, renovating the premises, and delivering and fixing equipment, while other relatives supplemented the entrepreneur's own savings with a loan, to provide some start-up capital.

The latter form of support was often mentioned by interviewees in case studies; one respondent describing this as being 'traditional for our family'. Examples of informal support range from advice on the business idea, and physical help in setting up the firm, to help in accessing financial resources, and assistance in finding customers and in obtaining supplies. Female entrepreneurs also often turn to informal contacts in authorities, either to access help in registering the firm or to solve problems with licences, tax payments and similar requirements. For example, 'My husband helped me through his personal contacts', illustrates how female entrepreneurship in transition conditions often needs to be interpreted in the household context. 'I set up informal contacts with the authorities' is another typical statement of female entrepreneurs in our case studies, illustrating the importance of being well connected with officials in order to do business (Ledeneva, 1998).

Some authors interpret this frequent reliance on male assistance from spouses and/or family as reflecting the 'renaissance of patriarchy' (Zhurzhenko, 1999: 246) in post-Soviet societies. In a traditional society, such as Uzbekistan, where widows and young women are not expected to act on their own, assistance from family sources becomes a necessity. This can be illustrated with reference to the case of a 34-year-old female entrepreneur, who set up a sewing firm in the Namagan region. Her mother accompanied her when she first registered her business with the authorities. However, as the business developed, and the female entrepreneur gained in confidence, as well as developing her own contacts, this aspect of social capital became less important.

At the same time, the diversity of female entrepreneurship needs to be stressed. Many women enter entrepreneurship in order to sustain themselves and their families; in some cases, despite disapproval from family and spouses. Some case evidence shows male spouses working in the firm in a subordinate role, having tacitly accepted their business wife. In one such Ukrainian firm, which was manufacturing and selling dresses, as well as running a retail outlet for survival reasons, the female owner described her husband as 'reliable, but without initiative', although he was acting as manager as well as being a driver. In a retail company selling flowers, the husband initially strongly opposed his wife's business activities, although she took the initiative to set up her business, despite this, in order to supplement the family income.

However, case studies also show a differentiated picture with regard to assistance from family and spouses. For example, in Ukraine, case-study evidence demonstrates that women with young children often find it difficult to combine running a business and raising children without any external help from the family. In Uzbekistan the specific local environment (so-called *mahallyas*, which are local neighbourhood communities) plays an additional role in enabling (or constraining) female entrepreneurs, mainly because of the attitude of neighbours towards them. Case studies from Uzbekistan illustrate an ambiguous picture. Some female entrepreneurs, who set up their business in the local neighbourhood, referred to envy being shown on the part of some neighbours ('they don't send their girls into my sewing school, but take them to another district'), although it is common for female entrepreneurs to support their community, for example, by training local girls, or by offering reduced prices. A similar pattern is reflected in research on ethnic minority businesses, which often emphasize the role that family and local communities play in relation to social capital (Fadahunsi et al., 2000). It is specifically the close nature of families or communities that allows ethnic, or in this case female entrepreneurs to access networks and networking contacts.

Case studies also demonstrate how female entrepreneurs assist others to set up their businesses, which in some cases is facilitated by membership of a women's business association. Most consider this as an implicit requirement if they are to receive assistance themselves. In this regard, our survey results show that men are more likely than women to turn to other entrepreneurs for assistance, especially in Uzbekistan and Moldova. As a consequence, business partners are an important source of social capital for both female and male entrepreneurs, based around the principle of reciprocity, but qualitative differences can be identified in the nature of the process by which assistance is received, as well as in the networking contacts they use.

CONCLUSIONS AND IMPLICATIONS

Similarities and Differences across Gender in a Transition Context

This chapter contributes to an ongoing debate about the role of gender in entrepreneurship, by bringing in a perspective from transition environments, where less research on female entrepreneurship has been conducted. On the whole, our exploratory analysis, which draws on our own survey and case material as well as on published studies for other transition countries, shows that in a transition context, there are more similarities than differences between female and male entrepreneurs and also in relation to their businesses, although in generalizing this we have to acknowledge the limitations of our three-country study and the methodology used in this chapter.

The main business obstacles mentioned by survey respondents, as well as in some of the other studies cited above, are less gender related, but instead refer more to an unfavourable external operating environment, where business conditions are volatile and changing quickly. Female entrepreneurs frequently perceived their gender to be an advantage in business relations; seldom considering it to be a disadvantage, although case evidence shows a rather mixed picture in this respect. Although female entrepreneurs referred to the non-discriminatory attitude of various institutions, they typically prefer to deal with people of the same gender, which is especially pronounced in the case of business consultants, where trust between client and consultant plays an important role. Where female entrepreneurs indicate a negative gender influence, these instances are often connected to a traditional upbringing and traditional values, which do not encourage girls to develop business-related attitudes and behaviours.

Both 'push' and 'pull' motives can be identified in transition environments, with regard to women starting entrepreneurial activity. Some female entrepreneurs are pushed by negative circumstances (that is, unemployment), while others are pulled by positive opportunities. The extent to which entrepreneurs (of both sexes) in transition environments are pushed into business, by a need to find some way of supporting themselves and their families, has led some authors to suggest that a majority are better described as 'proprietors' rather than 'entrepreneurs'. Entrepreneurs are characterized by the reinvestment of business profits for the purpose of business growth and ultimately further capital accumulation, while proprietors tend to consume the surpluses generated (Scase, 2003). This implies that a large share of female owners of small and medium-sized enterprises in the surveyed countries would fall into the 'proprietorship' category, at least when their businesses are started. However, a more dynamic view is needed, which would recognize the learning capacity of individuals over time, particularly where considerable human capital is involved, as well as possible changes in external circumstances. These can lead to changes in the aspirations of individuals and their ability to spot and exploit new business opportunities. Even if specific entrepreneurial actions or events, such as creating a venture, are primarily driven by necessity or opportunity, it is inappropriate to place entrepreneurs, regardless of gender, into such categories, because of the need to incorporate a dynamic element. This is an important point from a policy perspective, since it has implications for the entrepreneurial capacity of an economy and what needs to be done to enhance it (Smallbone and Welter, 2003).

Although studies in Western countries often show female entrepreneurs to have low growth orientation, the results from Ukraine, Uzbekistan and Moldova in this chapter show that a high proportion of female entrepreneurs are in fact growth orientated, which is supported by results from some other transition studies (for example, Wells et al., 2003; Welter and Kolb, 2006). However, in poor countries, such as Moldova, this phenomenon is closely connected to economic motives, such as the need to increase business income in order to provide a living for families. Our results also indicate that in a transition context the woman's decision to enter entrepreneurship is often affected by the needs of other members of her household, especially in cases where the woman is divorced, a widow or a single parent.

Implications for Research and Policy

The analysis has implications for future research, as it draws attention to the most appropriate unit of analysis to use. (Should it be the household instead of the entrepreneur?) The associated question for further research is how to re-define entrepreneurship to include the phenomenon of 'enterprising households', in which the needs and resources of more than one household member contribute to the entrepreneurial activity, whether led by a women or a man. In our understanding, the concept is different from that of a family business, but is similar to the family embeddedness perspective, which Aldrich and Cliff (2003) emphasize. Only recently have entrepreneurship scholars (for example, Wheelock, 1998; Aldrich and Cliff, 2003; Jennings and McDougald, forthcoming) started to draw attention to the embeddedness of entrepreneurship in family and household contexts, often discussing this in the context of work–life balance. In this regard, entrepreneurship researchers might explore the linkages between entrepreneurial activities and household matters in more detail.

Another avenue for further research concerns the role of social entrepreneurship in a fragile environment, as elements of social entrepreneurship are apparent in those cases where female entrepreneurs stress their social responsibilities, such as to their employees and incorporating this attitude into their behaviour.

Our results also illustrate the diversity of female entrepreneurs in and between transition countries, indicating the context specificity of entrepreneurship. A distinctive feature of female entrepreneurship in transition countries is a diversity of types, including the forced (often unregistered) female entrepreneurs mentioned above; former managers of previously state-owned companies that have been privatized, professionals (teachers, medical doctors, accountants), who changed the legal status of their activities, as well as entrepreneurial female owners of fast-growing companies. This emphasizes the heterogeneity that exists within the small business sector, which needs to be taken into account in any policy response. In this regard, Mirchandani (1999: 230) draws attention to the fact that there is 'little analysis of how gendered processes may shape the size of firms, or the tendency to focus on certain industries'. She raises the point that most research on female entrepreneurship is not based on feminist theories, which tends to result in gender differences being explained in terms of how female entrepreneurs deviate from a so-called 'male norm'. With regard to a transition context, this indicates a need to pay attention to the changing role of women (entrepreneurs) during the transition period, as well as to the role of external conditions in shaping patterns of women's entrepreneurship. As far as further research on female entrepreneurs is concerned, it emphasizes a need to look at (female) entrepreneurship within its social and economic context, thus stressing the embeddedness of entrepreneurship, which also might explain differences often taken as gender-related ones.

With regard to implications for policy, our exploratory results suggest that perhaps the main priority for female entrepreneurs in transition economies is to improve the overall environment for business, which will help both women and men. This includes measures to reduce corruption and the violation of rules at local level, which are among the most urgent issues identified by female entrepreneurs. It also includes capacity building and sensitization of administrations at national and local levels to the needs of entrepreneurs. State representatives need a better understanding of the issue of (female) entrepreneurship, while women's business organizations need to work in partnership with other business associations to lobby for improvements in the general business environment. Although the overall conclusion from our study suggests that the differences between males and females may be less striking in many ways than those identified in some studies in Western countries, the concentration of women (for example, in trade and other low-entry threshold activities) is a distinctive characteristic. It means, for example, that policies aimed at or influencing these sectors can have a disproportionate impact on women, even if this is not the intention of policy makers.

Our study also revealed a need for a 'joined-up' policy approach. A good example is the relationship between access to childcare provision and the ability of young women to engage in entrepreneurship. The case studies show that female entrepreneurs often can only combine business and family responsibilities provided that their relatives (mothers) help to raise children. In this regard, measures such as raising funds for childcare institutions, or benefits to private childcare institutions to reduce prices for their services are likely to have a positive effect on female business development at least in Ukraine and Moldova. This aspect is particularly important in view of the contribution made by female entrepreneurs to household incomes in situations where there are often few alternative opportunities. As in mature market economies, a variety of government policies and actions can impact on entrepreneurs and businesses, including some that are not directed at the business sector at all.

REFERENCES

Aculai, E., N. Rodionova and N. Vinogradova (2006), 'Women business owners in Moldova: proprietors or entrepreneurs?', in F. Welter, D. Smallbone and N. Isakova (eds), *Enterprising Women in Transition Economies*, Aldershot: Ashgate, pp. 67–91.

Aidis, R. (2006), 'From business ownership to informal market traders: the characteristics of female entrepreneurship in Lithuania', in F. Welter, D. Smallbone and N. Isakova (eds), *Enterprising Women in Transition Economies*, Aldershot: Ashgate, pp. 119–42.

Akiner, S. (1997), 'Between tradition and modernity: the dilemma facing contemporary Central Asian women', in M. Buckley (ed.), *Post-Soviet Women: From the Baltic to Central Asia*, Cambridge: Cambridge University Press, pp. 261–304.

Aldrich, H.E. (1989), 'Networking among women entrepreneurs', in O. Hagan, C. Rivchun and D.L. Sexton (eds), *Women-Owned Businesses*, New York: Praeger, pp. 103–32.

Aldrich, H. and J. Cliff (2003), 'The pervasive effects of family on entrepreneurship: toward a family embeddedness perspective', *Journal of Business Venturing*, **18**, 573–96.

Aldrich, H., B. Rosen and W. Woodward (1986), 'Social behaviour and entrepreneurial networks', *Frontiers of Entrepreneurship Research*, Wellesley, MA: Babson College, pp. 239–40.

Allen, W.D. (2000), 'Social networks and self-employment', *Journal of Socio-Economics*, **29**, 487–501.

Ashwin, S. (2000), 'Introduction: gender, state and society in Soviet and post-Soviet Russia', in S. Ashwin (ed.), *Gender, State and Society in Soviet and Post-Soviet Russia*, London: Routledge, pp. 1–29.

Babayeva, L. and A. Chirikova (1996), 'Women in business', *Sotsiologicheskie issledovanya*, (4), 75–80 (in Russian).

Baines, S. and J. Wheelock (1998), 'Working for each other: gender, the household and micro-business survival and growth', *International Small Business Journal*, **17** (1), 16–35.

Baygan, G. (2000), 'Improving knowledge about women's entrepreneurship', paper presented at the OECD Second Conference on Women Entrepreneurs in SMEs: 'Realising the Benefits of Globalisation and the Knowledge-Based Economy', 29–30 November, www.oecd.org/dsti/sti/industry/indcomp.

Bliss, R.T. and N. Garratt (2001), 'Supporting women entrepreneurs in transition economies', *Journal of Small Business Management*, **39** (4), 336–44.

Blundel, R. and D. Smith (2001), 'Business Network Report', Research Report to the Small Business Service, Glasgow.

Bruno, M. (1997), 'Women and the culture of entrepreneurship', in M. Buckley (ed.), *Post-Soviet Women: From Baltic to Central Asia*, Cambridge: Cambridge University Press, pp. 56–74.

Brush, C. (1992), 'Research on women business owners: past trends, a new perspective and future directions', *Entrepreneurship Theory and Practice*, **16**, 5–26.

Brush, C., N.M. Carter, E.J. Gatewood, P.G. Greene and M.M. Hart (eds) (2006), *Growth-oriented Women Entrepreneurs and Their Businesses: A Global Research Perspective*, Cheltenham, UK and Northampton, MA, USA: Edward Elgar.

Brush, C. and R. Hisrich (2000), 'Women-owned businesses: an exploratory study comparing factors affecting performance', Working Paper Series 00-02, RISEbusiness, Washington, DC.

Buttner, E.H. and D.P. Moore (1997), 'Women's organizational exodus to entrepreneurship: self reported motivations and correlates with success', *Journal of Small Business Management*, **35** (1), 34–46.

Caputo, R.K. and A. Dolinsky (1998), 'Women's choice to pursue self-employment: the role of financial and human capital of household members', *Journal of Small Business Management*, **36** (3), 8–17.

Carter, S., S. Anderson and E. Shaw (2001), 'Women's business ownership: a review of the academic, popular and internet literature', Report to the Small Business Service, Glasgow.

Carter, S. and P. Rosa (1998), 'The financing of male- and female-owned businesses', *Entrepreneurship and Regional Development*, **10** (3), 203–24.

Catley, S. and R.T. Hamilton (1998), 'Small business development and gender of owner', *Journal of Management Development*, **17**, 75–82.

Cliff, J. (1998), 'Does one size fit all? Exploring the relationship between attitudes towards growth, gender, and business size', *Journal of Business Venturing*, **13** (6), 523–42.

Cromie, S. (1987), 'Similarities and differences between women and men who chose business proprietorship', *International Small Business Journal*, **5**, 43–60.

Drnovsek, M. and M. Glas (2006), 'Women entrepreneurs in Slovenia: by fits and starts', in F. Welter, D. Smallbone and N. Isakova (eds), *Enterprising Women in Transition Economies*, Aldershot: Ashgate, pp. 143–70.

Du Rietz, A. and M. Henrekson (2000), 'Testing the female underperformance hypothesis', *Small Business Economics*, **14**, 1–10.

Fadahunsi, A., D. Smallbone and S. Supri (2000), 'Networking in ethnic minority entrepreneurship: an analysis of small minority owned firms in North London', *Journal for Small Business and Enterprise Development*, **7** (3), 228–40.

Fajth, G. (2000), 'Women in transition: themes of the UNICEF MONEE project', in M. Lazreg (ed.), *Making the Transition Work for Women in Europe and Central Asia*, World Bank Discussion Paper No. 411, Washington, DC: World Bank, pp. 89–101.

Fay, M. and L. Williams (1993), 'Gender bias and the availability of business loans', *Journal of Business Venturing*, **8**, 363–76.

Glas, M. and T. Petrin (1998), 'Entrepreneurship: new challenges for Slovene Women', paper to the 1998 Babson–Kauffman Foundation Entrepreneurship Research Conference, Gent, 20–24 May.

Greve, A. (1995), 'Networks and entrepreneurship – an analysis of social relations, occupational background, and use of contacts during the establishment process', *Scandinavian Journal of Management*, **11**, 1–24.

Hoang, H. and B. Antoncic (2003), 'Network-based research in entrepreneurship: a critical review', *Journal of Business Venturing*, **18**, 165–87.

Isakova, N. (2001), 'Gender similarities and differences in performance and evaluations of the Ukrainian entrepreneurs', *Sociology: Theory, Practice, Marketing*, (2), 144–53 (in Ukrainian and Russian).

Isakova, N., O. Krasovska, L. Kavunenko and A. Lugovy (2006), 'Entrepreneurship in the Ukraine: a male female comparison', in F. Welter, D. Smallbone and N. Isakova (eds), *Enterprising Women in Transition Economies*, Aldershot: Ashgate, pp. 17–43.

Ivaschenko, O. (1994), 'On the development of female entrepreneurship in Ukraine', *Filosofskaya i sotsiologicheskaya mysl*, (1–2), 250–53 (in Russian).

Jennings, J.E. and M.S. McDougald (forthcoming), 'Work–family interface experiences and coping strategies: implications for entrepreneurship research and practice', accepted for *Academy of Management Review*.

Jennings, J.E. and M. Provorny Cash (2006), 'Women's entrepreneurship in Canada: progress, puzzles and priorities', in Brush et al. (eds), pp. 53–87.

Jenssen, J.I. (2001), 'Social networks, resources and entrepreneurship', *Entrepreneurship and Innovation* (June), 103–9.

Jungbauer-Gans, M. (1993), *Frauen als Unternehmerinnen*, Frankfurt. Lang.

Jungbauer-Gans, M. and P. Preisendörfer (1992), 'Frauen in der beruflichen Selbständigkeit: Eine erfolgreiche Alternative zur abhängigen Beschäftigung?', *Zeitschrift für Soziologie*, **21** (1), 61–77.

Kalleberg, A.L. and K.T. Leicht (1991), 'Gender and organizational performance: determinants of small business survival and success', *Academy of Management Journal*, **34** (1), 136–61.

Kiblitskaya, M. (2000), 'Russia's female breadwinners: the changing subjective experience', in S. Ashwin (ed.), *Gender, State and Society in Soviet and Post-Soviet Russia*, London: Routledge, pp. 55–70.

Koncz, K. (2000), 'Transitional period and labor market characteristics in Hungary', in M. Lazreg (ed.), *Making the Transition Work for Women in Europe and Central Asia*, World Bank Discussion Paper No. 411, Washington, DC: World Bank, pp. 26–41.

Ledeneva, A.V. (1998), *Russia's Economy of Favours: Blat, Networking and Informal Exchange*, Cambridge: Cambridge University Press.

Lituchy, T.R. and M.A. Reavley (2004), 'Women entrepreneurs: a comparison of international small business owners in Poland and the Czech Republic', *Journal of International Entrepreneurship*, **2**, 61–87.

Lohmann, H. and S. Luber (2000), 'Geschlechtsunterschiede in der Struktur und den Determinanten beruflicher Selbständigkeit: Ein Vergleich zwischen der Bundesrepublik und dem Vereinigten Königreich', paper to 2nd Microcensus User Conference 'Forschung mit dem Mikrozensus. Analysen zur Sozialstruktur und zum Arbeitsmarkt', ZES, University of Mannheim, Mannheim, 12–13 October.

Lokar, S. (2000), 'Gender aspects of employment and unemployment in Central and Eastern Europe', in M. Lazreg (ed.), *Making the Transition Work for Women in Europe and Central Asia*, World Bank Discussion Paper No. 411, Washington, DC: World Bank, pp. 12–25.

Luber, S. and R. Leicht (2000), 'Growing self-employment in Western Europe: an effect of modernization?', *International Review of Sociology*, **10** (1), 101–23.

Manolova, T. (2006), 'Builders and leaders: six case studies of men and women small proprietors in the Bulgarian construction industry', in Brush et al. (eds), pp. 232–58.

McManus, P.A. (2001), 'Women's participation in self-employment in Western industrialized nations', *International Journal of Sociology*, **31** (2), 70–97.

Meyer, R. and N. Harabi (2000), *Frauen-Power unter der Lupe: Geschlechtsspezifische Unterschiede zwischen Jungunternehmerinnen und Jungunternehmern, Ergebnisse einer empirischen Untersuchung*, Fachhochschule Solothurn, Reihe A: Discussion Paper 2000–04, Solothurn.

Mirchandani, K. (1999), 'Feminist insight on gendered work: new directions in research on women and entrepreneurship', *Gender, Work and Organization*, **6** (4), 224–35.

Mrcozkowski, T. (1997), 'Women as employees and entrepreneurs in the Polish transformation', *Industrial Relations Journal*, **28** (2), 83–91.

Öczan, G. (2006), 'Djamila's journey from Kolkhoz to Bazaar: female entrepreneurs in Kyrgyzstan', in F. Welter, D. Smallbone and N. Isakova (eds), *Enterprising Women in Transition Economies*, Aldershot: Ashgate, pp. 93–115.

Renzulli, L.A., H. Aldrich and J. Moody (2000), 'Family matters: gender, networks, and entrepreneurial outcomes', *Social Forces*, **79**, 523–46.

Roberts, K. and J. Tholen (1999), 'Junge Unternehmer in den neuen Marktgesellschaften Mittel- und Osteuropas', in D. Bögenhold (ed.), *Unternehmensgründungen und Dezentralität – Eine Renaissance der beruflichen Selbständigkeit?*, Opladen: Westdeutscher Verlag, pp. 257–78.

Rosa, P., S. Carter and D. Hamilton (1996), 'Gender as a determinant of small business performance: insights from a British study', *Small Business Economics*, **8**, 463–78.

Rosa, P., D. Hamilton, S. Carter and H. Burns (1994), 'The impact of gender on small business management: preliminary findings of a British study', *International Small Business Journal*, **12** (3), 25–32.

Scase, R. (2003), 'Entrepreneurship and proprietorship in transition: policy implications for the SME sector', in R. McIntyre and B. Dallago (eds), *Small and Medium Enterprises in Transitional Economies*, Basingstone, UK: Palgrave, pp. 64–77.

Schutjens, V. and E. Stam (2003), 'The evolution and nature of young firm networks: a longitudinal perspective', *Small Business Economics*, **21**, 115–34.

Scott, C.E. (1986), 'Why more women are becoming entrepreneurs', *Journal of Small Business Management*, **4**, 37–44.

Shane, S., L. Kolvereid and A. Westhead (1991), 'An exploratory examination of the reasons leading to new firm formation across country and gender', *Journal of Business Venturing*, **6** (6), 431–46.

Smallbone, D. and F. Welter (2001), 'The distinctiveness of entrepreneurship in transition economies', *Small Business Economics*, **16** (4), 249–62.

Smallbone, D. and F. Welter (2003), 'Entrepreneurship in transition economies: necessity or opportunity driven?', paper presented at the Babson College–Kaufmann Foundation Entrepreneurship Research Conference, Babson College, Wellesley, MA, June.

Srinivasan, R., C.Y. Woo and A.C. Cooper (1994), 'Performance determinants for male and female entrepreneurs', *Frontiers of Entrepreneurship Research*, Wellesley, MA: Babson College, pp. 43–55.

Stevenson, L.A. (1986), 'Against all odds: the entrepreneurship of women', *Journal of Small Business Management*, **24** (4), 30–36.

Storey, D. (1994), *Understanding the Small Business Sector*, London and New York: Routledge.

Tabyshalieva, A. (2000), 'Revival of traditions in post-Soviet Central Asia', in M. Lazreg (ed.), *Making the Transition Work for Women in Europe and Central Asia*, World Bank Discussion Paper No. 411, Washington, DC: World Bank, pp. 51–7.

Verheul, I. and R. Thurik (2001), 'Start-up capital: "does gender matter?"', *Small Business Economics*, **16**, 329–45.

Wells, B., T. Pfantz and J. Bryne (2003), 'Russian women business owners: evidence of entrepreneurship in a transition economy', *Journal of Developmental Entrepreneurship*, **8** (1), 59–71.

Welter, F. and S. Kolb (2006), 'Women and entrepreneurship in Latvia', TeliaSonera Institute Discussion Paper No. 4, Riga: TSI and SSE.

Welter, F. and D. Smallbone (2003), 'Entrepreneurship and enterprise strategies in transition economies: an institutional perspective', in D. Kirby and A. Watson (eds), *Small Firms and Economic Development in Developed and Transition Economies: A Reader*, Aldershot: Ashgate, pp. 95–114.

Welter, F., D. Smallbone, E. Aculai, N. Isakova and N. Schakirova (2003), 'Female entrepreneurship in post-Soviet countries, in J. Butler (ed.), *New Perspectives on Women Entrepreneurs*, Greenwich, CT: Information Age, pp. 243–70.

Welter, F., D. Smallbone, D. Mirzakhalikova, N. Schakirova and C. Maksudova (2006), 'Women entrepreneurs between tradition and modernity – the case of Uzbekistan', in F. Welter, D. Smallbone and N. Isakova (eds), *Enterprising Women in Transition Economies*, Aldershot: Ashgate, pp. 45–66.

Wheelock, J. (1998), 'Working for each other: gender, the household and micro business survival and growth', *International Small Business Journal*, **17** (1), 16–35.

Zhurzhenko, T. (1999), 'Gender and identity formation in post-socialist Ukraine: the case of women in the shuttle business', in R. Bridgman, S. Cole and H. Howard-Bobiwash (eds), *Feminist Fields: Ethnographic Insights*, Ontario: Broadview Press, pp. 243–63.

Zhurzhenko, T. (2001), 'Free market ideology and new women's identities in post-socialist Ukraine', *European Journal of Women's Studies*, **8** (1), 29–49.

11. The impact of the venture capitalists' service and monitoring activities on control systems and performance of entrepreneurial firms

Frits H. Wijbenga, Theo J.B.M. Postma and Rebecca Stratling

INTRODUCTION

By being represented on the entrepreneurial firm's board of directors, the venture capitalist (VC) can play an active role in the strategy development and evaluation process of the entrepreneurial firm by offering value-adding activities (Gorman and Sahlman, 1989; MacMillan et al., 1989; Rosenstein et al., 1993; Sapienza et al., 1996; Fried et al., 1998; Deakins et al., 2000; Gabrielsson and Huse, 2002). Seminal work on the VC's added value (for example, MacMillan et al., 1989; Sapienza and Timmons, 1989; Rosenstein et al., 1993; Ehrlich et al., 1994) has reached a general consensus as to which value-adding activities are provided to entrepreneurial firms (Sapienza, 1992; Sapienza et al., 1996). However, there is little agreement in the literature as to whether the VC's board activities actually increase entrepreneurial firm performance (ibid.; Flynn, 2001).

This chapter attempts to resolve the VC 'added value' proposition by opening up the 'black box' between the VC's value-adding activities on the one hand, and the entrepreneurial firm's performance on the other. Previous research mainly focuses on partial relationships between either the impact of the VC's value-adding activities on the entrepreneurial firm's performance, or the impact of the VC's value-adding activities on the development of (control) systems present in the entrepreneurial firm. This study adopts a multi-theoretical approach and integrates both streams of research in order to get a more fine-grained insight into the VC value-added proposition, such as considering the impact of mediating and moderating mechanisms through which the VC may enhance or even erode the entrepreneurial firm's financial performance. The focal point in this study is to examine both mediating and moderating mechanisms which may impact on how the VC influences the entrepreneurial firm's performance by aligning its value-adding activities (that is, monitoring and service activities) to the entrepreneurial firm's control systems. As VCs tend to be short-term and efficiency-orientated investors (Ruhnka and Young, 1987; Gomez-Meija et al., 1990; Steier and Greenwood, 1995; Zahra, 1996b), the control systems of the entrepreneurial firm are supposed to help them safeguard their investment by holding the entrepreneurial team accountable (Ruhnka and Young, 1987). At the same time, these control systems enable the entrepreneurial firm to grow and expand more quickly (see also Churchill and Lewis, 1983; Flynn, 2001) as they promote the more efficient and effective use of the resources provided by the VC to the entrepreneurial firm.

The structure of the chapter is as follows. First we present the theories and hypotheses, and then we discuss the methodology and the data analysis techniques. Finally we report the results, and conclude with a discussion of the implications of our findings.

THEORY AND HYPOTHESES

Value-adding Activities

Board theory indicates that there are two generic types of value-adding activities that boards (Zahra and Pearce, 1989; Goodstein et al., 1994), and thus VCs (Gabrielsson and Huse, 2002), provide for the entrepreneurial firm: *service activities* and *monitoring activities*. According to the resource-based view (Peteraf, 1993), external board members provide service activities and add value to the firm through their engagement in the development and evaluation of company strategy (Stiles and Taylor, 2001). Strategic involvement varies from taking and shaping strategic decisions, to setting the strategic context (McNulty and Pettigrew, 1999). Resource dependency theory (Pfeffer and Salancik, 1978) emphasizes service activities of external board members who act as 'boundary spanners' and provide access to external networks. Board members' networking activities refer to interlocking and connecting activities on behalf of the firm in order to secure critical resources and develop and maintain long-term relationships (ibid.). Studies on VCs' post-investment service activities indicate that VCs provide service activities such as recruiting additional managers to the firm, acting as an interface with the investor group, providing assistance on operations, facilitating contacts with new finance partners, supplying the firm with advisers and providing assistance with the introduction of new products/services to the market (for example, MacMillan et al., 1989; Sapienza and Timmons, 1989; Harrison and Mason, 1992; Rosenstein et al., 1993; Ehrlich et al., 1994).

According to agency theory, board members, in particular those representing significant external investments, can add value to the firm by engaging in a wide range of monitoring activities (Fama and Jensen, 1983). These activities consist mainly of control tasks, such as evaluating strategic initiatives and appointing, disciplining or removing ineffective individual managers or management teams (see Barnhart et al., 1994). VC monitoring activities usually cover monitoring financial performance, monitoring operational performance, and the evaluation of the entrepreneurial firm's business strategy and product market opportunities (MacMillan et al., 1989; Sapienza and Timmons, 1989; Harrison and Mason, 1992; Rosenstein et al., 1993; Ehrlich et al., 1994).

The VC's Contribution to the Entrepreneurial Firm

Agency theory suggests that the VC can reduce the agency problem not only by monitoring, but also by forcing the entrepreneurial firm to use control systems (see Jensen and Meckling, 1976). From an agency perspective, these control systems may function as an efficient and time-consuming substitute for the VC's monitoring activities. The relevance of these control systems is that like monitoring activities they help the VC to reduce information asymmetry problems and prevent the entrepreneur from behaving opportunistically. Hence, the application of control systems by the entrepreneurial firm would increase organizational performance (ibid.).

VCs are short-term and efficiency-orientated investors (Ruhnka and Young, 1987; Gomez-Meija et al., 1990; Steier and Greenwood, 1995; Zahra, 1996b). Therefore, it is important for the VC that entrepreneurial firms pass their stages of development more quickly. Stages of development theory suggests that established control systems are a necessary requirement for entrepreneurial firms in order to expand, as they help the entrepreneurial firm to make more efficient and effective use of its resources (Churchill and Lewis, 1983; Scott and Bruce, 1987). The role of VCs aimed at the entrepreneurial firm passing life-cycle stages more quickly is also supported by Flynn (2001), who reports that VCs emphasize various control systems for both early-stage (seed or start-up) and later-stage investments (mezzanine or bridge investments). Flynn also suggests that because entrepreneurs or scientists are often primarily focused on innovative activities or the technical core, the VC's activities can help the entrepreneurial firm to establish effective control systems, thereby facilitating fast organizational growth (Flynn, 2001).

In the next paragraphs we shall explore how the VC board activities impact on the degree and nature of the entrepreneurial form's control systems (that is, quality system, incentive and reward system, and cost control system), and subsequently the entrepreneurial firm's performance.

The impact of the VC service activities

A quality system is a well-known tool for achieving this through workforce empowerment aimed at continuous improvement (Gordon, 1996, p. 478): 'In their empowered role, employees are expected to call attention to a specific quality problem in their normal work, look for ways to perform their jobs better, and identify ways to improve organizational functioning to create continuous improvement in organizational processes'. By implementing quality systems, entrepreneurial firms shape the conditions that enable them to expand and achieve high organizational performance. Based on Stiles and Taylor's (2001) remarks on quality indices, we suggest that the VC's representatives might add value to the entrepreneurial firm by making its management team aware of the benefits of quality systems, and by subsequently providing guidance to the entrepreneurial firm's management team with regard to the process of adopting and running quality systems. We therefore hypothesize:

H1: The degree of VC service activities is positively associated with the degree of sophistication of a quality system in the entrepreneurial firm.

The effectiveness of even highly skilled employees can be enhanced when they are motivated to perform (Huselid, 1995). Therefore, next to the firm's application of a quality system, the firm's utilization of an incentive and reward system is an effective instrument to increase the entrepreneurial firm's productivity, by making better use of the knowledge, skills and abilities of the firm's current and potential employees (ibid., p. 637). Since incentive and reward systems aim at increasing employees' motivation, they are also likely to reduce shirking and to enhance the retention of quality employees while encouraging non-performers to leave the firm (Huselid, 1995). As part of their service activities, VC-appointed directors are likely to add value by developing or reviewing the appropriateness of the entrepreneurial firm's system of performance measurement and compensation (see Andrews, 1980, p. 27). From the VC's perspective this serves to align the incentives of the entrepreneurial firm's employees with the firm's key success factors, that is, making them more productive. We therefore suggest that:

H2: The degree of VC service activities is positively associated with the degree of sophistication of an incentive and reward system in the entrepreneurial firm.

Since entrepreneurs are more orientated towards the primary process of the firm, the VC's expertise in cost control may help the entrepreneurial firm to operate more efficiently (Flynn, 2001). As short-term and efficiency-orientated investors (Ruhnka and Young, 1987; Gomez-Meija et al., 1990; Steier and Greenwood, 1995; Zahra, 1996b), the VC is likely to emphasize the importance of efficient production in order to direct the entrepreneurial firm towards relatively short-term goals. In doing so, VC service activities might encourage the entrepreneurial firm to employ information systems capturing its cost structures, thereby enabling the firm to improving its plant efficiency, competitiveness in the market and so on. We therefore hypothesize that:

H3: The degree of VC service activities is positively associated with the degree of sophistication of a cost control system in the entrepreneurial firm.

The relevance of the entrepreneurial firm's control systems is twofold. First, control systems are substitutes of the VC's monitoring activities, which hence reduce the moral hazard of the entrepreneur and subsequently have a positive impact on the entrepreneurial firm performance. Second, control systems are necessary requirements for entrepreneurial firms in order to expand, as they help the entrepreneurial firm to make more efficient and effective use of its resources (Churchill and Lewis, 1983; Scott and Bruce, 1987). In line with the previous hypotheses, it is thus likely that the effect of the VC service activities indirectly influence the entrepreneurial firm's performance via the set of control systems. In other words, we suggest that:

H4: The entrepreneurial firm's control systems positively mediate the effect of VC service activities on the entrepreneurial firm's financial performance.

The impact of the VC monitoring activities

Formal analyses of the agency problem show that the agency costs of monitoring (including the presence of control systems), bonding and residual losses are partly complementary in nature (Jensen and Meckling, 1976). While monitoring and bonding activities can lead to a reduction of residual losses, these activities themselves at the same time create both set-up and operating costs (Williamson, 1988a, 1988b). As a consequence, the cumulative use of various monitoring and bonding activities can lead to an increase in total agency costs. Particularly with reference to the debate about the impact of corporate governance mechanisms on corporate performance, research indicates that substitutional effects are likely to exist between internal and external mechanisms of corporate governance (Walsh and Seward, 1990; Weir et al., 2002) such as managerial ownership, outside block ownership, control by banks, capital structure, managerial remuneration, financial reporting and control as well as board structure (Beatty and Zajac, 1994; Weir et al., 2002; Hermalin and Weisbach, 2003). Consequently, we suggest that when VCs focus closely on monitoring and various control systems are already present in the entrepreneurial firm, an unnecessary duplication of efforts may occur.

If non-executive directors deal with relational risk by focusing on the use of control mechanisms mainly because they are suspicious of management, the consequential development of distrust between boards and managers is likely to reduce the ability of directors to contribute to strategy development and resource access (Roberts et al., 2005). This is because managers are becoming more concerned with justifying their managerial decisions to the board rather than using the directors' expertise and contacts to improve firm performance (Sundaramurthy and Lewis, 2003). Landström (1993) in particular criticizes the narrow focus on potential agency conflicts adopted by VCs, pointing out that monitoring mechanisms are likely to be counterproductive as they lower the level of trust between the VC and the entrepreneur. This also means that principals' and agents' perception of the risk of opportunistic behaviour and the appropriateness of the control systems is of great importance (Arthurs and Busenitz, 2003; Busenitz et al., 2004). If VCs overestimate the extent of agency problems, they might not only waste precious resources in developing and implementing superfluous monitoring mechanisms, but they might also damage the firm's performance by inhibiting the management team from utilizing their and the VCs' abilities and resources to the fullest potential. This implies that VCs monitoring activities are likely to have a negative effect on the relationship between both types of control systems and firm performance. These findings and arguments lead to:

H5: VC monitoring activities negatively moderate the effect of the entrepreneurial firm's control systems on its financial performance.

METHODOLOGY

Sample and Data Collection Procedure

We sent questionnaires to 441 Dutch venture capital-backed small firms, which we identified from the Reach database (for example, capturing business information from the Dutch chambers of commerce), annual reports and Internet sites of venture capitalists. The mail survey produced 93 usable questionnaires. The net response rate is about 21 per cent. Two Kolmogorov–Smirnov two-sample tests provide strong evidence (that is, the asymptotic significance (2-tailed) is 0.940 for the firm's age and 0.477 for the firm's industry) that both the respondent and the non-respondent firms come from the same distribution.

Measures

Dependent variables

The entrepreneurial firm's performance is assessed by a financial and a non-financial performance measure, which are based on the studies of Manigart et al. (1995) and Sapienza et al. (1996). The scales have a high disclosure rate, strong internal consistency, and relatively strong inter-rater reliability (Chandler and Hanks, 1993). Previous studies comparing VCs' and CEOs' assessments prove these measures to be highly reliable and valid (Sapienza, 1992; Sapienza and Gupta, 1994). The financial performance measure comprises: (i) sales growth; (ii) market share; (iii) gross margin; (iv) return on investment; (v) market value of company shares; and (vi) liquidity position. For each item, the entrepreneur's satisfaction score is multiplied by a corresponding importance score (see Zahra, 1996a). The importance items are measured by using a Likert scale from 1: Not important, to 6: Very important, and the satisfaction scores with 1: Not satisfied, to 6: Very satisfied. The scales are calculated by dividing the sum of items' weighted scores by the sum of the number of items. Cronbach's α is 0.76, which is well above the lower limits of acceptability of 0.50–0.60 (Nunnally, 1978).

The non-financial performance measure consists of: (i) development of new products and organizational processes; (ii) development of new target markets; (iii) operational efficiency; (iv) employees' development; (v) firm's stability; and (vi) preparation for exit of venture capitalist. The scale is computed in a similar manner as the financial performance measure. Cronbach's α is 0.56.

Independent variables

Table 11.1 provides an overview of the scales analysis and discriminant validity of the independent variables. The VC's board role scales are the VC service and monitoring activities. These items are based on previous studies (MacMillan et al., 1989; Sapienza and Timmons, 1989; Harrison and Mason, 1992; Rosenstein et al., 1993; Ehrlich et al., 1994). The entrepreneurs are asked to indicate the intensity by which they agree or disagree with a number of propositions about the value-adding activities provided by their venture capitalist(s). The propositions are measured by using a Likert scale from 1: Fully disagree, to 5: Fully agree. The two board role scales are computed by dividing the total sum of the item scores by the number of items. Cronbach's α of the VC service activities is 0.76, and of VC monitoring activities is 0.80.

The items of the cost control system scale are based on Miller (1988). The entrepreneurs are asked how important they perceive each item to be for their company by using a Likert scale from 1: Not important, to 7: Very important. The scale is calculated by summing the item scores, and then dividing the total sum by the total number of the items. Cronbach's α is 0.56.

The measures of the company's incentive and reward system and quality system are based on Huselid (1995). For each scale's items the entrepreneur has to indicate the percentage of his/her workforce to whom the particular work practices apply. The scales are computed by the sum of the items divided by the number of the items. Cronbach's α of the incentive and reward system is 0.68, and of the quality system is 0.51.[1]

Control variables

We use the following control variables: firm's age, firm's size, and two industry dummy variables, that is, information and communications technology (ICT) life science industries, and services/sales industries. These covariates take into account that VCs tend to be more involved in younger and smaller firms, and firms operating in emergent industries (Elango et al., 1995).

Common method variance

Harman's single factor test (cf. Podsakoff et al., 2003) provides evidence that the analysis is not subject to common method bias. The items of our measures and the construction of the scales are rather different from each other (Harrison and McLaughlin, 1996), which reduces the common method bias. Moreover, the questionnaire design separated measurements of the dependent and independent variables psychologically, and guaranteed the respondents' anonymity (see also Podsakoff et al., 2003 about common method bias strategies).

Table 11.1 *Overview of the scale analysis and discriminant validity of the independent variables*

VC's value-adding activities	Service activities	Monitoring activities
Recruit additional managers	**0.66**	0.13
Interface with the investor group	**0.64**	0.30
Assistance on introducing new products/services to the market	**0.72**	0.14
Assistance on operations	**0.68**	−0.15
Getting new finance partners	**0.64**	0.26
Contact with advisers	**0.63**	0.24
Financial monitoring	0.16	**0.81**
Evaluate our business strategy	0.13	**0.76**
Operational monitoring	0.24	**0.79**
Evaluate product-market opportunities	0.09	**0.77**
Percentage of variance explained (total: 54.72%)	27.52%	27.20%

Control systems	Incentive and reward system	Cost control system	Quality system
Formal information-sharing programme	**0.56**	0.23	0.10
Formal job analysis	**0.74**	−0.21	−0.14
Formal performance appraisals	**0.76**	0.02	−0.15
Performance appraisals determine compensations	**0.62**	−0.06	0.05
Attitude surveys on a regular basis	**0.63**	0.04	0.28
Use of cost centres	−0.07	**0.81**	0.10
Use of standard costs	0.29	**0.73**	−0.01
Minimization of advertising expenditures	−0.13	**0.64**	−0.16
Price cutting	−0.09	**0.34**	−0.65
Participation in quality of work life programmes, quality circles, and/or labour management teams	−0.07	0.01	**0.66**
Access to a formal grievance procedure and/or complaint resolution system	0.07	0.13	**0.80**
Percentage of variance explained (total: 53.28%)	21.30%	16.67%	15.31%

Data Analysis

Two-stage-least-squares (2SLS) estimation techniques are used for calculating the effect of the VC service activities on the entrepreneurial firm's control systems (hypotheses 1–3). The 2SLS technique is preferred to ordinary least squares (OLS) (see also Berry, 1984, p. 15), because of possible reciprocal effects between independent and dependent variables. Instruments for VC service activities are the percentage of shares held by the VC, and the frequency of contact with the VC. The instruments have a Pearson correlation of 0.41 ($p<0.01$) and 0.22 ($p<0.05$) with the VC service activities, respectively. OLS moderated regression techniques are used to calculate the interaction effects of the VC monitoring activities and the set of the entrepreneurial firm's control systems to the firm's performance (hypothesis 5). The main effects of the firm's set of control systems on its performance are used to test hypothesis 4.

RESULTS

Summary descriptive statistics and pairwise Pearson correlations are provided in Table 11.2. The VC monitoring activities have a high positive correlation with the entrepreneurial firm's cost control system ($p<0.01$) and with the ICT/life science industries ($p<0.01$). The latter might be explained by the VC's attempts to reduce information asymmetry in dynamic environments (Amit et al., 1998). Conforming to findings by Elango et al. (1995), VC service activities have a high negative correlation with firm size ($p<0.05$), firm age ($p<0.05$), and a positive correlation with ICT/life science firms ($p<0.01$). Finally, there is a positive correlation between both types of board activities ($p<0.01$), which is consistent with MacMillan et al.'s (1989) active and passive VC involvement types.

Table 11.3 shows the regression equations that are computed to test hypotheses 1–3. Since we do not find support for an effect of the VC service activities on the entrepreneurial firm's policy to adopt a quality system, hypothesis 1 is not accepted. However, hypothesis 2 is accepted, that is, entrepreneurial firms which apply an incentive and reward system are associated with VCs adding value through their service activities ($p<0.05$). Hypothesis 3 is also supported, that is, VC service activities help the entrepreneurial firms to enhance their cost control systems ($p<0.05$).

Table 11.4 reports the OLS results of the contribution of the entrepreneurial firm's set of control systems to its financial and non-financial performance. Hypothesis 4 about the indirect performance effects of VC service activities is only supported for the mediating effect of incentive and

Table 11.2 Descriptive statistics and Pearson correlations

Variables	Mean	SD	1	2	3	4	5	6	7	8	9	10	11
1. Firm age	21.87	31.25	–										
2. Firm size	49.47	56.99	0.52**	–									
3. ICT/life science industries	0.37	0.48	−0.31**	−0.07	–								
4. Service industry	0.27	0.45	−0.03	0.07	−0.46**	–							
5. Cost control system	4.14	1.16	0.12	0.04	0.02	−0.04	–						
6. Incentive and reward system	66.77	25.20	−0.07	0.15	0.31**	−0.23*	0.02	–					
7. Quality system	45.36	31.72	−0.09	−0.12	−0.09	0.23*	−0.11	0.05	–				
8. VC service activities	1.85	0.74	−0.22*	−0.21*	0.29**	−0.22*	−0.02	0.17	0.10	–			
9. VC monitoring activities	2.67	0.95	−0.16	−0.16	0.35**	−0.14	0.29**	0.20	0.01	0.42**	–		
10. Fin. performance	12.59	3.82	0.15	0.21*	−0.19	0.11	−0.06	0.12	0.28**	−0.14	−0.13	–	
11. Non-fin. performance	12.97	2.83	−0.01	0.02	−0.08	−0.12	0.00	0.30**	0.23*	0.10	0.02	0.42**	–

Note: ** $p<0.01$; * $p<0.05$.

Table 11.3 The effect of the VC service activities on the entrepreneurial firm's set of control systems (2SLS)

Dependent variable	Equation 1		Equation 2		Equation 3	
	Quality system		Inc. & reward system		Cost control system	
Intercept[a]	48.198***	(23.723)	18.474***	(20.032)	2.152**	(0.963)
Firm age	−0.032	(0.138)	−0.045	(0.116)	0.008	(0.006)
Firm size	−0.071	(0.073)	0.154**	(0.062)	0.001	(0.003)
ICT/life sciences	0.150	(8.974)	5.818	(7.578)	−0.157	(8.283)
Services/sales	16.721*	(9.312)	−5.018	(7.715)	−6.911	(0.389)
VC service activities[b]	−1.505	(9.136)	21.663**	(9.642)	0.963**	(0.475)
F-value	1.251		3.330***		1.046	
R-square	7.01%		16.71%		5.71%	

Notes:
a. Unstandardized regression coefficients with * $p<0.10$; ** $p<0.05$ and *** $p<0.01$, and standard errors in parentheses.
b. Instrumental variables: percentage of shares held by the VC, the frequency of contact of the entrepreneurial firm with the VC.

Table 11.4 The effect of the set of control systems on the entrepreneurial firm's performance (OLS)

	Equation 1		Equation 2		Equation 3	
Dependent variable: financial performance						
Intercept[a]	11.290***	(2.364)	11.387***	(2.466)	10.577***	(2.443)
Firm age	−0.003	(0.015)	0.001	(0.015)	0.002	(0.015)
Firm size	0.011	(0.008)	0.013	(0.008)	0.013	(0.008)
ICT/life sciences	−1.295	(0.984)	−1.685	(1.038)	−1.655*	(0.992)
Services/sales	−1.014	(1.029)	−0.740	(1.060)	−1.002	(1.045)
VC monitoring activities	−0.128	(0.490)	−0.032	(0.514)	−0.254	(0.504)
VC service activities	−0.896	(0.583)	−0.567	(0.591)	−0.690	(0.579)
Cost control system	0.196	(0.389)	−0.178	(0.372)	0.036	(0.378)
Incentive and reward system	0.021	(0.017)	0.023	(0.018)	0.022	(0.017)
Quality system	0.030**	(0.013)	0.036***	(0.013)	0.041***	(0.013)
VC monitoring × cost control system	−0.828**	(0.340)				
VC monitoring × incentive and reward system			0.010	(0.017)		
VC monitoring × quality system					0.026*	(0.013)
F-value	2.645***		1.945*		2.390**	
R-square	25.57%		20.16%		23.69%	

Dependent variable: non-financial performance						
Intercept[a]	9.799***	(1.816)	9.621***	(1.821)	10.179***	(1.847)
Firm age	−0.010	(0.012)	−0.010	(0.011)	−0.010	(0.011)
Firm size	0.001	(0.006)	0.002	(0.006)	0.000	(0.006)
ICT/life sciences	−1.818**	(0.756)	−2.021**	(0.767)	−1.826**	(0.750)
Services/sales	−1.565*	(0.791)	−1.557*	(0.783)	−1.415*	(0.790)
VC monitoring activities	−0.193	(0.377)	−0.126	(0.380)	−0.126	(0.381)
VC service activities	0.047	(0.448)	0.120	(0.436)	0.132	(0.438)
Cost control system	0.260	(0.299)	0.188	(0.275)	0.133	(0.286)
Incentive and reward system	0.038***	(0.013)	0.041***	(0.013)	0.038***	(0.013)
Quality system	0.018*	(0.010)	0.020*	(0.009)	0.017*	(0.010)
VC monitoring × cost control system	−0.132	(0.261)				
VC monitoring × incentive and reward system			0.012	(0.012)		
VC monitoring × quality system					−0.009	(0.010)
F-value	2.195**		2.279**		2.263**	
R-square	22.18%		22.84%		22.71%	

Note: [a] Unstandardized regression coefficients with * $p<0.10$; ** $p<0.05$ and *** $p<0.01$, and standard errors in parentheses.

reward systems. This means that by helping to set up incentive and reward systems (recall hypothesis 2), the VC service activities positively contribute to entrepreneurial firm performance, as incentive and reward systems are significantly associated with non-financial performance ($p<0.01$). Furthermore, it appears that entrepreneurial firms which have a quality system are highly associated with financial ($p<0.01$) and moderately with non-financial performance ($p<0.10$). However, as previously shown (recall hypothesis 1), entrepreneurial firms do not appear to be stimulated to adopt quality systems by VCs who provide service activities. These findings suggest that hypothesis 4 is only supported with regard to a VC's influence on the entrepreneurial firm to enhance an incentive and reward system.

Hypothesis 5 is moderately supported for the interaction effect between VC monitoring activities and entrepreneurial firms employing quality systems with regard to financial performance ($p<0.10$). However, contrary to our expectations it appears that this effect is positive, which suggests that quality systems and VC monitoring activities are not complementary but more synergetic in nature. Furthermore, as expected, entrepreneurial firms which have implemented a cost control system are negatively associated with financial performance when receiving VC monitoring activities ($p < 0.05$). Too much emphasis on costs and short-term profits is likely to erode the entrepreneurial firm's profitability. Finally, there is no significant support for the interaction effect of VC monitoring activities and an incentive and reward system on organizational performance.

DISCUSSION

In this study, a multi-theoretical approach was used in order to resolve the VC 'value-added' proposition by taking account of the entrepreneurial firm's control systems as intermediary factors. In doing so, we simultaneously analysed whether the VC enhances the entrepreneurial firm's control systems, and accordingly contributes to entrepreneurial firm performance. We therefore incorporated two board activities (service and monitoring) and three control systems (quality system, incentive and reward system, cost control) into a set of multivariate regression models.

Our results indicate that VCs play an enabling role for the establishment and the effective use of the entrepreneurial firm's control systems in order to facilitate the entrepreneurial firm's stability and efficiency. We find that VC service activities facilitate the entrepreneurial firm's utilization of cost control and incentive and reward systems. Since such systems are positively significantly related with entrepreneurial firms' non-financial performance, VC service activities can have an indirect effect on organizational performance. Moreover, entrepreneurial firms employing quality systems which additionally receive VC monitoring activities are moderately associated with high financial performance. Since quality systems produce more transparency about the strengths and weaknesses of the entrepreneurial firm's operational processes, VCs who are keen on monitoring may provide more valuable support by fine-tuning their expertise to the needs of entrepreneurial firms. In doing so, VCs who have a high proficiency in monitoring activities may enhance organizational learning (see Larsson et al., 2000).

We find a negative interaction effect of VC monitoring activities and the use of cost control systems on the entrepreneurial firm's financial performance. This suggests that VCs who rely on these control systems in order to emphasize financial outcomes through their monitoring activities may erode the entrepreneurial firm's performance. Thus, in terms of control, more is not necessarily better. Due to the not only substitutive but also complementary relationship of monitoring mechanisms, principals can increase agency costs by excessive monitoring. The development, implementation and use of control and incentive systems come at a cost not only in terms of their operation but also potentially with regard to behavioural incentives of managers. If the overemphasis of managerial control leads to a loss of trust between entrepreneurial teams and VCs, managers may become mainly concerned with justifying their decisions rather than receiving support from the VC.

The results suggest that VCs tend to pay too little attention to the establishment of quality systems in entrepreneurial firms. This appears to be a failure in the VC's involvement policy, since the adoption of a quality system is strongly related to high organizational financial and non-financial performance. Since quality systems create empowerment and enhance communication in the entrepreneurial firm, VCs who help entrepreneurial firms in setting up such systems may benefit in two ways. First, through empowerment VCs become less dependent on the entrepreneur, since through empowerment firm-specific knowledge rests not solely in the head of the entrepreneur. Second, through picking up firm-specific knowledge created by more advanced communication processes in the entrepreneurial firm, VCs are better able to fine tune the services they provide to the needs of the entrepreneurial firm.

NOTE

1. We are aware that there are different views about the (arbitrarily chosen) level of acceptability of constructs. These views, among others, depend upon the nature of the domain

that the construct attempts to measure or whether the construct in question is in an explorative stage or not (see also Nunnally, 1978). For the present study, the domains of the constructs are rather broad, particularly given the heterogeneous character of our sample (that is, in terms of the different industries the firms of our sample compete in). From a psychometric perspective, the constructs are rather more explorative measures than repeatedly tested established measures. Van de Ven and Ferry (1979) suggest that Cronbach's αs should fall between 0.55 and 0.70 for a moderately broad construct, and between 0.35 and 0.55 for three-items scales of a very broad construct. From this perspective, the Cronbach's αs of our constructs are reasonable. Furthermore, from a statistical point of view, it is important to note that relatively low Cronbach's α's are more likely to work *against* this study's findings, because measurement errors may lead to the failure to detect significant effects that are actually present in the population (see also Jaccard et al., 1990: 38). So, our findings are based upon a conservative test.

REFERENCES

Amit, R., J. Brander and C. Zott (1998), 'Why do venture capital firms exist? Theory and Canadian evidence', *Journal of Business Venturing*, **13** (6), 441–66.

Andrews, K.R. (1980), *The Concepts of Corporate Strategy – Revised Edition*, Homewood, IL: Richard D. Irwin, Inc.

Arthurs, J.D. and L.W. Busenitz (2003), 'The boundaries and limitations of agency theory and stewardship theory in the venture capitalist/entrepreneur relationship', *Entrepreneurship Theory and Practice*, **28** (2), 145–63.

Barnhart, S.W., M.W. Marr and S. Rosenstein (1994), 'Firm performance and board composition: some new evidence', *Managerial and Decision Economics*, **15** (4), 329–40.

Beatty, R.B. and E.J. Zajac (1994), 'Managerial incentives, monitoring and risk bearing: a study of executive compensation, ownership and board structure in initial public offerings', *Administrative Science Quarterly*, **39** (2), 313–35.

Berry, A. and L. Perren (2000), *The Role of Non-executive Directors in United Kingdom SMEs*, Research Report 63, London: Certified Accountants Educational Trust.

Berry, W.D. (1984), *Nonrecursive Causal Models*, Newbury Park, CA: Sage.

Busenitz, L.W., J.O. Fiet and D.D. Moesel (2004), 'Reconsidering the venture capitalists' "value-added" proposition: an interorganizational learning perspective', *Journal of Business Venturing*, **19**, 787–808.

Chandler, G.N. and S.H. Hanks (1993), 'Measuring the performance of emerging businesses: a validation study', *Journal of Business Venturing*, **8** (5), 391–408.

Churchill, N.C. and V.L. Lewis (1983), 'The five stages of small business growth', *Harvard Business Review*, **61** (3), 30–50.

Deakins, D., E. O'Neill and P. Mileham (2000), 'The role and influence of external directors in small, entrepreneurial companies: some evidence on VC and non-VC appointed external directors', *Venture Capital*, **2** (2), 111–27.

Ehrlich, S.B., A.F. De Noble, T. Moore and R.R. Weaver (1994), 'After the cash arrives: a comparative study of venture capital and private investor involvement in entrepreneurial firms', *Journal of Business Venturing*, **9** (1), 67–82.

Elango, B., V.H. Fried, R.D. Hisrich and A. Polonchek (1995), 'How venture capital firms differ', *Journal of Business Venturing*, **10** (2), 157–79.

Fama, E.F. and M.C. Jensen (1983), 'Separation of ownership and control', *Journal of Law and Economics*, **26** (2), 301–25.
Flynn, D. (2001), 'Life cycles of new ventures organizations: different factors affecting performance', *Journal of Developmental Entrepreneurship*, **6** (1), 41–58.
Fried, V.H., G.D. Bruton and R.D. Hisrich (1998), 'Strategy and the board of directors in venture capital-backed firms', *Journal of Business Venturing*, **13** (6), 493–503.
Gabrielsson, J. and M. Huse (2002), 'The venture capitalist and the board of directors in SMEs: roles and processes', *Venture Capital*, **4** (2), 125–46.
Gomez-Mejia, L.R., D.B. Balkin and T.M. Welbourne (1990), 'Influence of venture capitalists on high tech management', *Journal of High Technology Management Research*, **1** (1), 103–18.
Goodstein, J., K. Gautam and W. Boeker (1994), 'The effects of board size and diversity on strategic change', *Strategic Management Journal*, **15** (3), 241–50.
Gordon, J.R. (1996), *Organizational Behavior: A Diagnostic Approach*, Englewood Cliffs, NJ: Prentice-Hall.
Gorman, M. and W.A. Sahlman (1989), 'What do venture capitalists do?', *Journal of Business Venturing*, **4** (4), 231–48.
Harrison, D.A. and M.E. McLaughlin (1996), 'Context, cognition, and common method variance: psychometric and verbal protocol evidence', *Organizational Behavior and Human Decision Processes*, **68** (3), 246–61.
Harrison, R.T. and C.M. Mason (1992), 'The roles of investors in entrepreneurial companies: a comparison of informal investors and venture capitalists', in N.C. Churchill, S. Birley, W.D. Bygrave, D.F. Muzyka, C. Wahlbin and W.E. Wetzel (eds), *Frontiers of Entrepreneurship Research*, Babson Park, MA Babson College, pp. 388–404.
Hermalin, B.E. and M.S. Weisbach (2003), 'Boards of directors as an endogenously determined institution: a survey of the economic literature', *Economic Policy Review*, **9** (1), 7–26.
Huselid, M.A. (1995), 'The impact of human resource management practices on turnover, productivity, and corporate financial performance', *Academy of Management Journal*, **38** (3), 635–72.
Jaccard, J., R. Turrisi and C.K. Wan (1990), *Interaction Effects in Multiple Regression*, London: Sage.
Jensen, M.C. and W.H. Meckling (1976), 'Agency costs and the theory of the firm', *Journal of Financial Economics*, **3**, 305–60.
Landström, H. (1993), 'Agency theory and its application to small firms: evidence from the Swedish venture capital market', *Journal of Small Business Finance*, **2** (3), 203–18.
Larsson, R., L. Bengtsson, K. Henriksson and J. Sparks (2000), 'The interorganizational learning dilemma: collective knowledge development in strategic alliances', *Organization Science*, **9** (3), 285–306.
MacMillan, I.C., D.M. Kulow and R. Khoylian (1989), 'Venture capitalists' involvement in their investments: extent and performance', *Journal of Business Venturing*, **4** (1), 27–47.
Manigart, S., H.J. Sapienza and W. Vermeir (1995), 'Venture capital: méér dan enkel financiering? – een vergelijkend onderzoek in vier landen', *Mando: Tijdschrift voor Organisatiekunde en Sociaal Beleid*, **49** (2), 72–90.

McNulty, T. and A. Pettigrew (1999), 'Strategists on the board', *Organization Studies*, **20** (1), 47–74.
Miller, D. (1988), 'Relating Porter's business strategies to environment and structure: analysis and performance implications', *Academy of Management Journal*, **31** (2), 280–308.
Nunnally, J.D. (1978), *Psychometric Theory*, New York: McGraw-Hill.
Peteraf, M.A. (1993), 'The cornerstone of competitive advantage: a resource-based view', *Strategic Management Journal*, **14** (3), 179–91.
Pfeffer, J. and G.R. Salancik (1978), *The External Control of Organizations*, New York: Harper & Row.
Podsakoff, P.M., S.B. MacKenzie and J.Y. Lee (2003), 'Common method biases in behavioral research: a critical review of the literature and recommended remedies', *Journal of Applied Psychology*, **88** (5), 879–903.
Roberts, J., T. McNulty and P. Stiles (2005), 'Beyond agency conceptions of the work of the non-executive director: creating accountability in the boardroom', *British Journal of Management*, **16** (S1), S5–S26.
Rosenstein, J., A.V. Bruno, W.D. Bygrave and N.T. Taylor (1993), 'The CEO, venture capitalists, and the board', *Journal of Business Venturing*, **8** (2), 99–113.
Ruhnka, J.C. and J.E. Young (1987), 'A venture capital model of the development process for new ventures', *Journal of Business Venturing*, **2** (2), 167–84.
Sapienza, H.J. (1992), 'When do venture capitalists add value?', *Journal of Business Venturing*, **7** (1), 9–27.
Sapienza, H.J. and A.K. Gupta (1994), 'The impact of agency risks and task uncertainty on venture capitalist–CEO interaction', *Academy of Management Journal*, **37** (5), 1618–32.
Sapienza, H.J., S. Manigart and W. Vermeir (1996), 'Venture capitalist governance and value added in four countries', *Journal of Business Venturing*, **11** (6), 439–69.
Sapienza, H.J. and J.A. Timmons (1989), 'The roles of venture capitalists in new ventures: what determines their importance?', *Academy of Management Best Papers Proceedings*, 74–8.
Scott, M. and R. Bruce (1987), 'Five stages of growth in small business', *Long Range Planning*, **20**, 45–52.
Steier, L. and R. Greenwood (1995), 'Venture capitalist relationships in the deal structuring and post-investment stages of new firm creation', *Journal of Management Studies*, **32** (3), 337–57.
Stiles, P. and B. Taylor (2001), *Boards at Work*, Oxford: Oxford University Press.
Sundaramurthy, C. and M. Lewis (2003), 'Control and collaboration: paradoxes of governance', *Academy of Management Review*, **28** (3), 397–415.
Van de Ven, A. and D.L. Ferry (1979), *Measuring and Assessing Organizations*, New York: Wiley.
Walsh, J.P. and J.K. Seward (1990), 'On the efficiency of internal and external corporate governance mechanisms', *Academy of Management Review*, **15** (3), 421–58.
Weir, C., D. Laing and P.J. McKnight (2002), 'Internal and external governance mechanisms: their impact on the performance of large UK public companies', *Journal of Business Finance and Accounting*, **29** (5/6), 579–611.
Williamson, O.E. (1988a), 'The logic of economic organization', *Journal of Law, Economics and Organization*, **4** (1), 65–93.
Williamson, O.E. (1988b), 'Corporate finance and corporate governance', *Journal of Finance*, **43** (3), 567–91.

Zahra, S.A. (1996a), 'Technology strategy and new venture performance: a study of corporate-sponsored and independent biotechnology ventures', *Journal of Business Venturing*, **11** (4), 289–321.

Zahra, S.A. (1996b), 'Governance, ownership, and corporate entrepreneurship: the moderating impact of industry technological opportunities', *Academy of Management Journal*, **39** (6), 1713–35.

Zahra, S.A. and J.A. Pearce (1989), 'Boards of directors and corporate financial performance: a review and integrative model', *Journal of Management*, **15** (2), 291–334.

Index

Titles of publications are in *italics*.